The free speech wars

The free speech wars

How did we get here
and why does it matter?

Edited by Charlotte Lydia Riley

Manchester University Press

Published by Manchester University Press
Altrincham Street, Manchester M1 7JA
www.manchesteruniversitypress.co.uk

British Library Cataloguing-in-Publication Data
A catalogue record for this book is available from the British Library

ISBN 978 1 5261 5254 1 hardback
ISBN 978 1 5261 5116 2 paperback

First published 2021

Typeset by Servis Filmsetting Ltd, Stockport, Cheshire
Printed in Great Britain by TJ Books Limited, Padstow, Cornwall

Contents

Contents

Contents

Contributors

Charlotte Lydia Riley is Lecturer in Twentieth-Century British History at the University of Southampton. She is a feminist historian of twentieth-century Britain, with particular focus on decolonisation, the Labour Party and overseas aid and development programmes. More broadly, she is interested in the culture of British politics and identity in the twentieth century.

Jodie Ginsberg is a free speech and media freedom campaigner. She is the former CEO of UK-based freedom of expression charity, Index on Censorship.

Edward Packard is Lecturer in History at the University of Suffolk, where he teaches international history. His research is mainly focused on interwar Britain and the histories of refugee children, albeit he also has a long-standing interest in the history of Speakers' Corner from its Victorian origins to the present.

Sam Popowich is a Canadian librarian and a postgraduate researcher in political science at the University of Birmingham. His research focuses on political theory, social justice and librarianship from a broadly Marxist perspective.

Emma Harvey is CEO of Trinity Community Arts, a charity formed to manage the Trinity Centre, Bristol – a grade II* listed building, community arts centre and independent live music venue. She is interested in localism, and in developing inclusive spaces, platforms and technologies.

Edson Burton is a writer, historian, programme curator and performer based in Bristol. His academic specialisms include Bristol and the transatlantic slave trade, Black history in the USA, and cultural continuities between Africa and the New World.

Victoria Stiles is an independent researcher specialising in the interplay between aspects of fascism and colonialism, especially within public discussions of history and morality. Her PhD research at the University of Nottingham examined the shifting pressures on non-fiction publishing and bookselling in Nazi Germany.

Andrew Phemister is currently an Irish Research Council Postdoctoral Fellow at NUI Galway, having previously held postdoctoral positions at Oxford and Edinburgh. He studies nineteenth-century Ireland, agrarian radicalism and transatlantic republicanism, and has published work on Henry George, the international contexts of the Irish Land War, and religion in Irish political thought. He is working on a history of boycotting.

Omar Khan was director of the Runnymede Trust from 2014 to 2020, in which capacity he wrote his chapter for this volume. He has written widely on race and racism in the UK for two decades, and has a doctorate in political theory.

Neville Morley is Professor of Classics and Ancient History at the University of Exeter. He writes and teaches on a range of topics in ancient economic and social history, the modern reception and influence of classical antiquity, and historical methodology and theory.

Imen Neffati is a Junior Research Fellow in Religion at Pembroke College, University of Oxford. She is a historian of contemporary France and North Africa with a special focus on Islam, modernity and secularism. Her PhD (University of Sheffield) explored the history of the French satirical magazine *Charlie Hebdo* and studied its anti-clerical style and its rhetoric against Islam and Muslims.

Nina Lyon is a writer and PhD candidate in philosophy at the University of the West of England, where she is writing about nonsense in the work of Lewis Carroll. She is interested in the intersections of philosophy, culture and the mind and is the author of *Mushroom Season* (Vintage, 2014) and *Uprooted: On the Trail of the Green Man* (Faber, 2016).

Janna Kraus is a historian and lecturer at the Zurich University of Applied Sciences. Her courses focus on the history of science and technology with regard to economic exploitation, societal stratification and discrimination, as well as the emancipatory potential that so-called progress has brought and might still bring about. In addition, she is a committee member of Transgender Network Switzerland (TGNS).

Contributors

Aaron Ackerley is a module leader and teaching associate at the University of Sheffield. He is a historian of modern Britain and the British Empire, focused on elite and popular political cultures and the creation and dissemination of knowledge, information and ideologies. In particular, his research has explored the intersections between politics, economics and the press in interwar Britain.

Shaun McDaid is Senior Lecturer in the Division of Criminology, Politics and Sociology at the University of Huddersfield. His research focuses on political violence and its prevention. He is the author of *Template for Peace: Northern Ireland, 1972–75* (Manchester University Press, 2013) and co-author of *Radicalisation and Counter-Radicalisation in Higher Education* (Emerald, 2018).

Catherine McGlynn is Senior Lecturer in Politics at the University of Huddersfield. Her research focuses on conflict resolution and counter-terrorism with a particular focus on party politics in Northern Ireland and counter-radicalisation strategies in the UK and elsewhere.

Gabriel Moshenska is Associate Professor of Public Archaeology at UCL. He works on the archaeology of recent conflicts, the history of archaeology, and the public understanding of the past.

Grace Lavery is Associate Professor of English, Critical Theory, and Gender and Women's Studies at the University of California, Berkeley, where she teaches Victorian literature, cultural studies and trans feminist studies. Her current research focuses on modern and contemporary conceptualisations of efficacy in Britain and the United States.

Contributors

Paul Whickman is Senior Lecturer in English at the University of Derby. As well as censorship and 'free speech', his research interests lie in the Romantic period, particularly the work of Byron, Shelley and Keats. His book, *Blasphemy and Politics in Romantic Literature: Creativity in the Writing of Percy Bysshe Shelley*, was published by Palgrave in 2020.

Adam Standring is a postdoctoral research fellow in the Environmental Sociology section of Örebro University, Sweden. His research focuses on the political sociology of expertise and the politics of knowledge in international organisations. His current research looks at notions and practices of expertise and knowledge production in the International Panel on Climate Change (IPCC) and his other research interests include the moral politics of austerity, housing and drug policy.

Daniel Cardoso is an Assistant Professor in Politics and International Relations at the Autonomous University of Lisbon and a researcher at Observare – Observatory of Foreign Relations in the same university. He is interested in public policy and governance. His specific research interests include EU multi-level governance during the Eurozone crisis, Portuguese politics and emerging countries' foreign policy.

Marta Santiváñez is a journalist and social policy researcher based in London. Her work explores questions of migration in regard to gender, climate change and labour, with a particular focus on migrant unions and activism. She engages in writing that brings together her experience in the field with strong analysis of policy frameworks. She is one of the co-founders and editors of the *jfa* human rights journal, in which she raises questions about notions of citizenship and recognition.

Contributors

Ben Whitham is Senior Lecturer in International Politics at De Montfort University, Leicester. His research explores the global political economy of (in)security, and intersecting global inequalities. In particular, his recent work has focused on Islamophobia, austerity and racial capitalism, and on the cultural politics of crisis.

Henry S. Price is a PhD student in political science at the University of Birmingham. Using incel subculture as a case study, his thesis examines the ways in which contemporary anti-feminism is entangled with neoliberalism. More broadly, he is interested in the ambivalent effects of the incorporation of select feminist ideas into institutional cultures, and in understandings of gender relations today.

Penny CS Andrews is a writer, researcher, broadcaster and performer at the University of Sheffield. They work on politics, media and popular and internet cultures and use fandom as a lens for examining emotional and identity-driven attachments to political and parapolitical actors and campaigns. They also write about *Doctor Who*, pro wrestling, drag, queer culture and pop music.

Helen Pallett is a lecturer in human geography in the Science, Society & Sustainability group in the School of Environmental Sciences at the University of East Anglia. She is a human geographer and STS scholar interested in interactions between democracy and developments in science and technology. Her current research both uses digital tools to map diverse forms of democratic participation, and investigates the digital technologies that shape this participation.

Introduction
Telling people things that they do not want to hear: free speech debates and contemporary culture wars

Charlotte Lydia Riley

In early 2020 a new organisation, the Free Speech Union (FSU), was launched with much fanfare across the British right-wing press. Toby Young, the organisation's founder and director, has been associated with the cause for some time, having fallen back on the 'free speech' defence to justify, for example, making salacious remarks about female politicians' breasts.[1] The organisation aims to defend people who are the target of a 'digital outrage mob', or who face calls to be fired from their jobs, or who are being no-platformed by a university or criticised by 'newspaper columnists and broadcasting pundits'.[2] At the bottom of the FSU's 'Statement of Values' on its website is a line from George Orwell: 'If liberty means anything at all, it means the right to tell people what they do not want to hear.'[3]

The words come from a short essay that Orwell wrote towards the end of the Second World War, entitled 'The Freedom of the Press'.[4] This was intended to act as a preface to his novel *Animal Farm*; in the end it was not included in the book, and remained undiscovered until 1971. In the piece, Orwell explained some of the difficulties in getting *Animal Farm* published, and made the central message of the book – a critique of Stalinism specifically, rather than socialism generally – more explicit. But the essay was also a bigger exploration of the idea that there exists a right to freedom of speech and thought. In the context of wartime, Orwell grappled with the realities of censorship, both as official government policy, and – worse, he believed – as the result of groupthink among publishers and editors. In fact, he derided the 'intellectual cowardice' of these people as the worst enemy of any writer or journalist.

Orwell argued that the war had shown that 'unpopular ideas can be silenced, and inconvenient facts kept dark, without the need for any official ban'.[5] Instead, the liberal intellectuals who controlled publishing and journalism themselves agreed to avoid publishing on certain topics. In an environment where saying some things was simply 'not done' (as, Orwell argued, it was once 'not done' for a man to mention trousers in the presence of a lady), there did not need to be any particular censorship by states themselves. And the censorship in question was not about protecting state secrets or preventing criticism of the government. Rather, it was self-imposed and was predominantly intended to prevent criticism of the USSR, and to parrot Stalinist ideas.

Orwell argued that people self-censored, not only in their writing but also in their thoughts, out of a 'cowardly desire to keep in with the bulk of the intelligentsia'; people were too afraid and uncertain to acknowledge what was right or wrong themselves. He thought, too, that this extended beyond refusing to publish material. For example, he saw this tendency in the liberal outrage that greeted Oswald Mosley's release from internment in 1942, an act that Orwell believed to be entirely legitimate given the diminished threat from Nazi invasion. As he argued, despite Mosley's obviously repugnant far-right views, imprisoning anyone without trial was a dangerous precedent: 'make a habit of imprisoning Fascists without trial, and perhaps the process won't stop at Fascists'.[6]

Orwell has become a figurehead for a particular strand of liberalism. The Free Speech Union is far from the only group to mobilise him in support of telling people what they do not want to hear. These words have been quoted and commodified (on fridge magnets, notebooks and tea towels) beyond all meaning, as a catch-all defence of the right to say anything and everything. But Orwell's arguments about freedom of speech cannot be accepted without question.

The essay repeats the tendencies towards English exceptionalism seen in his earlier wartime writing. In 'The Lion and the Unicorn: Socialism and the English Genius', published in 1940, Orwell paints a picture of a gentle, liberty-loving nation of people who cannot be forced into goose-stepping or gestapos.[7] In 'The Freedom of the Press', Orwell continues this theme, arguing that 'tolerance and decency are deeply rooted in England'; but this is not, strictly, accurate. Nor does his claim that British 'civilisation over a period of four hundred years' has been 'founded on' the 'freedom of thought and speech' really hold up to scrutiny.[8] There was no free speech in the British Empire for most of its subjects; even in the Westminster Parliament, speakers might be free from accusations of libel, but it is forbidden to label your opponent a liar.

Orwell simply refuses to engage with the critiques of freedom of speech, writing that 'I am well acquainted with all the arguments against freedom of thought and speech – the arguments which claim that it cannot exist, and the arguments which claim that it ought not to. I answer simply that they don't convince me.' But we need to take these critiques seriously. Why might people – even supposedly intelligent, liberal, well-meaning people – demand limits on speech? Why might people feel that freedom of thought or speech might fundamentally be impossible – what do people mean when they claim that these things simply 'cannot exist'?

We need to think about who gets to make claims for freedom of speech, and whose rights to free speech are defended by institutions. And we should question what sort of speech is tolerated within the bounds of free speech and what is seen as off limits. This book seeks to explore these ideas.

When Orwell was writing, the UN Declaration of Human Rights had not yet been conceived. Adopted in Paris in 1948, the declaration is the founding document of the international human rights regime. In the context of the 'barbarous acts' of the Second World War, it sets out the rights that should be granted to all people and upheld by all nations.[9] In the preamble, the declaration states that the 'advent of a world in which human beings shall enjoy freedom of speech and belief and freedom from fear and want has been proclaimed as the highest aspiration of the common people'. Freedom of speech was written into the very heart of the post-war settlement. It is further guaranteed in Article 19: 'Everyone has the right to freedom of opinion and expression; this right includes freedom to hold opinions without interference and to seek, receive and impart information and ideas through any media and regardless of frontiers.'[10] There exists, therefore, an international and universal right to 'free speech', the defence of which is critical to democracy and free political expression around the world.

There remain many people and communities around the world who do not currently enjoy the freedom of speech: journalists who cannot publish their reports because their newspapers are controlled or censored by the government; writers who cannot express their criticism of regimes without being thrown into prison; poets and playwrights who risk ending their careers, or even their lives, if they speak the wrong words that express the wrong ideas. There are communities who cannot practise their religion freely for fear of persecution, and there are political parties that are banned or violently opposed. Across the world, there are people whose speech rights are limited or denied and governments whose power comes from denying their people's right to criticise or condemn them.

When Orwell was writing, of course, this was also the case. The Nazis banned and burned books, locked up and murdered their opponents; but European imperialists, too, closely controlled the press and the publication of critical literature across the colonies, and imprisoned nationalist leaders. In Britain, too, there was censorship: not just the wartime measures imposed by the Ministry of Information, and described in Orwell's essay as mostly sensitive and light-touch, but also blasphemy laws, obscenity laws and theatre censorship that meant that every play performed had to be approved by the Lord Chamberlain. Most of this domestic censorship was removed by the raft of permissive legislation passed by Home Secretary Roy Jenkins in the 1960s, except for blasphemy, which remained an offence until 2008, and remains a common law offence in Northern Ireland today.

Freedom of speech, then, was no simple thing to guarantee in 1948, even in democracies that expressed a general desire to uphold it for their citizens. And in the twenty-first century, its meaning is contested and complex. The ability of people to 'seek, receive and impart information and ideas through any media and regardless of frontiers' has been dramatically increased with the invention of the internet; people can seek information from across the world and broadcast their ideas, too, globally. Governments still try to shut this down with censorship and firewalls: citizen journalists use anonymous accounts and VPNs to get their message out regardless. People can say what they want, and read what they want, and nobody can stop them. Or can they?

We are, at this moment, in the middle of a culture war: in Britain, certainly in America, across Europe, throughout the world. It is easy to blame this on the rise of 'populism', or on the fracturing of political consensus in democracies, or on the rise of dictatorships. In some ways, the world in 2020 does not look so different from the interwar world when Orwell was thinking and writing – the far right in ascendance, and a global pandemic bringing economies to their knees. But in some ways – empires have fallen, the internet has risen – it is dramatically different.

The culture war right now is framed mostly around identity (as they always are): a backlash, perhaps, against the civil rights movements, women's rights movements, LGBTQ activism, disability activism, post-colonial and Indigenous rights campaigns of the last fifty or sixty years. The political right is angry, empowered around the world by electoral gains and successful campaigns. In many ways this is still the establishment, the people who hold the power, regardless of their attempts to pose as 'populist' voices. But at the same time they feel under threat from a world where the parameters of acceptable behaviour have gradually shifted. When you have been used to dominance, equality feels like oppression, and when you have been used to pushing other people around with no regard for their feelings, any limits on your own behaviour feels like an assault on your rights.

A lot of this perceived threat comes from anxieties and concerns around speech and language. There is a worry, often expressed, that you cannot say anything these days. And this worry turns into anger: how dare you tell me what I can and cannot say. People are enraged by the argument that their speech might be offensive, or even damaging, to others. They are furious at the idea that their speech might constitute something that needs to be stopped or silenced.

This manifests itself partly as a generational divide, with the 'boomer' generation less tolerant of calls to moderate their language, impatient with what they see as the oversensitivities of millennials and Generation Z. Given that baby boomers were actors in some of the twentieth century's most dramatic fights for civil rights – for women, people of colour and LBGT people – this generational divide can sometimes be overemphasised. But millennials and younger people are much more likely to tolerate limits on freedom of speech, if it means a reduction in hate speech or the protection of minorities. For example, a University of Chicago survey from July 2017 found that only 16 per cent of 18–34 year olds surveyed thought that people on a university campus had the absolute right to use slurs or other language that was intentionally offensive to certain groups, and only 33 per cent thought that people had the absolute right on campus to express political views that were offensive or upsetting to certain groups.[11] Plenty of younger people are free speech absolutists: plenty of older people are happy to see limits in certain circumstances. But broadly, the tone of the debate might be different for different generations.

Perhaps the generational divide also explains the resurgence of a retro complaint: that of the scourge of 'political correctness'. The sense that it is a desire to be politically correct that is somehow dampening free speech, preventing people from saying what they really think or mean, is alive and well within this culture war. Orwell, with his concerns about the development of 'an orthodoxy, a body of ideas which it is assumed that all right-thinking people will accept without question', and the timid intellectuals who self-censored in order to fit into this orthodoxy, very probably would have railed against the politically correct. (Mind you, Orwell was frequently antisemitic, racist and misogynistic, so it's possible that his views here aren't important.)

People are also resistant to the idea that speech might sit within a context, without which it cannot be properly understood. When people want to be able to say certain slurs, for example, they often cite the fact that these slurs have been 'reclaimed' by the people who were once their targets. But this is irrelevant: the fact that it is socially acceptable for some people to say some words does not mean that everyone should be allowed to do so. Words, and the way that we put them together as sentences, are not neutral tools of communication; they all carry baggage as well as meaning. And we already censor ourselves, all the time, in order to avoid causing offence or hurting people: we do not, usually, scream expletives in the middle of funerals. Words are powerful when they are put down on a page or when they become speech acts – pretending that they are 'only' words is disingenuous.

The point at which speech tips over into action is a difficult one to identify. At my least tolerant, I am tempted to argue that beliefs are only beliefs when they remain inside someone's head; when I know about your beliefs, that has crossed over into an active behaviour. This means that I do not, for example, really and truly support freedom of speech for people who wish to stand outside abortion clinics and scream insults at the people trying to go inside. I don't care about the freedom of speech of people who make placards showing foetuses and labelling abortion doctors murderers. I have tried, as a philosophical exercise, and a political one too – as Orwell says, ban that form of protest and who knows what protest will be banned next – but I just can't bring myself to want to protect the right to do and say such violent, unpleasant things.

Freedom of speech, of course, does not mean freedom from the consequences of that speech. Much of the time, when people demand freedom of speech, what they want is the latter. They want to be able to insult people, or shout slogans, to tell deliberate untruths or incite violence, without facing any repercussions. So a demand for 'freedom of speech' has often taken on a more nebulous meaning, which is as much to do with asserting freedom from criticism as it is to do with defending the right to freedom from censorship by governments.

Trying to work out the line here is also tricky: a government can hardly claim that its citizens have freedom of speech by arguing that people are free to say anything they like but that they might be imprisoned for their words. But at the same time, there is a need to balance one person's freedoms against another's well-being. There is also a requirement to think critically about degrees of freedom and degrees of harm: someone's personal freedoms are not infringed that severely because they cannot say the n-word, and the violence behind the word is such that it is worth giving up some freedom to keep people safe from harm.

There also needs to be a clear understanding of how and why people weaponise demands for free speech. Why do some figures find the call for freedom of speech so seductive? Why is it some people's automatic get-out-of-jail-free card? How do some ideological fights descend into battles over the meaning of free speech, rather than the initial topic under discussion, and how can this be avoided or worked out? This book focuses on the balancing of free speech rights and the ways in which free speech rights are increasingly invoked to try to defend speech or behaviour that should be critiqued or challenged.

As somebody who is currently working in a British university as an academic, I have watched the free speech wars with interest and trepidation. Universities and academia have become spaces in which debates around freedom of speech are increasingly focused.

Some of the key spaces and concepts around which British freedom of speech arguments have coalesced – 'safe spaces', 'trigger warnings' and 'no-platforming' – are seen as newly central to university life. A safe space is one in which a particular vulnerable group can feel secure: so, for example, spaces for the support of victims of sexual violence, or of racial prejudice. The idea is that these people might want to come together and have conversations without, for example, someone turning up who wants to argue from the perspective of the rapist or the racist. Trigger warnings are a clinical tool that allows survivors of trauma to avoid being 'triggered' into re-experiencing that trauma. Teachers, therefore, often use trigger warnings or 'content notes' to highlight when a book or film being used in a class includes depictions of upsetting topics. This is exactly the same as the announcement that points up 'adult content' or 'strong language' in a TV show, or the short text descriptions on a film's age-rating certificate. Both of these feel, to me, fairly non-controversial, but they have been heralded as proof that we are educating a new generation of 'snowflake' students, who cannot handle their views being challenged or their ideas being undermined.

In fact, both policies are aimed at being as inclusive as possible and allowing as many people as possible to participate in conversations. Trigger warnings, certainly, do not stop anybody from being allowed to say anything: rather, they help people who might be affected negatively by that speech to prepare themselves or choose not to expose themselves to that material. Safe spaces prevent people from speaking about a topic in a particular setting, but they do not prevent people from having these conversations in other places, and they only exclude people in order to better enable vulnerable groups to speak freely.

No-platforming means refusing to provide a platform for a speaker because of their views or affiliations. Student unions are especially implicated in this: for example, refusing to platform speakers who have expressed racist, homophobic or transphobic views. Often this leads to a debate about whether these views are acceptable, as well as a wider discussion about whether students can police the views and words of people in this way. The point is, of course, that nobody has a particular right to speak in a particular place, especially not a private space. I remain, as yet, sadly uninvited from giving the keynote speech at the Conservative Party conference or presenting the Oscars, but this does not mean that either organisation has actually no-platformed me. Questions might be raised about which groups within (for example) student unions are dominant, and who gets to invite or disinvite speakers; but the fundamental act of not inviting a speaker is not itself an assault on free speech. Efforts to address this have descended into the farcical: proposals to ban student unions from 'no-platforming' raised the spectre of every student union in Britain having to host every person in the world to speak on any topic they desire.

The other point to make here is that I have encountered all three of these topics far more frequently off campus than on it: the only place, in fact, where I have seen safe spaces discussed in detail has been in the British press, despite having worked in British universities for over a decade. There are absolutely limits and threats to free speech in British academia, but they are not the tabloid spectres haunting campuses; right-wing journalists digging up academics' personal opinions, university administrators monitoring their lecturers' tweets, and the Prevent duty turning academics into Home Office police are far more pernicious.

Orwell dismissed liberal qualms about whether free speech is possible as unconvincing. But it is perfectly legitimate to question whether it is possible for us to live in a world that grants freedom of speech to every person equally. This is especially true when we start to probe into what 'speech' actually entails in this context.

Orwell did not want the right only to speak, as such: he was arguing for the right to write, and not only to write, but to be published. His argument that even bad books get published, even those full of 'scurrility and slipshod writing', might be comforting or enraging to many budding writers. But of course, not every book gets published, or at least not by a prestigious publishing house, not because of censorship but because publishing is an extremely competitive industry and book contracts are not simply handed out to everybody who wants them. In 2017 Simon and Schuster dropped Milo Yiannopoulos's $255,000 book contract when a recording came to light that appeared to reveal the author endorsing paedophilia, and Yiannopoulos subsequently sued the publishers, saying that they should 'pay for silencing conservatives and libertarians'.[12] But this claim of silencing was complicated by the leaking of the editorial notes on the manuscript, which described the book as 'unclear, unfunny' and 'a sea of self-aggrandisement and scattershot thinking'.[13] It is unclear why a book described in such terms – by its own editor – was deserving of publication in the first place.

Not everybody writes a book; not everybody has the cultural or social capital to do so, or to get their book published, or publicised. If everyone has the theoretical right to freedom of speech, not everybody has the actual ability to be heard. And it is a truism that the people complaining that their freedom of speech has been attacked or denied are often the ones with the loudest voices and biggest platforms.

In 2017 Bruce Gilley, an associate professor of political science at Portland State University, published a piece in the academic journal

Third World Quarterly entitled 'The Case for Colonialism'. In it, Gilley called for the 'orthodoxy' that gave Western colonialism 'a bad name' to be questioned and instead argued that empires had been 'both objectively beneficial and subjectively legitimate'.[14] The piece was met with a furious response; fifteen members of the editorial board of *Third World Quarterly* resigned and a petition asking for a retraction from the journal garnered over 7,000 signatures. And the article was, indeed, removed from the journal website: not because of its controversial content, but because its publication apparently led to 'serious and credible threats of violence' against the editor.[15]

In an editorial for *The Times* in November 2017, headlined 'Don't Feel Guilty About Our Colonial History', an Oxford professor of theology, Nigel Biggar, defended Gilley's 'courageous' intervention, argued that the history of the British Empire was 'morally mixed' and concluded with a call for the British to 'moderate' their 'post-imperial guilt'.[16] He also announced a new research project, with himself at the head, which would explore the 'ethics' of empire and seek to learn lessons from imperialism that could be applied to the modern world. (Nigel Biggar is also one of the directors of the Free Speech Union.) Imperial historians reading this project proposal were baffled and angry. An open letter, signed by 58 historians from the University of Oxford, set out some key objections. It was, they argued, ill-conceived, ignorant and deeply problematic: why would an academic project seek to rehabilitate empire in this way? What possible lessons about, for example, 'the cohesion of multicultural societies' could be drawn from the violent and exploitative histories of imperialism?[17] This letter was interpreted by some as an attack on Biggar's freedom of speech; a *Daily Mail* article referred to the letter as an act of 'collective online bullying' and described Biggar as the 'latest in a long line of eminent academics to be shamed online for expressing their views'.[18]

Biggar is keen to portray himself as a victim of censorship, a brave martyr set upon by political-correctness-gone-mad imperial historians who are unwilling to countenance alternative viewpoints. The *Daily Mail* continued its campaign by naming and shaming a cabal of 'loud mouthed, Tory-loathing, anti-Israel academics' who propagate an 'ugly totalitarianism' of safe spaces and trigger warnings.[19] But this fundamentally doesn't make any sense. Biggar has been able to share his views across a variety of media platforms, including national newspapers, and his project is still going ahead, despite the serious issues that have been raised. Historians (such as myself) who object to Biggar's research are entitled to share our critiques of his ideas and his practice, and – given the political context – do so at risk of personal attack from an often hostile media, which is quick to interpret any critique of British history as a criticism of Britain today. But by crying out that his 'free speech' has been threatened, Biggar has rallied a portion of the press to his defence, and has succeeded in gaining an even larger platform for his views.

There are lessons to be learned from this; Orwell, with all his empire apologism, might argue again that it shows that it is the 'liberals who fear liberty and intellectuals who want to do dirt on the intellect'.[20] But the lessons I draw from this is that free speech is often only available to those who are already powerful; that the people who shout loudest about their speech being denied are still, at the end of the day, the ones whose voices carry furthest. Freedom of speech is an essential right and a powerful duty, but it is not the only thing that matters; the free speech wars are taking part on a much wider cultural battleground.

The book

This book is split into four sections. First, it considers some of the threats to free speech historically and in the present day, and some of the efforts that have been or are being made to protect it. How has the freedom of speech been contested and challenged throughout history? What are the longer roots of claims to freedom of speech? Jodie Ginsberg, the former CEO of Index on Censorship, opens this section with a powerful defence of the right to free speech, and a call for people to work harder to defend it in practice as well as in principle. Ed Packard explores the history of Speakers' Corner in Hyde Park, and argues that a historical space for freedom of speech has become a meta battleground for the alt-right. Sam Popowich examines how the issue of 'de-platforming' writers and speakers has exposed a significant rift among librarians and library communities. Emma Harvey develops these ideas, by exploring some of the practical issues around free speech through her experience of running a community arts centre. Victoria Stiles examines the history of Nazi publishing policies to explain how controlling the publication of ideas and arguments can be just as destructive to freedom of speech as burning books. Finally, Andrew Phemister examines the history of the 'boycott', and argues that, far from limiting freedom, the ability to enact boycotts is in fact a vital tool within democracies.

Second, it explores some of the ways that claims to free speech can be critiqued and challenged. How has 'free speech' been weaponised? When is it a claim made in bad faith? This section begins with Omar Khan, the former head of the Runnymede Trust, exploring how anti-racist activists can support freedom of speech, while simultaneously rejecting the premise that racists themselves are merely upholding or defending these freedoms. Neville Morley examines how Socrates is evoked in debates around freedom of speech and what the people who wish to identify themselves as 'Socratic' are really trying to achieve. Imen Neffati examines the case of the attack on the *Charlie Hebdo* offices in 2015 to examine how arguments around *laïcité* have privileged some rights over others. Turning the idea of 'speaking truth to power' on its head, Nina Lyon argues that power often resists speaking truth, and shows how these tactics affect public and political discourse. Janna Kraus uses Switzerland as a case study to examine what happens when a polity believes itself to be 'neutral' in these debates. Finally, Aaron Ackerley explores media history to argue that newspapers and journalists have used claims to freedom of speech to justify unethical or morally dubious journalistic practices and to escape external oversight.

The final two sections explore two spaces in which the free speech wars are currently being fought. First, it examines the role of universities and campuses in this debate. As outlined in this introduction, the university and the space of academia more widely has a particular salience for the issue of free speech today. Shaun McDaid and Catherine McGlynn open this section with an exposition of their research into British university campuses and the Prevent duty, the counter-radicalisation measures that form part of the British Home Office's counter-terrorism strategy. Gabriel Moshenska recounts a moment when his own teaching became the centre of a 'trigger warning' controversy, and reflects on how this fits into wider media debates about academia. Grace Lavery argues that academic freedom should not be extended to the right to 'deadname' or misgender academics or students, and proposes a baseline protocol for scholarly discourse with trans and non-binary students and faculty. Paul Whickman writes about his experience in teaching a course on the history of censorship and free speech, and how to approach this topic in a way that encourages a multiplicity of voices in the classroom. Adam Standring and Daniel Cardoso use the Nova Portugalidade affair as a case study to explore how these issues play out in campus politics in Portugal. Finally, Marta Santivánez examines some of the recent British discussions around freedom of speech on university campuses, especially exploring moments when students have had their own right to speak or protest curtailed by universities themselves.

Finally, the book explores the internet as the new Wild West of free speech. Ben Whitham looks at the rise of a transnational racist, misogynist, homophobic and transphobic far-right movement, and how figures such as Jordan Peterson have used calls for freedom of speech to push this movement into new spaces seemingly beyond criticism. Henry Price considers the 'Red Pill' phenomenon to examine how men's rights activists (MRAs) have used a free speech argument to try to defend 'truths' about their reactionary gender politics. Penny Andrews examines the ways in which 'fandoms' of particular charismatic figures have become, on the internet and in the wider media, increasingly vociferous, and how they have used the freedom of speech to launch and sustain campaigns against groups that they perceive as threats. Finally, Helen Pallett explores how the promise of the internet as a 'marketplace of ideas' has created a particular context for speech acts, and argues that this metaphor has in fact become increasingly unhelpful as a democratic ideal.

This book is intended not just a set of empirical chapters about contexts and events, but as an intervention that attempts to help the reader navigate the debates in this culture war. Not every chapter shares the same perspective: in fact, the authors frequently disagree among themselves about these issues. But what this book hopes to make clear is that this is not a binary issue, and nor is it one that can be rationalised out of existence; people's feelings about this topic are as important as their arguments. We need, above all, to be wary about how this debate is being weaponised, and to be suspicious – or at least sceptical – of the claims that people are making. I hope that this intervention might help to equip readers, not necessarily to take a specific side in or route out of this free speech war, but to understand the shape of the terrain, and to defend themselves and aid others where needed.

Notes

1 Ashley Cowburn, 'Toby Young deletes thousands of tweets amid row over his universities regulator appointment', *The Independent*, 3 January 2013, https://www.independent.co.uk/news/uk/politics/toby-young-twit ter-delete-tweets-universities-regulator-appointment-ofs-office-for-stu dents-a8139841.html (accessed 10 July 2020).
2 'About', Free Speech Union, https://freespeechunion.org/about/ (accessed 10 July 2020).
3 'Statement of Values', Free Speech Union, https://freespeechunion.org/about/statement-of-values/ (accessed 10 July 2020).
4 George Orwell, 'The Freedom of the Press', c. 1945, proposed preface to *Animal Farm*, *Times Literary Supplement*, 15 September 1972, https://www.orwellfoundation.com/the-orwell-foundation/orwell/essays-and-other-works/the-freedom-of-the-press/ (accessed 10 July 2020).
5 Ibid.
6 Ibid.
7 George Orwell, 'England, Your England', in *The Lion and the Unicorn: Socialism and the English Genius* (London: Searchlight Books, 1941), https://www.orwellfoundation.com/the-orwell-foundation/orwell/essa ys-and-other-works/the-lion-and-the-unicorn-socialism-and-the-engl ish-genius/ (accessed 10 July 2020).
8 Orwell, 'The Freedom of the Press'.
9 The United Nations, Universal Declaration of Human Rights (1948), https://www.un.org/en/universal-declaration-human-rights/ (accessed 10 July 2020).
10 Ibid.
11 'GenForward July 2017 Toplines', Gen Forward, University of Chicago, http://genforwardsurvey.com/data/ (accessed 10 July 2020).

12   Clark Mindock, 'Milo Yiannopoulous sues Simon & Schuster for can-
     celling his book deal: "They have to pay for silencing conservatives"',
     The Independent, 11 July 2017, https://www.independent.co.uk/news/
     world/americas/us-politics/milo-yiannopoulos-sues-simon-schuster-da
     ngerous-book-deal-cancellation-court-a7835766.html (accessed 10 July
     2020).
13   Martin Belam, '"Unclear, unfunny, delete": editor's notes on Milo
     Yiannopoulos book revealed', *The Guardian*, 28 December 2017, https://
     www.theguardian.com/books/2017/dec/28/unclear-unfunny-delete-edit
     ors-notes-on-milo-yiannopoulos-book-revealed (accessed 10 July 2020).
14   Bruce Gilley, 'The case for colonialism', *Third World Quarterly*, https://
     doi.org/10.1080/01436597.2017.1369037 (accessed 10 July 2020). As this
     article has now been withdrawn from publication, this reference is to
     the withdrawal notice.
15   Ibid.
16   Nigel Biggar, 'Don't feel guilty about our colonial history', *The Times*,
     30 November 2017, https://www.thetimes.co.uk/article/don-t-feel-gu
     ilty-about-our-colonial-history-ghvstdhmj (accessed 10 July 2020).
17   'Ethics and empire: an open letter from Oxford scholars', *The
     Conversation*, 19 December 2017, http://theconversation.com/ethics-
     and-empire-an-open-letter-from-oxford-scholars-89333 (accessed 10
     July 2020).
18   Eleanor Harding, 'Oxford academics accused of bullying Empire-
     defending don', *Daily Mail*, 21 December 2017, https://www.dailymail.
     co.uk/news/article-5200381/Oxford-academics-accused-bullying-Empi
     re-defending-don.html (accessed 10 July 2020).
19   Guy Adams, 'Oxford University is home to Tory-loathing, anti-Israel
     academics', *Daily Mail*, 23 December 2017, https://www.dailymail.co.uk/
     news/article-5207687/Oxford-home-Tory-loathing-anti-Israel-academi
     cs.html (accessed 10 July 2020).
20   Orwell, 'The Freedom of the Press'.

Protecting freedom of speech

1

Protecting the freedom of speech

Jodie Ginsberg

Freedom of speech is in peril. It is facing an unprecedented pincer movement in which governments and big business are ramping up greater controls on private speech while populist and nationalist movements – intolerant of expressions of difference and dissent – are on the rise worldwide. At the same time, the traditional opponents of censorship are becoming its greatest cheerleaders – seeing in restrictions over speech a means to achieve tolerance, inclusion and the genuine diverse representation of voices at all levels of society that remains sorely lacking.

How did we get here? For most people, even in the twenty-first century when censorship has taken on so many new and varied forms, censorship still largely conjures images of state control of speech: the banning of independent newspapers, the control of music, of theatre and of art. When Index on Censorship was founded in London in 1972, state censorship of the theatre in the United Kingdom had only just ended. A new liberalism was being introduced in western Europe but authoritarianism loomed large elsewhere. Franco was still in power in Spain, Greece was ruled by a military junta, and

Soviet authoritarian rule dominated eastern Europe. Indeed, Index was created in response to a request from Soviet dissidents who asked what their counterparts in the West could do to support those facing censorship behind the Iron Curtain.

For the next twenty-five years, pro-democracy movements campaigned to end these oppressive regimes, regimes that were all characterised by their brutal suppression of free speech. In 1989, with the fall of the Berlin Wall and the ending of apartheid in South Africa, so enthusiastic were some Index supporters that they genuinely believed the organisation would no longer be needed. Authoritarian regimes appeared to be collapsing from South America to south-east Asia. With their fall, it was thought censorship would collapse too.

For a brief period, democracy – and with it the plurality of voices that is the characteristic of a flourishing democracy – flowered. But 1989 did not mark the end of authoritarian regimes. And one of the hallmarks of the past decade has been growing authoritarianism within supposed democracies, authoritarianism that is characterised by increasing suppression of speech. The example most often cited is Turkey: a democracy that is also the world's largest jailer of journalists. It is a country where insulting the president can end in a prison sentence. But Turkey is by no means the only democracy that in recent years has clamped down on free speech in the name of protecting its population or for the promotion of supposed societal harmony. Using laws meant to deal with terrorists, countries from Australia to the UK are using national security powers in a way that could seriously impinge on the media's ability to investigate matters of national importance. Laws meant to deal with hate speech, harmful speech online and fake news in countries from Singapore to Germany are already scooping up political criticism and satire. Even the United States, which prides itself on being the flag bearer for free speech, demonstrates less than unfettered commitment to freedom of expression when its leader sees fit to brand the press as the 'enemies of the people'.

Meanwhile, authoritarian states such as China and Saudi Arabia continue to exercise more traditional means to suppress critics. The murder of journalist Jamal Khashoggi by agents of the Saudi government in 2018 indicated how far some governments are still willing to go to silence their opponents. The fact he was murdered on Turkish soil – and with no resulting international sanction on Saudi Arabia – indicates how perilous the situation for free speech is globally.

It might seem counterintuitive that freedom of expression should be under threat at a time when we have more ways to communicate than ever before. The rise of the internet was heralded – like the pro-democracy movements of the 1980s before it – as a great democratic tool. Certainly, it has provided platforms through which minority groups can exercise their rights to speak and organise as never before. Anonymity has allowed gay rights campaigners, religious minorities and political activists to speak out in countries where to do so publicly would mean jail – or death. Relatively low financial barriers to entry have enabled a host of new voices to access global audiences in a way that was unimaginable even a decade ago.

Yet this unfettered, and largely unmoderated, marketplace of voices has also unleashed hateful speech. It has created an environment in which a crass joke intended for a small audience can go viral and reach thousands within minutes. Until very recently, this vast internet content was largely regulated by social media platforms themselves through terms of service. Users signed up to rules (that most people never read) and the platforms were responsible for ensuring users followed those rules.

Initially, it seemed like there were no rules. Abusive material – racist, homophobic and misogynistic content – was everywhere, and with apparently little way to stop it. Now, we are swinging in the other direction as social media companies – nervous about government regulation and the prospect of swingeing fines for anyone who fails to deal with harmful content – introduce new rules on an almost daily basis in an effort to clean up discourse online.

We should be careful what we wish for. The growing power of social media platforms to control what we say has profound implications for social discourse. It not only allows unelected corporations to be the final arbiters of 'good speech', but it also creates a mob mentality in which the majority opinion on any platform risks becoming the ultimate censor. Nor are technical solutions to be embraced without serious caution. The volume of content being uploaded and shared on social media every day means it is impossible for human beings to sort every item of content for potential harm, and so algorithms take this on. This has already led to anti-racism campaigners having their Facebook accounts suspended for calling out the abuse they received, to women's rights campaigners being suspended from Twitter for raising concerns about new government proposals on gender recognition, and to human rights groups having videos documenting war removed for having violated policies related to violent content.

The confusion over what content should and should not be removed is not just a result of a machine's inability to understand nuance. Rather this confusion is reflective of a wider confusion about what does and does not constitute free speech, both legally and morally. What we are permitted to say – by law, or by our social media provider's terms of service – is often poorly understood, including by those who enforce the law. And beyond the legal barriers and protections for freedom of expression, there are widely differing opinions among all sectors of the population about what we should and should not be able to say in public. This confusion is manifest in the

UK laws that cover so-called 'hate speech'. It is illegal in the UK to stir up hatred against a person or group based on certain protected characteristics, such as race, religious beliefs or sexual orientation, but views on precisely what constitutes the 'threatening, abusive or insulting words or behaviour' that might denote stirring up of hatred differ widely.

Labelling someone as a person who engages in 'hate speech' – regardless of whether they have been found to be so in law – is now a common way of discrediting anyone with difficult or opposing views. This has seeped into discourse into universities, where individuals who express opinions that one group on campus has deemed 'hateful' are disinvited from speaking. Women's rights campaigners such as Julie Bindel and human rights activists such as Maryam Namazie are among those who have been no-platformed in this way.

This labelling of individuals extends way beyond the denial of a platform, however. Individuals are also being reported to employers for lawfully expressing their own opinions: freelancers in the arts in particular report a growing number of incidences in which they are accused – often anonymously – of 'hateful' speech and then find work cancelled. In 2019 a Christian actress was dropped from the lead role of *The Color Purple* at Birmingham Hippodrome because of comments she made about homosexuality, and an Asda worker was sacked (although subsequently reinstated) after sharing a Billy Connolly video on his personal Facebook page that a colleague considered Islamophobic.

Undoubtedly, too many hurdles exist to ensuring that all voices have an equal chance to be heard. In the media, in the arts, in academia there is still a woeful lack of diverse voices and decision makers. It would be wrong to focus on issues such a no-platforming as the leading censorship challenge in countries such as the UK. We need to pay more attention to the very many avenues through which voices are silenced, not least in considering how government policies such as Prevent – in which universities and others are mandated to prevent people being draw into terrorism – impact individuals' willingness and ability to express themselves.

However, addressing these imbalances through censorship is not the answer. Indeed, the greatest threat to our free speech at present might not be growing global authoritarianism or populism, but rather the abandoning of their posts by the traditional defenders of free speech. In 2015 twelve people were murdered at the offices of French satirical magazine *Charlie Hebdo* by religious extremists. Immediately following the killing, politicians, political commentators and artists from across the political spectrum declared their solidarity, quick to proclaim 'Je Suis Charlie' (I am Charlie) and their belief in free speech. But in the five years since, we have seen fewer and fewer people willing to speak out in defence of views with which they disagree: views that shock, offend or disturb. And we have seen more and more people – in the name of tolerance – call for laws and regulations that would not only silence those who incite violence, but a broad sweep of individuals who simply disagree with another's point of view.

This has created a vacuum into which those with extremist – and intolerant – views have stepped and cloaked themselves in the mantle of free speech. In abandoning its traditional defence of free speech, those on the political left and liberal spectrum have allowed 'free speech' to become the rallying cry of the far right, of all those who would use free speech to shut down the speech of others. In so doing, freedom of speech has become a dirty word.

Freedom of expression needs to be reclaimed as a good. Free speech – which must include views that others find offensive, troubling, even hateful if it is to mean anything at all, needs to find new and varied champions from all sides of the political spectrum.

We need to reignite a dialogue about the value and importance of freedom of expression in building a more tolerant and inclusive society – and we need to do this by raising up the voices of those who are not heard. Index on Censorship sought to do this with a scheme launched in 2019 called 'Free Speech Is For Me', which brought together individuals from diverse political and cultural backgrounds to debate the value of freedom of expression, and discuss what being able to talk openly meant to them. We gave individuals a 'safe space' (which, like 'free speech', is a phrase that has been much abused of late) to talk taboos, and to disagree.

Free speech is not simply a theory. It is a principle that can be proved in practice. And, like most things, it can be improved with practice. To do this, we must defend it. Without free speech, the rest is silence. For all of us.

2

Open-air free speech: the past, present and future of Speakers' Corner

Edward Packard

For most of the week Speakers' Corner in London's Hyde Park is an unremarkable expanse of concrete paving, railings and trees near the Marble Arch. On Sundays the site is transformed by crowds of regulars, tourists and curious passers-by, who gather around the platforms of numerous orators to listen, heckle and debate. It becomes a noisy and fluid place: audience members can become speakers, and vice versa. Crucially, anybody is permitted a platform without having to obtain prior permission. The tradition originated in the nineteenth century and since then the site has maintained a curious and paradoxical identity. On the one hand, those who speak there are frequently stigmatised as eccentric or mentally ill. For example, George Orwell wrote in 1945 that he had encountered 'a large variety of plain lunatics' speaking in the park. As a result, much of what is said there is deemed trivial by mainstream opinion. On the other hand, Speakers' Corner is a powerful and celebrated symbol of free speech, often used to support perceived notions of British tolerance and democracy. Orwell described it as 'one of the minor wonders of the world' and noted that he had known continental European visitors to be 'astonished and even perturbed by the things they had heard Indian or Irish Nationalists saying about the British Empire'.[1] More recently, in a 2014 speech to the Houses of Parliament, the German Chancellor Angela Merkel recalled her first visit to London in 1990, shortly after the fall of the Berlin Wall: 'We walked through Hyde Park looking for Speakers' Corner, which – especially for us as East Germans – was legendary, the very symbol of free speech.' Perhaps aware of the other side of its reputation, she added: 'I hope that is not an insult to you, the members of the British Parliament.'[2]

Speakers' Corner has also become a peculiarly 'meta' battle-ground in the free speech wars. Madsen Pirie, the founder of the neoliberal Adam Smith Institute, blogged in 2019 that '[y]ou can stand on a soapbox and say what you like at Speakers' Corner, but if you try to do that at most UK universities, people will stop you'.[3] Pirie blamed this situation on 'snowflakes' rather than the (hope-fully) obvious differences between Hyde Park and higher education institutions. The far-right activist Stephen Yaxley-Lennon, known as Tommy Robinson, is no stranger to campus bans and has capitalised on Speakers' Corner's symbolic value as part of his supposed crusade for 'free speech'. In reality, the far right and alt-right are using 'free speech' as a somewhat hypocritical cloak for their extreme politi-cal agendas. For instance, when Yaxley-Lennon spoke at Speakers' Corner in March 2018 his speech was written by Martin Sellner, the Austrian leader of the anti-Islam and anti-immigrant group Generation Identity, who had been refused entry into the UK the previous week.[4] A placard wielded by a supporter in the crowd, bear-ing the slogan 'Censor Islam, Not Speech', encapsulated the tone of the heavily policed and disorderly gathering. The criminologist Dev Maitra witnessed the event and suggested '[w]e have now created a vacuum in which the polemicists, the extremists, the contrarians can all claim victory by shouting, or booing, the loudest'. He contrasted this with a previous visit in 2004, when he had observed how 'spontaneous debates abound in Speakers' Corner, something so fundamental to a working democracy'.[5] Similarly, the journalist Hussein Kesvani likens present-day Speakers' Corner to a 'real-life 4chan' (a chaotic website linked to the alt-right).[6] Supporters of the radical Islamist Anjem Choudary, including some connected to terrorists, have also spoken in the park in recent years.[7] These developments have all contributed to the sense, articulated by many of the Corner's regular attendees, that the tradition of free speech in Hyde Park is in decline.

If Speakers' Corner has been hijacked by extremists who exercise free speech there without believing in the right of others to do so, is the future of this famous landmark in peril? In order to understand the present situation, and what is at stake, it is necessary to delve into the site's history – or histories. For Speakers' Corner, as a heritage site and tourist attraction, has become associated with a specific historical narrative, which is used to amplify and preserve its powerful symbolic reputation. This has two dimensions: the first draws attention to the vast number of public hangings at the Tyburn gallows, near the Corner's present location, which occurred between the twelfth and eighteenth centuries. The condemned were traditionally allowed to make a final speech from the platform.[8] The second dimension focuses on a series of mass political demonstrations held at Hyde Park in the mid-nineteenth century, particularly the 1855 Sunday trading protest, which Karl Marx reported on, and the 1866 Reform League meeting, when a large crowd pushed down the railings to gain access to the park after the police closed the gates.[9] Such 'monster' meetings were usually publicised in advance by organising committees, and often occurred without the consent of the authorities or in direct violation of official prohibitions. Some passed off peacefully, but several involved violence from the crowd and police.

In response, the government sought to regulate future meetings. A lengthy debate in Parliament and the press ensued, while Hyde Park itself hosted a demonstration against the government's 'tyrannical' proposals.[10] Eventually, the 1872 Royal Parks and Gardens Regulation Act introduced the concept of park rules for public addresses. Today a paving stone near Speakers' Corner commemorates the Act as allowing 'for regulations governing free speech in Hyde Park'.

Although the government intended the new regulations to deal with mass meetings, often involving tens of thousands of people in a large open area of the park, the Act has become firmly associated with the emergence of Speakers' Corner. It is a compelling narrative: the masses winning the right to meet and speak in what was increasingly viewed as 'the people's park' rather than the aristocratic playground of previous generations. There are two problems with this interpretation. First, the phrasing of the 1872 Act was prohibitive rather than permissive: it stated that no public address was permitted unless it was in accordance with the park rules. The right to speak was not entirely forced from below, but continued to be regulated – and policed – from above.[11] Second, this narrative does not explain how the specific tradition of Speakers' Corner emerged. Undoubtedly the Act's provisions helped it take root, but there are important differences between occasional mass political demonstrations and the smaller, more idiosyncratic types of regular meeting held at the Corner. The history of the latter is hard to ascertain: big protests and government decision making leave significant marks in the historical record, while Speakers' Corner orators appear less frequently, as a relatively marginal phenomenon. Theirs is a fragmented story but enough material survives to force a reassessment of the traditional narrative of the site's origins.

Speakers' Corner emerged out of a voracious appetite for oratory across the social spectrum of Victorian London. According to the historian Anna Davin, outdoor debate provided 'a significant form of intellectual activity for numbers of people, especially in London's poorest quarters and in parks to which the poor had access'.[12] It also reflected what the political scientist Stephen Coleman has identified as a historic 'common regard for the public space as a free site for the unofficial communication of ideas for which no other forum existed'.[13] Before the main protest at the 1855 Sunday trading demonstration, parts of the crowd 'divided into little knots of listening spectators around groups of orators, who held forth upon what they called this fresh attempt to crush the industrious classes'.[14] Later that year, in possibly the earliest recorded example of a Speakers' Corner-style marketplace of ideas in Hyde Park, several thousand people listened to a number of orators scattered around the park as part of a series of Sunday meetings protesting bread prices. According to *The Times*, one man described proceedings as a 'Jackdaw's parliament'. The newspaper suggested that 'everybody tried to talk and nobody listened, because in point of fact, nobody had anything to say worth listening to'.[15] Disorderly conduct prompted a police crackdown on the use of Hyde Park as a popular forum, although further meetings on political issues occurred in 1859, with the crowd, on occasion, forming into smaller discussion groups.

At the same time, religious preachers attempted to use Hyde Park. For example, the Revd Thomas Crybbace, worried about the influence of continental 'Popery and Despotism', repeatedly petitioned the government for permission to preach in the London parks.[16] In 1859 the Ministry of Works, which was responsible for the Royal Parks, presciently argued that allowing the 'principles of religious freedom would necessitate the expansion of such permission to Professors of all Creeds and Opinions, and thus the parks would become the scene of polemical strife, if not attacks upon religion'.[17] Yet after William Cowper became Minister of Works in 1860, he

allowed preachers to use Hyde Park unless they used 'shocking language' or 'blasphemy'.[18] The park therefore became part of the battle
for hearts and minds that raged between noisy 'infidel' orators and
establishment clergy across the open spaces of mid-nineteenth-
century London.[19] Cowper later explained that he had hoped that the
'mental exercise' of public discussion would 'produce good results,
and that truth would prevail'.[20]

Cowper's policy catalysed the embryonic Speakers' Corner, with
the *Morning Chronicle* lamenting in August 1860 that Hyde Park
had become 'the arena of political, religious and social discussion'.[21]
The following summer, the author James Payn wrote: 'You see the
knots of people scattered up and down yonder: each has its favourite
orator; and a frequenter of the place knows pretty well what tenets
are being inculcated by the position occupied by each.' Regular
speakers became part of the park's fabric, with 'the Infidel tree, and
the Mormon bench, and the bare spot of ground where the people
collect around the Temperance man who preaches from the top of
his friend's shoulders'.[22] Entertaining or notorious individuals drew
large crowds. On a Sunday in September 1860 at least one thousand people gathered around the radical orator Samuel Owen, who
possessed a powerful voice, while several other speakers attracted
audiences of up to eight hundred people.[23] Orators fielded serious
questions, dealt with humorous heckles, and argued against rival
platforms. Audiences might not have agreed with the speakers' idiosyncratic views, but they certainly provided intellectual stimulation
and entertainment.

Much of the contemporary printed commentary on park oratory
was layered with condescension. Accent, grammar, pronunciation
and vocabulary were easy targets for professional writers, and the
Saturday Review was not atypical in describing speakers as 'fervid
but ungrammatical apostles'.[24] The dropped aspirate attracted

frequent comment. For example, James Payn remarked of a temperance lecturer: '[w]hat power there is in simple truth, even when the man who presents it leaves out his *hs*!'[25] Whatever criticisms were levelled at Hyde Park speakers, they had to be interesting to compete against rival platforms. Their audiences, whether cheering, heckling, laughing, asking questions or quietly listening, were engaged and empowered, and speakers had to be prepared to clarify or defend their views. The crowds browsed and sampled different speakers and, by mingling in an atmosphere of open discussion, were able to learn about and critique different views and the people who held them. Hyde Park oratory in the early 1860s was therefore not dissimilar to what eventually became known as Speakers' Corner.

Contemporary commentators generally did not perceive individual political speakers as a revolutionary threat and some argued that permitting the airing of radical views constituted a safety valve, or 'an instance of that freedom which a form of government too secure for fear can venture to permit'.[26] Unorthodox religious speakers prompted greater anxiety: not only did they diminish 'real religion', but their brimstone and indecorum provided an easy target for socialist speakers, who could potentially 'win for infidelity and error the greatest triumph of the whole'.[27] On the other hand, Payn suggested that the 'healthy love of religious liberty makes the people dislike an orator who attacks anybody's faith' and quoted comments from a strident atheist's audience: 'Why don't he let other people bide? Why, that 'ere beggar flies at everybody!'[28]

A Hyde Park demonstration in support of Italian unification ended in disorder and violence in October 1862. The police prohibited any further 'public discussion of popular and exciting topics' in London's parks, and the nascent Speakers' Corner was temporarily halted.[29] The government used the prohibition to ban the Reform

League meeting at Hyde Park in 1866 but, as that demonstration showed, the state could not indefinitely prevent people from meeting and speaking in open spaces where the habit had taken root.[30] The government began to move away from the unworkable prohibition and towards the 1872 Parks Regulation Act. Political and religious speakers continued to use Hyde Park and, by the start of the twentieth century, they were a well-established tradition. The author Ethel Tweedie wrote in 1908: 'You will find them at the same spots year in year out, proclaiming theology or agnosticism, socialism, and a dozen other "isms," beating the air with their fists, exhausting their physical powers by gesticulating, and not infrequently shouting repartees at one another.'[31]

An awareness of this early history of Speakers' Corner, or what might be called the 'eccentric' narrative, prompts a reassessment of the perceived difficulties facing the site today. In the first place, it challenges the notion that Speakers' Corner is a shadow of its former self. Both the Royal Parks, who manage Hyde Park, and contemporary Speakers' Corner regulars, two groups who rarely agree on much else, typically locate the site's origins within the symbolic and somewhat romanticised radical political narrative of the Tyburn martyrs, Karl Marx and the Reform League.[32] This grand history naturally casts the present-day Speakers' Corner in a less spectacular light. If more attention was given to the 'eccentric' narrative revealed in this chapter, the obvious historical continuities could challenge declinist arguments by showing the important role played by marginalised and obscure figures in Speakers' Corner's history. For instance, the long-ignored but crucial role of religious speech in the site's origins undermines the argument that the rise of religious speakers in recent decades has contributed to the Corner's decline. The use of Hyde Park by extremists and others with fringe beliefs, who are unable to access platforms elsewhere, perhaps signifies that it continues to fulfil its historic function as a safety valve. It is also worth indicating that exaggerated reports of the site's decline have been issued regularly since at least the 1930s, when the popular orator Bonar Thompson, bemoaning the rising tide of left-wing 'scummunist' speakers, suggested that the site was no longer the 'speakers' paradise' of the previous century.[33]

It is certainly a valid concern that radical Islamic speakers and the far right are weaponising Speakers' Corner, not least by undermining the traditional relationship between speakers and their audiences. Violence, whether threatened or explicit, undermines the exercise of free speech although it does echo the historical scenes of disorder that accompanied some of the larger organised Hyde Park demonstrations. In this regard, the March 2018 Yaxley-Lennon meeting was clearly not an attempt to spark genuine debate in the spirit of Speakers' Corner, but rather a publicity stunt, faintly echoing Oswald Mosley's 1934 British Union of Fascists rally in Hyde Park. For all of Yaxley-Lennon's complaints of being silenced, he claimed that his speech was broadcast to 45,000 people online.[34] Indeed, the internet, and particularly social media, have transformed Speakers' Corner. In particular, YouTube hosts countless hours of amateur video from the site. As one regular has observed, 'what happens at Speakers' doesn't stay at Speakers' like it did before'.[35] Yet this is arguably an evolution of an existing trend: in the nineteenth century journalists and writers reported on Hyde Park oratory, followed by analogue sound and video recording in the twentieth century. Speakers' Corner will have to evolve and adapt to twenty-first-century technology.

The most crucial issue in terms of the future of Speakers' Corner is the continued tension between those who use the site and the authorities who are responsible for it. While mid-nineteenth-century governments felt that the parks were not suitable venues for oratory, they ultimately could not contain popular enthusiasm for the speakers who frequented them. Public spaces must continue to exist in the digital age, where people can meet and talk face-to-face, and experience all the nuances of tone, expression and all the non-verbal cues that are often absent from social media communication. Such spaces might also help combat alienation and loneliness. While it is almost unthinkable that the government would ban Speakers' Corner, the authorities can make it more difficult to speak there. A recent campaign, led by Heiko Khoo, a Marxist speaker and Hyde Park veteran, contended that the Royal Parks has 'by intent or incompetence systematically undermined Speakers' Corner'. Complaints included allegations of a reduction in the size of the speaking area, and an assertion that a lack of policing had encouraged intolerance and violence.[36] The Corner also overlaps with an area used for large concerts in the summer and these commercial ventures are typically prioritised over the historic tradition of public oratory. These points raise important questions about who really 'owns' Speakers' Corner and highlight issues surrounding access to and use of public space for gathering, speaking, listening and debate. It is hard to sympathise with controversial public figures who claim to have been 'no platformed' when their grievances are amplified by tens of thousands of people online, but restricting access to Speakers' Corner genuinely robs ordinary people of a platform. The overriding concern is that the park authorities will seek to preserve Speakers' Corner as a sanitised heritage site, based on symbolic myths, rather than allowing it to evolve and adapt from below, in line with its less comfortable, yet more authentic, historical roots.

Notes

1 G. Orwell, 'Freedom of the park', in *The Collected Essays, Journalism, and Letters of George Orwell Volume IV: In Front of your Nose 1945–1950*, ed. S. Orwell and I. Angus (London: Secker and Warburg, 1968), p. 39.

2 'Speech by Federal Chancellor Angela Merkel in London', 27 February 2014, www.parliament.uk/documents/addresses-to-parliament/Angela-Merkel-address-20130227.pdf (accessed 31 January 2020).

3 M. Pirie, 'Speakers' Corner still has free speech', 14 October 2019, www.adamsmith.org/blog/speakers-corner-still-has-free-speech (accessed 19 January 2020).

4 J. Mulhall, 'Tommy Robinson delivers Generation Identity leader's speech', 19 March 2018, www.hopenothate.org.uk/2018/03/19/tommy-robinson-delivers-generation-identity-leaders-speech/ (accessed 26 January 2020).

5 D. Maitra, 'I thought that by attending a Tommy Robinson speech I could understand his arguments – but there were none, only hate', *The Independent*, 12 July 2018, www.independent.co.uk/news/long_reads/tommy-robinson-arrest-jail-leeds-breach-peace-freedom-speech-islam-edl-a8408441.html (accessed 19 January 2020).

6 H. Kesvani, 'How a historic corner of London became a real-life 4chan' (2018), www.melmagazine.com/en-us/story/how-a-historic-corner-of-london-became-a-real-life-4chan (accessed 29 January 2020).

7 K. Burgess and J. Simpson, 'Extremists hijack Speakers' Corner', *The Times*, 18 August 2018, p. 17.

8 S. Coleman, *Stilled Tongues: From Soapbox to Soundbite* (London: Porcupine Press, 1997), pp. 25–30; J. M. Roberts, 'The enigma of free speech: Speakers' Corner, the geography of governance, and a crisis of rationality', *Social and Legal Studies*, 9.2 (2000), pp. 278–82.

9 B. Harrison, 'The Sunday trading riots of 1855', *Historical Journal*, 8.2 (1965), pp. 219–45; J. M. Roberts, 'Spatial governance and working class public spheres: the case of a Chartist demonstration at Hyde Park', *Journal of Historical Sociology*, 14.3 (2001), pp. 308–36; Coleman, *Stilled Tongues*, pp. 30–7.

10 For a report of this protest, see 'Demonstration in Hyde Park', *The Times*, 4 March 1872, p. 10.

11 Roberts, 'The enigma of free speech', pp. 284–8.

12 A. Davin, 'Socialist infidels and messengers of light: street preaching

and debate in mid-nineteenth-century London', in T. Hitchcock and
H. Shore (eds), *The Streets of London: From the Great Fire to the Great
Stink* (London: Rivers Oram Press, 2003), p. 166.

13 Coleman, *Stilled Tongues*, p. 9.
14 'Demonstration in Hyde Park', *The Times*, 25 June 1855, p. 11.
15 'Meeting in Hyde Park', *The Times*, 22 October 1855, p. 8.
16 'Open air preaching in the parks', *The Times*, 17 September 1856, p. 9;
   'Park preachings', *Standard*, 29 April 1857, p. 1; The National Archives,
   London (hereafter TNA), HO 6794/1, letter from Crybbace to Derby, 13
   May 1859.
17 TNA, HO 6794/2, draft reply by Ministry of Works, 21 May 1859 (communicated 26 May 1859).
18 S. Gilley, 'The Garibaldi riots of 1862', *Historical Journal*, 16.4 (1973),
   p. 708.
19 Davin, 'Socialist infidels'.
20 *Hansard Parliamentary Debates*, 3rd series, 189 (1867), col. 388.
21 'Sunday afternoon in Hyde-Park', *Morning Chronicle*, 13 August 1860,
   p. 6.
22 'Meliboeus among the peripatetic preachers', *Chamber's Journal*, 12
   October 1861, p. 234.
23 'Hyde Park oratory', *Examiner*, 8 September 1860, p. 571.
24 'Sunday preaching in the parks', *Saturday Review*, 24 May 1862,
   p. 590.
25 'Meliboeus among the peripatetic preachers', p. 236.
26 'The Hyde Park preachings', *All The Year Round*, 27 April 1861, p. 120.
27 'Preaching in the parks', *Era*, 19 August 1860, p. 9.
28 'Meliboeus among the peripatetic preachers', p. 234.
29 Gilley, 'Garibaldi riots'.
30 Davin, 'Socialist infidels', pp. 180–1.
31 E. Tweedie (as Mrs Alec Tweedie), *Hyde Park: Its History and Romance*
   (London: Eveleigh Nash, 1908), p. 298.
32 The Royal Parks website currently promotes the Tyburn–Marx–Reform
   League–1872 Act narrative: www.royalparks.org.uk/parks/hyde-park/
   things-to-see-and-do/speakers-corner (accessed 31 January 2020). An
   archived copy of this page exists at web.archive.org/web/20191004135930/
   www.royalparks.org.uk/parks/hyde-park/things-to-see-and-do/speake
   rs-corner (accessed 31 January 2020).
33 B. Thompson, *Hyde Park Orator* (London: Jarrolds, 1934), p. 281.
34 Mulhall, 'Tommy Robinson'.

35 Y. Serhan, 'A physical public square in the digital age', *The Atlantic*, 16 September 2018, www.theatlantic.com/international/archive/2018/09/speakers-corner-london-freedom-of-speech/568963 (accessed 19 January 2020).
36 'Speakers' Corner Movement press release: Save Speakers' Corner', www.speakerscorner.net on 27 January 2020. An archived copy of this page exists at web.archive.org/web/20200103230424/www.speakerscorner.net (accessed 30 January 2020).

3

The problem of neutrality and intellectual freedom: the case of libraries

Sam Popowich

Intellectual freedom in libraries

The issue of de-platforming – the denial of a real-world or virtual public venue to controversial speakers – has exposed a significant rift in the library profession. In 2019 and 2020, for example, transphobic speakers used libraries' commitments to neutrality and intellectual freedom (the equivalent of free speech and free expression in librarianship) to disseminate views harmful to trans communities in North America. By booking rooms at public libraries these speakers leverage the trust our communities have in libraries in order to win a certain legitimacy for their views. When the community pushes back, challenging libraries to uphold values of community and equality, and when librarians themselves criticise the dominant place intellectual freedom holds in library policy, they are dismissed as confused, naive or authoritarian. James Turk, director of the Ryerson Centre for Free Expression, and one of the main exponents of intellectual freedom in Canada, argues that de-platforming is equivalent to state censorship, and that 'censoring offensive expression, attractive as it may seem, is not a road to equality or an end to marginalisation, nor does censorship ever lead to equality'.[1]

For libraries, de-platforming appears to run counter to the profession's ethics, enshrined in the core values of the American Library Association (ALA, in North America) and the Chartered Institute of Library and Informational Professionals (CILIP, in the UK). Like Turk, both the ALA and CILIP equate de-platforming with censorship, and draw no distinction between the kind of state censorship involved, say, in imprisoning dissident writers, and the bottom-up community decision to exclude particular perspectives from the legitimacy of a public forum. The legal context for what I call the 'maximalist' or 'absolutist' view of intellectual freedom derives in part from Article 19 of the Universal Declaration of Human Rights, which reads:

> Everyone has the right to freedom of opinion and expression; this right includes freedom to hold opinions without interference and to seek, receive and impart information and ideas through any media and regardless of frontiers.[2]

Additionally, both the First Amendment of the US Constitution and the Canadian Charter of Rights and Freedoms protect freedom of speech/expression from government control or censorship. While the specifics differ in both countries, there is broad agreement that some speech/expression – child pornography, for example – is not protected by either the Constitution or the Charter. Since many university libraries and most public libraries are state-run or state-funded organisations, libraries have typically seen their role as fostering an unimpeded flow of ideas, opinions and expression both as part of their core mission and as government institutions legally obliged to uphold freedom of speech/expression. In practice, this tends to give intellectual freedom primacy over all other values or ethical principles enshrined in the various codes of ethics or values statements across the profession. It should be noted that the ALA has no legal authority over anyone in the profession: the association cannot 'disbar' a librarian for violating the code of ethics or the Library Bill of Rights.

The absolutist intellectual freedom position which gives intellectual freedom priority over other values – community relations, for example – has been dominant in the profession since the 1930s when works such as John Steinbeck's *The Grapes of Wrath* were considered improper for libraries to collect.[3] The Library Bill of Rights of 1939 enshrined the absolutist position in North American librarianship, but it also gave rise to a counter-tradition, often simply called 'social responsibility'. This tendency argues that libraries have social commitments beyond the unquestioning support of unlimited speech/expression, for example to promote equality and diversity, and therefore a responsibility to exclude certain works from library collections. Periodically, the debate between the two positions comes to a head, often at times of civil and political crisis. The tension between the responsibility of librarians towards their communities – especially towards marginalised and under-represented groups – and the protection of intellectual freedom is an unresolved contradiction within the profession.

With the rise of right-wing populism across the globe, this tension has become more acute. In 2017 Toronto Public Library was criticised for allowing right-wing sympathisers to book a room to host a memorial service for a lawyer who had represented Holocaust deniers and neo-Nazis. In the wake of this criticism, Toronto Public Library changed its room-booking policy to allow denial of a booking to groups likely to provoke hate. In 2018, in an attempt to make its compliance with the First Amendment explicit, the ALA's Office of Intellectual Freedom (OIF) proposed an amendment to the ALA's own room-booking policy (on which many library policies are based) to specifically include 'hate groups' among the kinds of groups permitted to book space at public libraries. This caused outrage in the profession and, while the OIF held firm to its absolutist position, the wording change was eventually overturned.

More recently, in 2019 and 2020 Vancouver Public Library, Toronto Public Library and Seattle Public Library all came under fire for allowing 'gender-critical' or 'trans-exclusionary' women's groups to hold public lectures in library spaces. In all three cases, the libraries had prided themselves on their relations with local queer and trans communities. These communities, as well as librarians, raised concerns that by protecting the freedom of expression of people with views not just unpopular or offensive, but actively harmful to members of the community (in this case, trans people specifically), the library is seen as supporting the normalisation and spread of these views, and indirectly promoting harm to their own community.

Each of the libraries includes community relations and community-led policy making alongside intellectual freedom in their value statements, but faced with community and professional criticism, the library administrations took the usual absolutist stance, arguing that intellectual freedom took precedence over any question of community well-being or social responsibility. The libraries took great pains to explain that by providing a platform they were not condoning the views expressed by various speakers, that libraries are 'neutral', and that they are legally obliged to provide such a platform for ideas no matter how harmful (up to the limits of constitutionally protected speech). The legal obligation, however, is far from clear, and ongoing court cases are being used to determine the level of obligation.

As in many other professions – journalism, for example – the concept of neutrality has long been part of the dominant conception of the professional practice of libraries and is closely connected to the idea of intellectual freedom. However, like intellectual freedom, the purported neutrality of libraries has been challenged within the profession for just as long, typically by those who embrace a 'social justice', 'progressive' or 'critical' perspective. Librarians who tend to see libraries as organisations embedded in unjust societies (whether in terms of race, class, gender, sexuality, disability or any combination of these) argue that an adherence to 'neutrality' is at best spurious, and at worst upholds the injustice that library values claim to challenge.

However, with transphobia, a conception of intellectual freedom that takes ideology and social justice seriously would recognise that transphobia is not *accidental*, not simply a misunderstanding that can be cleared up through recourse to more information or better arguments. Rather, they are reflections of real inequalities and oppressive structures integral to capitalism. Transphobia, racism, sexism – none of these can be extinguished simply through debate or an exhortation to *think differently*. They can only be overcome through a change in economic and social relations. This poses a particular problem for librarianship, where the dominant culture is one of an apolitical neutrality.

Social responsibility

The contradiction between intellectual freedom and social responsibility – between neutrality and commitment to social justice – is often framed simply as one of competing values. For example, intellectual freedom is one of Vancouver Public Library's (VPL) core values, but so are 'community-led planning' and 'community-partnerships'. By sticking firmly to a 'neutral' stance giving priority to intellectual freedom, VPL undermines and contradicts its own community values. In response to the booking of a transphobic speaker at VPL, the Vancouver Pride Society – organisers of the city's Pride parade – banned VPL from marching as an organisation in the 2019 parade (individual library workers were allowed to participate).[4] Vancouver Pride banned the University of British Columbia (UBC) for similar reasons. The banning of VPL and UBC was divisive within the library profession. Some librarians adhered to the absolutist intellectual freedom line, suggesting that Pride was attempting to force VPL and UBC to go against their own core values. Others suggested that VPL and UBC had to weigh intellectual freedom against community interests; if they chose to prioritise intellectual freedom then, as with all decisions, there would be consequences. The tension between community and free speech/expression came to a head in late 2019 when Toronto Public Library allowed the same transphobic speaker to book a meeting room at one of their library branches. After a contentious library board meeting in which board members who had been vocal in their support of trans rights refused to listen to what trans people were telling them, a thousand people protested peacefully in front of the library branch. The library – purportedly committed to both community and intellectual freedom – called the police, and a number of protesters were 'kettled' inside. This is a good indication of the role the library plays as an institution of state order and control and the library's reliance on state power whenever its authority is threatened.

A partnership between the library and police at Winnipeg Public Library in 2019 also raised concerns within the profession. As with many central or downtown library branches in North America, Winnipeg Public Library's downtown location was heavily used by all sectors of society, including marginalised communities (in particular Indigenous people) who, after decades of austerity, had nowhere else to go. Citing staff safety concerns, and without consulting community groups, the library took police advice to implement airport-style security upon entrance to the library. Citing class and race discrimination, many community members in Winnipeg and many librarians across the country have criticised this approach. In particular, this combination of library and state power is seen as evidence of libraries abandoning intellectual freedom principles when it suits the purposes of the capitalist state.

By reducing the tension between intellectual freedom and social responsibility to a debate simply about competing values, however, we risk losing sight of the historical and political dimensions of the problem. Rather than being at odds with each other, we can understand *both* intellectual freedom and social responsibility as core components of a particular social and political world view, a world view that arises from social and political realities. In order to resolve the contradiction, then, it is not enough simply to change our perspective to accommodate the differences; the world itself must be transformed.

Ideology

The idea that our understanding of the world arises from social and political realities, and is dependent on those realities, forces us to deal with the question of *ideology*. In his first political book, *Social Justice and the City*, David Harvey draws a distinction between two kinds of ideology. The usual definition of ideology, he argues, is 'the aware and critical exposition of ideas in their social context', which covers political ideologies such as liberalism, conservatism, anarchism, etc. On the other hand, there is also ideology 'as an unaware expression of the underlying ideas and beliefs which attach to a particular social situation'.[5] This second definition is the one I want to focus on: ideologies that arise out of the social relationships prevailing in a given society. These relationships are specific to a particular economic organisation of society; in our case, this is a society in which some people can only live by selling the one commodity they own – labour power – to the people who own everything else. Ideologies, in this view, are the ways in which people make sense of the complex, rich, hidden realities of social life, especially when those realities contain unpalatable truths or run counter to people's own values, stories and images of themselves.

The absolutist intellectual freedom position is derived from classical liberalism, and it tends to deny outright the definition of ideology I am interested in. Liberalism sees ideas, thoughts and values as a free choice of free, independent individuals. When a person reaches the 'age of discretion' they then, as self-determining adults, decide for themselves what they think about things, what they consider important, what their values are. Intellectual freedom is the *defence* of this individual self-determination, the result of a taken-for-granted individual agency (liberty). It is the (presumed) freedom of intellectuals to engage with information, ideas, thoughts, data, and so on.

But non-liberal theories argue that such individual liberty is an illusion, and as a result they take the structuring effects of social relations – and ideology itself – seriously. Our intellectual activity, in this view, is *always* structured by forces and relationships outside ourselves; we are not *free* in any absolute or unqualified sense. We cannot, for example, choose to speak a different mother tongue. There are some things which are *necessary*, and our conception of freedom must always take that into account. As Friedrich Engels put it, 'freedom is the appreciation of necessity'.[6]

An alternative intellectual freedom

The necessity imposed by social structures, the structuring effect of social relationships, means that the self-directed intellectual activity of the liberal individual is a myth, like the self-sufficiency of Robinson Crusoe.[7] Everything librarians think of as upholding intellectual freedom in fact only upholds the subtle, unconscious ideology of liberal capitalism. This is why intellectual freedom and 'neutrality' hold absolute sway in the profession and occupy such a central place in the rhetoric and discourse of librarianship: because their function is to enable the ideological reproduction (and thereby the social reproduction) of capitalist society. Challenging absolutist intellectual freedom in the name of alternative values is not enough; critics of the absolutist position, defenders of de-platforming, argue that we must challenge the hegemony of absolutist intellectual freedom itself.

To return to the example of transphobia, we can see how interminable debate and argument is not enough, especially when such debate calls into question the identity or the humanity of trans people themselves. In such instances, engaging in debate and trying to change people's minds risks doing more harm than good.

This could be read as an argument for quietism, for inaction, for waiting for a revolution, but that is not what I am advocating. The relationship of economic relationships to ideology is not a one-way, simple determinism. Ideas feed back into our collective lives, our collective struggles, into how we relate to the world. What I am arguing for is a conception of intellectual freedom that takes this situation seriously, that recognises that transphobia, for example, is not just ignorance, not just misunderstanding, not amenable to debate and discussion, but serves a specific purpose (social control, scapegoating) which must be confronted and challenged. The version of intellectual freedom I am proposing, against the absolutist position that objects to de-platforming, is less of a static noun, a defence of the status quo, and more of a verb: intellectual freedom must mean *the freeing of the intellect* rather than assuming that the intellect is already free. It means education in its broadest sense. Liberal intellectual freedom is passive, it waits to be manipulated by charlatans and bigots, and it calls this neutrality. The kind of intellectual freedom I am calling for is active, a commitment to an intellectual life shared by all and lived in common. The decision of a community to de-platform, to violate the liberal principles of free speech where the community considers it necessary, is an integral part of this common intellectual project.

Notes

1 James Turk, 'Social justice requires intellectual freedom – why the Toronto Public Library should refuse to deplatform Meghan Murphy', *Centre for Free Expression*, 17 October 2019, https://cfe.ryerson.ca/blog/2019/10/social-justice-requires-intellectual-freedom-why-toronto-public-library-should-refuse (accessed 10 July 2020).

2 United Nations, 'Universal Declaration of Human Rights' (1948), https://www.un.org/en/universal-declaration-human-rights/ (accessed 10 July 2020).

3 Toni Samek, *Intellectual Freedom and Social Responsibility in American Librarianship, 1967–1974* (Jefferson, NC: McFarland, 2001), p. 7.

4 Tiffany Crawford, 'Vancouver Pride Society Pulls Public Library From Parade', *Vancouver Sun*, 24 July 2019, https://vancouversun.com/news/local-news/vancouver-pride-society-pulls-public-library-from-parade (accessed 10 July 2020).

5 David Harvey, *Social Justice and the City*, rev. edn (Athens, GA: University of Georgia Press, 2009), p. 18.

6 Frederick Engels, *Anti-Dühring: Herr Eugen Dühring's Revolution in Science* (Moscow: Progress Publishers, 1969), p. 136.

7 Karl Marx, *Grundrisse: Foundations of the Critique of Political Economy (Rough Draft)* (London: Pelican, 1973), p. 83.

4

In a diverse society, is freedom of speech realisable?

Emma Harvey, co-written and edited by
Edson Burton

Inclusion is the watchword of our free society, one where progressive movements have used free speech as a tool to champion equal rights, shaping policy and legislation over 800 years, and culminating most recently in the Equality Act 2010. Ten years on from this, things have become a little muddled. Groups that the Act was meant to protect find themselves in conflict with one another over culture, values and identity clashes. These conflicts fuel a much wider societal divide, one where warring factions demand that we choose between two seemingly competing notions of inclusion and free speech. Can we have both? What responsibilities might those who manage the physical and virtual spaces where this debate manifests itself bear? Could revisiting the principles that these spaces were founded on help bring about a resolution?

Like everyone, my identity is a negotiation between my past and present self and the rest of the world. I'm a working-class, free-thinking, free-speaking, secular humanist, passionate about freedom of expression, equality and inclusion. My experiences have helped shape the ethos of the community arts centre I run. More and more people like me, guardians of shared spaces, find ourselves as reluctant arbitrators.

The single framework provided by the Equality Act has thrown up unexpected intersectional paradigms. Where more than one protected characteristic is at stake, inclusion is threatened, freedoms and rights become fragmented, and intersectionality and free speech are seen as incompatible.[1] We need to enable as many compatible goods from as many different incompatible positions as is possible, says philosopher Julian Baggini.[2] Not so straightforward in practice, as found out when I tried (and failed) to explain to a stakeholder who wanted to run a single-sex activity that she couldn't exclude transwomen. In her eyes, transwomen are not women and she felt their inclusion would alienate other women from her group on faith grounds. As a woman of colour, she herself had faced discrimination and victimisation.

The journeys of transwomen are fraught with obstacles, in a battle for basic rights that most of us take for granted. I want to provide a place where people feel both safe and free. I tried and failed to do anything other than insist forcefully on the law. The woman decided to leave the centre. Some would see this as a victory, but for me this felt like a failing because, when we insist forcefully, we are not changing minds; we are just leaving people behind to seek out alternative spaces to have their views affirmed.

As civic spaces are founded on a committment to equality and diversity, it can be risky to stick our necks out too far in taking responsibility for negotiating between the competing truth claims of equalities groups. With many spaces dependent on public funding, we're all justifiably petrified given how even the most reasoned and measured response might be received in the current landscape. This is a fear well documented by the work of Index on Censorship, as cultural leaders like me are making our decisions based around mitigation of reputational risk, rather than providing people with the safe spaces they need to explore difficult themes and express themselves openly. This is a shame because, as we saw when members of a mosque in York encountered the EDL, it's our real-world civic spaces that hold the potential to reduce the distance between opposing sides. It becomes much harder to hold on to our fables when we join with our enemy for tea, biscuits and a game of football.

But secular spaces where we have a chance to meet and interact with people from different backgrounds are dwindling in number as local authorities across the country flounder from one funding crisis to the next.[3] With less space to explore, competing equality agendas can become compounded by escalating discourse across online platforms. Positions quickly become entrenched and it feels more difficult to find a resolution to satisfy all parties when intersectional conflicts arise.

At the beginning of 2019, LGBT+ rights collided with the beliefs of faith communities over proposed changes to relationship and sex education (RSE) in the National Curriculum; the absence of clarity placed responsibility for resolving these issues at the feet of teachers and community leaders. When the debate began to manifest in Bristol, our centre was asked to host a meeting of concerned parents. Mindful that this was a sensitive matter and wanting to uphold our commitment to both communities, we reached out to statutory and voluntary agencies for support. A 'multi-faith, multi-agency round-table' was arranged for May as the discourse continued to play out within communities and online. By the time the Department of Education published its guidance in June, it was too late. While insisting on the importance of the teaching materials being introduced into schools, the guidance also offered parents the right to withdraw their children.

With strong leadership absent and the statutory guidance offered being extensive and contradictory, conversations quickly move away from physical to virtual platforms. People, like my stakeholder or concerned parents, fill the void with a myriad of myths, conspiracies and digital echoes that go unquestioned and unchecked. These are closed, antagonistic spaces, which we're turning to as our secular avenues for open discourse diminish – spaces that, instead of compensating for our loss of human interaction, allow grievances to fester and embolden groups to find new strategies with which to persevere in their battle to win over everyone else to their absolute truth. Nothing gets resolved in an online world where the free software principles of net neutrality have been superseded by platforms that have sprung up in the absence of any definable authority.

Tim Berners-Lee gifted us with a free internet to provide us with something that was universally held and owned without any large companies or governments having total control.[4] But in reality this has just created a power vacuum, which has been quickly filled by platforms that benefit from monetising the information flow, regardless of its accuracy or consequences. Rather than a place to build a better understanding, in this new online world we find ourselves drawn to those who validate our existing position. Our view of ourselves and everyone else is focused through a narrow prism of what human identity is, which distorts our perspective of what commonality looks like. The virtual world allows us to be the villain and the hero simultaneously, with little to no recompense. This is a freedom that clashes with libertarian thinking, discouraging convergence and nuance in favour of conflict and cruelty. Our words are not to intended to liberate but to galvanise, reinforce and build like-minded supporters. In the war of identity, this speech has become a digital commodity. We accept the spaces we're left to battle in, their rules and the commodification of the speech we use in order to feel 'free'. It is free. But free as in beer, not free as in freedom.

We have willingly signed up to a gladiatorial, digital communication era that helps to float a bloated, dying broadcast and print media that sucks up the latest feud to regurgitate it as news. While we're busy fighting one other, control of what we can say and to whom is becoming more centralised and monolithic. We're moving away from a mixed, responsive, grassroots multiplicity towards a slick, functioning, homogeneous, closed-source way of life – a singular-societal framework to prevent war and cooperate peacefully. It's safe(ish) and works (mostly), as well as generating (for a few people) wealth and prosperity. This imperialistic social ordering provides us with a world in which, if you're not the 'we' deciding on what game's being played, you're the 'them' that needs to be bound by a set of rules that you have no say in.

Rather than resisting, libertarians like me have assimilated and now we're stuck in a power struggle where there can be only one victor. It's unlikely to be us, given that we're sacrificing our own values of complexity and nuance in favour of insisting forcefully that everyone sign up to our world view, and being disappointed and angry when someone doesn't catch on quick enough.

It's the law! Transwomen and women have shared spaces for years! Nothing I did or said mattered. I couldn't shift my stakeholder's belief that she was being asked to compromise her own hard-fought rights in order for someone else's to be furthered.

We hoped our rules would suffice, but there's a lot of information that now sits between the rule of law and everyday life. We have tried to hold a moral high ground, but we haven't done anything except disenfranchise and make enemies of a whole swathe of people who think that we either don't understand or don't care about their concerns and fears. People will always find a way to subvert any imposed narrative, even one that comes from a place of good intention.

Bit by bit, we're edging towards a societal model that embraces open speech, but one that doesn't feel very free. A distinction between the open and the free – says free software programmer and activist Richard M. Stallman – is critical to safeguarding freedom overall. For software to be free, you have to be able to run the program for any purpose, access the source code to study how it works, redistribute it to help others and distribute modified versions so that everyone can benefit from the evolution of the original program. It's purposeful. A constant journey of discovery that is not owned or controlled by any single faction.

If we want to continue to adapt and improve, we need to accede to a freedom that enables everyone's advancement, not just the furthering of our own agenda. If we applied this distinction to the type of speech we use, we would very quickly see a lot of examples of open speech – favouring a practical advantage for only one section of society – but not a lot of speech that is free in a philosophical sense.

If we want 'free', it seems silly to think that this could be achieved by any one group maintaining control over what we do or say. As comedian Ken Cheng outlined in his 2018 BBC podcast *Game Over, Humans*, AI can easily beat even the best human at games such as chess, but the program cannot be inspired by its win to develop a passion to learn how to play other games. An algorithm is yet to beat the power of our many human minds, and our diverse perspectives are integral to a prosperous society. As with law, this is only as effective as the diversity of perspectives involved in its creation and application. We are (sort of) getting to a place where we're beginning to understand this in business, with evidence that companies with more diverse workforces regularly and dramatically outperform less diverse competitors.[5] Conversely, when we see brands make costly mistakes by launching ill-thought products that lead to public backlash, this leaves us scratching our heads, wondering whether this would have happened had there been more diversity among their decision makers.

As with free software, at the heart of this 'diversity is good for business' message is the 'many minds' principle, weaving together the fine threads of our heritage, interests and lives and really connecting. Rather than having to insist through authority, these threads organically intertwine during our everyday experiences, separating myth from reality and allowing our enemies to take the shape of real people. As with our centre, it's our shared real-world spaces that bring out the best of us and teach us what it means to be human. Sharing mundane and extraordinary moments of life with those who aren't 'us' can be beneficial both to society and to the individual in immeasurable ways. These interactions, when we permit them to happen, hold the propensity to rehabilitate, liberate, empower and inspire even those most lost and disenfranchised. It takes a village to raise a child and a community to save a soul.

It feels as if we know this, that people are more complex than we like to give our enemies credit for. Yet we have become distracted, playing a game that has not been designed with us in mind. The platforms and algorithms that have been built to interpret our behaviour have segmented us in a way that sits unnaturally with our messy humanness. While it can be easy to offer simple notions of a left-liberal inclusion agenda butting heads with a right-wing nationalist free speech agenda, the reality is far more complex. As some of the battles around RSE revealed, there can be some odd bedfellows when political discourse and identity battles intertwine.

Free speech has become a tool to be bartered for and a blockade used to safeguard one's personal freedom. The muddy waters between open and free speech help to mask who is really being silenced; no-platforming cries from those who traditionally hold power conceal deeply ingrained discrimination across online, academic and broadcast platforms, most notably of black women.[6] We are forcing our academics and activists to remove themselves from the debate altogether, with alarming ferocity and speed, and we are allowing this to play out online because we see no other way.[7] Politicians and programmers point at one another to take responsibility for regulation. Rather than any moral pursuit, those who hold on to power play to the gallery for votes and clicks. They are intentionally vague and non-committal with their guidance, to keep us guessing, confused and disconnected.

GNU free software principles warned us of the consequence of this over fifteen years ago. Stallman's 'Four Freedoms' of free software make the distinction between the free and the open to protect our freedoms and provide us with a universally held and owned, neutral, virtual world, as per Berners-Lee's intention.

The problem is, we have got a bit stuck; as Stallman says, 'control of our software by a proprietary company means control of what we can say and to whom. This threatens our freedom in all areas of life.'[8] The false sense of freedom provided to us by our free (as in beer) platforms is threatening our freedom. Those who hold the most power are wielding a type of weaponised open speech hidden under a guise of free speech and using it to silence any dissenting voice in the crowd. That such speech mainly guarantees a practical advantage for the dominant society, while making it open, doesn't make it very free.

Pitting freedom and inclusion as incompatible robs us of a tool that has been traditionally used by every activist, civil rights movement and artist throughout history to challenge and hold power to account. It's such a sublime misdirection, so akin to the fable of the

Emperor's new clothes, that it's a wonder we're not all jumping up down and yelling in unison at this naked truth.

So what can we do to redefine, reclaim and defend free speech, in its original sense? I'd love to say I've come up with a toolkit or framework to make it easier to find resolution between two opposing truths. But even the best laws and platforms need human beings to interpret, apply and adapt them. As liberal thinkers, if all we do is attempt to refine the principles of our programmers and lawmakers by replacing one rigid set of rules with our own competing set of demands, we're just trying to occupy a space that's already overloaded. We don't need any more rules, we just need a reboot to reconnect with our values.

If every villain is a hero in their own story, it's up to those who care the most about equality to enable as many competing goods as possible to flourish. We can make other people's negotiations between their identity and the rest of the world that bit easier by approaching competing truth claims with sufficient openness so as to reduce the fragmentation between differing perspectives. We can try to insist less forcefully on our own narrative and extend an open hand of invitation, rather than delivering our message with a closed fist.

Given how long it's taken us to get to this point, we might have to accept that the pace of change might feel slow and not all that satisfying. If we want to ease the rubbing-up against one another in the messy pluralism of our world today, sometimes tolerance rather than celebration might be the best we can hope for. We have to resist the urge to pick at the loose threads that make us human, catch a glimpse of ourselves in the other, and embrace diversity as a whole, not just the bits we like.

But that's why we have arts and community centres in the first place; it gives us a taste of what is missing of the human, between the law and the algorithm. So, before we lose our voices, it's time for us to come together to break bread with the enemy who, like us, might have the most to lose if we let our freedoms fail.

Notes

1 Andrew Torba, 'There's nothing "intersectional" about free speech', *Quillette*, 7 February 2019, https://quillette.com/2019/02/07/theres-noth ing-intersectional-about-free-speech/ (accessed 15 June 2020).
2 Julian Baggini, *The Edge of Reason: A Rational Skeptic in an Irrational World* (New Haven, CT: Yale University Press, 2016).
3 Gareth Davies, Charles Boutaud, Hazel Sheffield and Emma Youle, 'Revealed: the thousands of public spaces lost to the council funding crisis', *Bureau of Investigative Journalism*, 4 March 2019, www.theburea uinvestigates.com/stories/2019-03-04/sold-from-under-you (accessed 15 June 2020).
4 Tim Berners-Lee, 'Internet freedom must be safeguarded', *The Guardian*, 26 June 2013, www.theguardian.com/technology/2013/jun/26/tim-bern ers-lee-internet-freedom (accessed 15 June 2020).
5 Sheree Atcheson, 'Embracing diversity and fostering inclusion is good for your business', *Forbes*, 25 September 2018, www.forbes.com/sites/sher eeatcheson/2018/09/25/embracing-diversity-and-fostering-inclusion-is-good-for-your-business/#5494796f72b1 (accessed 15 June 2020).
6 Nesrine Malik, 'There is a crisis on campuses – but it's about racism, not free speech', *The Guardian*, 13 October 2019, www.theguardian.com/ commentisfree/2019/oct/13/universities-crisis-racism-not-political-corre ctness (accessed 15 June 2020).
7 GNU principles, www.gnu.org, 2005.
8 GNU principles, www.gnu.org, 2005.

5

Training readers as censors in Nazi Germany

Victoria Stiles

The destruction of a book can provoke an almost instinctive negative reaction. It is an act which has come to symbolise the suppression of knowledge and an intolerance of education or enlightenment. In fictional portrayals such as Ray Bradbury's *Fahrenheit 451* and Roald Dahl's *Matilda*, destroying books is an authoritarian attack on freedom, as well as an indication of ignorance and philistinism. Similarly, reverence for books is seen as a sign of good character and open-mindedness. When Nazi Germany appears as a historical example in free speech debates, there is a natural inclination to emphasise the more intimidating measures employed by the party and state apparatus to suppress dissenting voices and inconvenient information. Methods such as public book burnings or the blacklisting of works and creators loom large in our imaginations because they are so dramatic and draconian in themselves, and because we know the escalation of oppression and its end results. The destruction of Jewish literature, records and artefacts was part of a deliberate attempt to erase an entire culture and people, while the exclusion of authors and academics from their professions had a devastating

impact on many fields. The colossal human cost of the regime's policies and actions justifiably serves as an important warning from history, and the shocking images of bonfires of books in May 1933 set
the tone for the period.

In order to apply this warning to modern-day debates around
freedom of speech, we need to appreciate the impact of cultural
policies in Nazi Germany, taking into account not only the more
spectacular acts of destruction but also the more mundane, day-to-
day business of creating a national culture along National Socialist
lines. Book burnings were not an expression of philistinism as such
but were a declaration that certain books did not belong in German
cultural and intellectual life. These works were being excluded from
something which was revered as vital to the nation. In other words,
certain books were burned to symbolise their worthlessness compared to other books. The public book burnings of 1933 can also be
read as an expression of triumph and as a statement of intent. They
were an open celebration of having gained an advantage in the escalating 'culture war' which had been taking place in Europe throughout the 1920s and early 1930s. They were also a brazen announcement
that in Germany under Hitler, this war against cosmopolitanism,
communism and other philosophies which ran counter to National
Socialism (including the wrong kind of conservatism) was to become
more intense and unopposable.

Nazi cultural policy was therefore not focused only on the destruction of undesirable elements and influences, but on the building of
a more unequivocally dominant German-nationalist (*völkisch*) culture. The methods used to achieve this – with the semi-voluntary
compliance of many creators and custodians of culture – existed
alongside overt methods of control and censorship and brought
about dramatic, devastating change in only a few years. If we are
to recognise similarly harmful processes at work today, we need to

appreciate how these policies presented at different levels, how their effects were overlapping and interconnected, and how creators and audiences were made complicit in their own intellectual confinement. The exact details of the ways in which each type of media was controlled by the institutions of party and state would take multiple volumes to describe fully, but there are factors which all had in common. The examples which follow come from the area I know best from my research: publishing and bookselling.

Limitations of state and party control

Changing the reading habits of an entire country was a Herculean task for the new regime, but many people in the literary world were eager to make the attempt. Even before any territorial expansion, Germany had a highly literate population of over 60 million people, served by a thriving market for books (new and second-hand), newspapers and periodicals, as well as public and commercial libraries. Germany's self-image as the 'land of poets and thinkers' had been a part of the national identity long before the state's formation in 1879. In one sense, this tradition was a blessing for a regime wanting to control what the reading public had access to. Mechanisms for the 'protection' of German literature had existed before 1933, as had campaigns regarding what should and should not be read by impressionable people. Like-minded individuals and groups were quickly incorporated into the party apparatus, often as willing volunteers. On the other hand, overt, top-down methods of censorship could not have a transformative effect on reading habits without destroying this cherished impression of intellectual freedom. This is turn could risk a backlash or might have the opposite of the intended effect by drawing attention to suppressed works and ideas. Maintaining and feeding the idea that Germany was still an intellectual powerhouse, feeding the curiosity of discerning readers, also had its uses as a positive and enticing message that was flattering to its target audience.

There was also the problem of who would oversee this policy area. Control of the press, radio, film and theatre was the remit of the Ministry for Propaganda and Public Enlightenment under Joseph Goebbels, and this included responsibility for combating *Schund und Schmutz* (obscene or trashy material) and promoting national literature and the publishing industry as a whole. Within this ministry was the Reich Chamber of Literature, which incorporated existing professional organisations, some of which had already been campaigning against 'un-German' material and had supported the book-burning events spearheaded by the Association of German Students. Membership of the Chamber was compulsory for anyone involved in the creation and distribution of books. In effect, this gave the Propaganda Ministry the power to end careers and shut down whole publishing houses. At the same time, it suffered from a lack of sufficient funds and personnel to conduct systematic reviews of all new manuscripts.

Goebbels was by no means the only minister active in this area, and no institutional fiefdom was happy to concede power to any of the others. Alfred Rosenberg was given the unhelpfully broad remit of supervising 'the entire intellectual and ideological instruction' of the party, which included the promotion of German literature. Meanwhile the Ministry for Science, Education and Public Instruction, which had the ability to determine which books were suitable for use in the classroom, in school and research libraries, and in adult education programmes, was under Bernhard Rust. There was also an office within the party whose job was to check all publications to do with the history and ideology of the party itself, which began in part as a type of brand-protection exercise but quickly increased in scope. This is only a sketch of an administrative situation which is confusing enough on paper before taking into account the overlapping loyalties of individual bureaucrats, informal collaborations, a lack of accurate information, petty rivalries, corruption and incompetence.[1] The twelve-year lifespan of the regime was not long enough to put into place a planned, efficient system of control over all publishing activities. However, as in many areas of governance in Nazi Germany, redundancy and in-fighting did not entirely prevent progress towards the regime's core aims.

How those aims could be served by any particular manuscript was not always clear to those bureaucrats responsible for overseeing literary activities. For many topics, there was no single, clear party line, and decisions rested on matters of personal taste. Such was the case with the novels of Karl May, which were deemed to be of little value by some reviewers, but escaped official censure due to Hitler's personal enjoyment of them. A similar situation arose in the theatre world with the works of George Bernard Shaw. Such matters were rarely escalated so far up the hierarchy, however. It is certainly not the case that everything published in Nazi Germany had the explicit, wholehearted approval of the regime. Significant though the more overt measures of censorship were, they nevertheless left large areas of intellectual life – and publishing – under a plausibly deniable level of state control, albeit with an increasing sense of unease and a heightened drive towards self-censorship and risk-avoidance.

Support, control and self-censorship

As the risks became more severe, the intense and intimidating pressure towards conformity meant that existing decision-making mechanisms within publishing houses, bookshops and libraries became 'voluntarily' more restrictive. Avoiding denunciation or censure and maintaining access to professional networks and publicity mechanisms was crucial to both personal and professional survival. For some, there was also the thrill of new opportunities. Published books were, after all, a commercial product and market forces still played an important role in their success or failure.

Government guidance for publishers and booksellers took many forms, with support and supervision going hand in hand. The trade publication *Bücherkunde*, produced by a branch of Rosenberg's office, contained lists of books arranged by subject matter which were 'to be promoted' or 'not to be promoted'. These lists were different in tone to the 'blacklists' of dangerous literature, which were limited in scope and acted as an intimidation tactic against high-profile targets of the Nazi culture war. The 'unpromotable' books on the *Bücherkunde* lists might still exist on the market but were relegated to a second-class status, cut off from many avenues of publicity.

In spite of the lack of clear governing hierarchy in the area of literary policy, the number of organisations and individuals on the lookout for ideologically transgressive or valueless manuscripts meant that there was ample opportunity for scrutiny and judgement. Rivalries and grudges between individual writers and publishers also played their part. In February 1935 the Chamber of Literature mediated a dispute between the publishers of two new scholarly works on the same topic. One book was by a German research group and had the explicit support of Rosenberg's office. The other, under contract with German publisher Felix Meiner, was a collaboration between a French scholar and a Jewish scholar in exile. Each publisher took issue with how the two books were being publicised and reviewed, claiming that they were being sabotaged by the other. The German group's arguments were aggressively nationalist and antisemitic, while Meiner argued that the attacks on his publication were harming Germany's scholarly reputation abroad. The Chamber ruled that Meiner would be allowed access to its advertising channels and that the German research group should tone down their public attacks against the French/Jewish work. In spite of this victory, Meiner passed the contract on to a Swiss publisher the following year. Although the precise reason for the Chamber's decision is unclear, this example of bureaucratic wrangling indicates the balance which was struck in the early years of the regime between controlling the field and maintaining an outward appearance of freedom. Sadly, it also shows how some people were willing to bring disputes to the attention of the authorities in the hope of gaining a commercial advantage. As filtering mechanisms at different levels became increasingly coordinated – deliberately or otherwise – to exclude the same writers and works, it became almost impossible for riskier projects to survive without the protection of a suitably influential official.

At the same time, the Propaganda Ministry and Rosenberg's office upheld their promises to act as promoters of the book trade. Having brought the German Booksellers' Association under its control, the Propaganda Ministry used the Association's existing channels to offer suggestions for themed bookshop windows, including providing posters. Themes could be something relatively benign such as anniversaries of the births or deaths of cultural figures, or they might be more overtly political. Themes might also tie in with the annual 'German Book Week', a festival intended to promote sales of German books at home and abroad. Here as elsewhere, there was no contradiction between the promotion of reading and the regime's aggressive, expansionist aims. For example, the slogan in 1938 was 'A home library for every home', while a key focus of the exhibitions was German literature from Austria and the Sudentenland, both of which were annexed that year.

The dutiful reader

As well as being a vehicle for the regime's own propaganda, this assistance with advertising showed booksellers how to market their stock to the new type of consumer who was being moulded: the dutifully patriotic reader. The role of the reader in this more 'purposeful' literary world was described in a book produced by a subsidiary of the Propaganda Ministry and was reinforced through many channels, including literary magazines.[2] The German people were described as having a special connection with literature, and the *Volk* were seen as being both the foundation and the end users of all German literature. The publishing industry's customers were offered an aspirational vision of how being patriotic and well-read could coexist. What was discouraged, alongside these appeals to buy more books, was the trend of 'indiscriminate reading'.

The categories set by the promoted/unpromoted lists were part of a drive to define not only the ideological stance but also the utility of each book, and publishers made use of these classifications to show cooperation and to attract buyers. Desirable messages from literature might include the display of 'Germanic' heroism, family values or patriotism. In some cases, changing this framing meant that older material could be reissued with a new regime-friendly purpose, with a better chance of making it on to promoted lists or, after wartime rationing was introduced, of being granted a paper permit. For example, books relating to French and English studies were reclassified as 'enemy' studies at the start of the Second World War, creating an opportunity for material from the First World War to be repackaged and brought back on to the market. This shift was also reflected in the publicity for new books and series, and in their blurbs and introductions. To some extent, these guided how a book should be read. The books themselves might contain extensive quotes, even whole primary sources, from nationals of hostile countries, giving readers the impression that they were being granted access to unfiltered information which was being allowed to 'speak for itself'. However, the overall framing made it clear that a true National Socialist would read this material critically and come to the 'correct' assessment of its worth.

The encouragement to build home libraries of 'must-read' literature worked alongside these mechanisms of categorisation and contextualisation to give the field the appearance of completeness. When every series of books from every publisher, or every contents page of individual compendiums, contains essentially the same entries in slightly different guises, it becomes impossible to imagine what might be missing. Some perspectives become labelled as inherently blinkered, outdated, hypocritical or otherwise dismissible. The strongest common message of Nazi-guided culture was the belief that a hierarchy of races – and the supposed superiority of the Germanic/Nordic/Aryan race – was the key to understanding the world. With this repeated framing, no amount of 'outside' voices could push back, as all were painted as blind to the truth and so were stripped of legitimacy. There is no point in having a voice if the audience has been trained not to understand or believe your words. In short, the aim was to make readers complicit in creating a national literature which was inspired by the right kind of people, for the practical use of those people, to the exclusion of others.

Conclusion

Personally, I find the resulting image from all of the above to be more disturbing than the bonfires of books. In many areas, censorship in Nazi Germany was fractious, underfunded and subject to unclear and incomplete guidance and ad hoc procedures. It is an example of how efficiency, single-mindedness and total authoritarian control are not necessary to create an environment where freedom of speech and the range of perspectives offered for public consumption are both devastatingly restricted. Even when dissenting opinions were presented, giving the impression of open debate and real intellectual value for audiences, framing these voices as 'un-German' or hostile, and redefining the very words they used, left them effectively mute.

Perhaps, in a climate of concern regarding 'de-platforming' on campuses, it is all too easy to focus on the image of students happily participating in the mass destruction of books. There is certainly something more naturally outrageous about a book that already exists being destroyed, or removed from circulation, or having its publication cancelled, than there is about an author's work quietly being turned down by a publisher or denied effective publicity. Mere commercial pressures on the effective deployment of speech rarely receive the same sort of focus as a 'ban' or an act of 'de-platforming'. Our instincts tell us that any deliberate intervention is straying into draconian measures and a slippery loss of individual choice and expression. Far safer, surely, to allow the market to regulate itself? But as we have seen, two or more filtering mechanisms working in the same direction can have a dramatic effect on the shape of the field, and commercial pressures can create a push away from the 'risk' of minority perspectives. We should also consider which voices are being excluded through a lack of promotional activities, such as inclusion on book club reading lists or nomination for prizes. If we define freedom of speech purely in terms of a lack of overt government or institutional restrictions, we risk underestimating the more subtle pressures placed on publications which need to be commercially viable and have mainstream appeal, in a crowded and competitive market. Passive, seemingly neutral arbitration is not able to act as a counterbalance to the mutually amplifying effects of dominant narratives, politics and tastes.

At the same time, we need to look at which voices are being distorted beyond comprehension or palatability even as they are being broadcast. The mere existence of a book does not indicate that the voice within it has been granted a fair hearing, just as the rejection of a proposal or cancellation of a talk does not equate to an absolute denial of a person's freedom to air their views. Freedom of speech includes the right of intermediaries to curate their output by choosing not to platform, promote or amplify any and all voices with the confidence to put themselves forward. The active preservation of space for voices less often heard, and more frequently misunderstood, is often the only guarantee against a monotonous, static, *unfree* conversation.

Notes

1   A comprehensive overview of the field is offered by Jan-Pieter Barbian, *The Politics of Literature in Nazi Germany: Books in the Media Dictatorship*, trans. Kate Sturge (London: Bloomsbury, 2013).
2   Hellmuth Langenbucher (ed.), *Die Welt des Buches: Eine Kunde vom Buch* (Ebenhausen bei Munchen: Langewiesche-Brandt, 1938).

6

Is boycotting for or against free speech?

Andrew Phemister

Impotent fury is never in short supply in the dyspeptic world of social media, but it is rarely more pronounced than when boycotts are condemned for inhibiting 'free speech'. It is not hard to find such complaints. For anyone committed to a vision of detached individualism, being confronted with their dependence on the social acceptance of others is clearly a disorientating experience. It's all very well valorising individual rationality and achievement, freed from the unnecessary encumbrances of society, but if you're made to feel uncomfortable at the theatre, or a publisher abandons plans to publish your book, it soon becomes evident that we can only speak when others are willing to listen.[1] As the recent Stop Funding Hate and Grab Your Wallet campaigns have shown, the boycott remains a powerful tool for reasserting social interdependence; a classic moral economy 'weapon of the weak', updated for a global and (perhaps) digital age. Boycotts are inherently incorporating, forcing us all to make a moral choice, and therefore damaging to the belief in political neutrality that sustains ostensibly 'free' speech. The history of the tactic reveals that the wide-eyed confusion of the modern 'classical liberal' has its historical antecedents, and that the boycott has long been a fundamentally destabilising force for both classical liberalism and free market capitalism. By tracing the strained history of boycotting with modern liberalism, this chapter argues that the practice is inseparable from democracy, and indeed necessary for any notion of a public sphere on which free speech can rest.

Today, the legitimacy or illegitimacy of boycotting is often understood to rest on its relationship to 'free speech', or to broader claims for freedom of action and association. Indeed, since 'free speech' itself comes tied with a bundle of other rights claims that notionally reside in the rational and autonomous individual, and which, together, underwrite an intellectual defence of the 'free market', the social right to free speech is also entangled with the role of democracy in capitalism. While critics of boycotts often frame them as a socially coercive restriction on free speech, supporters note that calling for or joining a boycott is itself an example of 'free speech'. And in the US, at least at the time of writing, boycotting remains protected as a First Amendment right. Neither of these positions are novel or historically unfamiliar, however, and much can be learned from the parallel responses elicited by boycotting in the 1880s, the decade of its birth.

The word itself originated in Ireland during the Land War (1879–82), though shunning and ostracism, alongside the supporting cast of gossip, ridicule and other mechanisms of social shaming, have been used to enforce collective solidarity (and indeed conformity) for millennia. Ostracism formed part of the Athenian demos, for instance, and was central to the powers of medieval Westphalian *Vehmgerichts*, the community courts that Marx famously recalled as a parallel for the coming proletarian revolution. Forms of folk justice, which often involved the 'rough music' of hooting and jeering, or semi-ritualised processions, were common across early modern

Europe. While not usually progressive in intent, these non-alienated forms of collective retribution were a means by which communities could enforce social norms and punish transgressions such as domestic violence, sexual assault and economic profiteering of various types. In many places across Europe these social enforcements survived until the late nineteenth century, when increasingly powerful states were finally able to fully exert their judicial authority. It was at just this juncture, where rural communality confronted liberal individualism, that the term 'boycott' was coined.

The story of how the boycott got its name reveals the transformative and powerful political principles at its heart. 'Captain' Charles Cunningham Boycott was born in the English county of Suffolk. The son of a Protestant clergyman, Boycott had enjoyed a short career in the British Army before taking up a position as a land agent for the Anglo-Irish aristocrat Lord Erne. A stern and resolute figure for his tenants and labourers, Boycott had been in Ireland for twenty years when he found himself at the centre of a political storm. Since late 1879, tenant farmers in Ireland had been organising to demand changes to the land laws. A broad cross-section of Irish rural life had come together in an often uneasy coalition to fight for greater rights to Irish land under the suitably malleable banner of 'Land for the People'. On 23 September 1880 the conflict came, quite literally, to Boycott's door when around a hundred local men arrived at his house near Ballinrobe in Co. Mayo and informed him that his labourers would no longer work for him. Boycott soon found himself and his family completely isolated. Unable to buy food and supplies, harvest his own crops, or collect rents from tenant farmers, and subjected to constant jeers from the locals, Captain Boycott complained that 'the spirit of terrorism' had come over the community.[2]

Although not a man of immense talents, Boycott certainly had a flair for publicity. His letters to the London *Times* garnered a great deal of international attention, as well as financial support for his plight. It was in these first weeks and months that the terms and metaphors used to conceptualise 'boycotting' as an infringement on freedom were crystallised, and this discursive frame continues to shape our understanding of it today. Boycott cast himself as the innocent victim of an uncivilised and irrational conspiracy against the rights of property, despite his tenants' retort that he had 'made it the business of his life to torment us with the very worst forms of feudalism'.[3] His righteous anger was also directed at the state for not doing more to intervene and compensate him, even though he had been afforded the protection of an infantry regiment to guard him from the stares and passive hostility of the local community. Right from the first 'boycott', the refusal of boycotters to engage socially and economically was constructed as a threat to private property and to individual freedoms. Like many who would follow him, Captain Boycott demanded the intervention of the state to secure an expanded version of property rights and a narrowed conception of free expression – not simply the right to possession but also to profits; not simply the right to speak freely, but to be obeyed.

At the core, the argument centred over whether boycotters were themselves acting 'freely'. Commentators in Britain and the US followed Captain Boycott's lead in blaming a small group of malicious conspirators for terrifying a weak-willed and largely irrational peasantry into acquiescence. This argument was central to the British government's efforts to secure prosecution of several Land League leaders on the grounds of constructive conspiracy. The Irish Attorney General, Hugh Law, noting that 'personal liberty consisted […] of freedom of mind and will', argued that the boycotters were not exercising free will, but had been 'made the tools of men more crafty and designing than themselves'. In response, the defence naturally framed the government's prosecution as itself a 'blow at freedom of speech, at the sacred right of public meeting', a view echoed by the League's supporters, who saw 'the prosecutions instituted by the Government as an attempt […] to deprive the people of the indisputable birthright of every free man – freedom of speech'. In his attempt to secure a prosecution for boycotting, as an editorial in the *Washington Post* observed, the Attorney General had tried to spread 'the meshes of the law wide enough to catch almost any man who has said anything against high rents'.[4] There were, however, few other responses available to critics of the boycott, since almost any legal avenue involved an attack on the fundamental liberal principle of 'free speech'.

Understanding the boycotters as 'irrational' was an attempt to circumvent this free speech problem, and was a prominent approach as the practice spread beyond the west of Ireland. And spread it did. This 'new social peril', a 'subtle and mischievous rebellion', according to the press, elicited copious comment and concern about its remarkable efficacy. Scrabbling around for parallels, the boycott was seen as pre-modern and pre-enlightened, a relic of medieval Europe and the 'Middle Ages'. The *New York Times* worried breathlessly that if a means of stamping out the practice was not found, 'industry, trade, civilisation itself […] would be as precarious […] as they were in medieval Europe'.[5] Within months the practice had been transplanted to the United States through the networks of Irish nationalists and labour radicals who populated the transatlantic branches of the Irish National Land League and the Knights of Labor, and would drive forward the labour movement in the US by causing conflict and consternation in the courts.

Today we tend to think of the boycott in narrowly economic terms, being primarily the exercise of consumer choice, or possibly institutional pressure, to effect change. In its early years during the 1880s it encompassed a broad palette of possibilities, but despite its variety, there remained two necessary features of any boycott: the renunciation of violence, and the existence of commonly shared moral norms. It depended on there being, as Irish nationalist leader Charles Stewart Parnell explained, 'no man so full of avarice, so lost to shame, as to dare the public opinion'. Early boycotts, both in Ireland and the US, took on several forms that aimed to reinforce such shame, such as hooting, jeering and ridicule, as well as public denunciation. One Tipperary farmer, who had rented the land of an evicted family, had his crimes 'proclaimed though the town' by a bellman. Similarly, during the 1882 freight handlers' strike in New York, union president Jeremiah Murphy explained how boycotted men would 'have circulars containing their names printed and distributed over the city, and sent home to Ireland, too'.[6] This public shaming was of course socially coercive, making use of the interlocking sentiments of duty, loyalty, guilt and shame. But it was also rooted in the rights of individuals to verbalise and express their moral anger at those who had violated shared ethical commitments.

In both Ireland and the US the power of the boycott, as was immediately obvious to critics and supporters alike, lay in the fact that it involved 'no infraction of the laws, even the unjust laws'. On mass platforms in Ireland, the rural population was reminded that 'a landlord could not compel a man to work for him, or to buy or sell from him'.[7] Courts on both sides of the Atlantic struggled to define, let alone prosecute, boycotting without jettisoning the liberal rights to free speech and free association that underpinned the democratic notion of a 'public sphere'. For owners of property, however, being compelled to behave in accordance with the expectations of the wider community appeared as an unbearable imposition, and one that was often described as an imposition on their own rights: 'All the rights of property as hitherto understood are in the balance' was the fevered declaration of one Irish landlord who was struggling to sell his cattle.

The Cork Defence Union, a landlord organisation formed to combat what it called 'infringements on liberty', solemnly detailed the case of a carpenter called James Sullivan, whose liberty was apparently infringed simply by being 'hooted' at whenever he was outside.[8] It was in this way that free speech was reframed as intimidation, a slippery term which the House of Commons spent three full days trying to define. It was soon clear that there was no way to distinguish between people who had been intimidated and those who had been simply persuaded to join a boycott, and the increasing awareness of the ambiguity between definitions of social pressure, persuasion and coercive behaviour made many liberal thinkers question the viability of participatory democracy itself. How could liberal values and property rights be protected if democracies were populated not by autonomous, rational individuals, but by social animals, interdependent on each other and prone to speaking and acting collectively?

The conflict between expansive property rights and democratic freedoms is a familiar one for us today, when boycotts still draw their discordance into dramatic relief. Indeed, there is a remarkable symmetry between criticisms of the boycott in the 1880s and those that can be heard today. Rhetorically, it was construed as a 'reign of terror', or, in the words of Californian railroad millionaire Charles Croker, a 'tyrannical practice', just as contemporary conservatives have referred to boycotters as 'economic terrorists who hate free speech'.[9] The large numbers who might support a particular boycott were characterised as either 'deluded people' in thrall to zealots and demagogues, or victims themselves, browbeaten by 'this *Vehmgericht* which nevertheless they are afraid to disobey'.[10] Today, we are familiar with similar complaints that boycotters and protesters are morally coercive, cowing a silent majority into submission for fear of public ridicule and condemnation. In this way, the notion of a democratic public sphere becomes unpalatable, since popular opinion itself is reframed; instead of being understood as an inhibitor of socially damaging behaviours, it comes to be seen as a nebulous restriction on the free speech of an unidentifiable majority.

The political responses to the boycott and the role of 'free speech' in the 1880s are hugely instructive for understanding the modern political distemper prompted by similar questions, not least because our understanding of democracy itself was shaped by these issues. Nineteenth-century liberals, on both sides of the Atlantic, had to make a choice between their conceptions of personal liberty and the capitalist social order. Many classical liberals became increasingly sceptical about the prospects for democracy, viewing only an educated elite as rational enough to possess truly free speech.[11] In a similar fashion, contemporary libertarians are often led down this authoritarian and anti-democratic path when confronted by boycotting. Trying to keep the right to economic exploitation free from social restrictions, they find it difficult to explain why social coercion should be opposed and economic coercion ignored.

Others, it must be said, like the Liberal MP for Orkney, Samuel Laing, defended the principle if not the practice of the boycott, asserting that the state would become overbearing if there was not 'unlimited liberty [...] of moral coercion'. But for most, the intervention of the state against boycotters was to be welcomed. In doleful voices, liberal politicians and theorists quickly abandoned notions of free speech and a democratic public sphere on the basis that government coercion was preferable to coercion by 'an irresponsible and ferocious mob'.[12] If civilisation was to be maintained, then liberty as it was previously understood would have to be redefined. The power of the boycott was finally halted in the US by the use of court injunction, which, in the case of the famous Pullman boycott of 1894, sought to prohibit compelling another's actions by 'persuasion'. Prompted by the perceived dangers of the boycott, the freedom to speak and to be heard moved further from popular grasp – away from what Woodrow Wilson described in critical terms as 'the democracy of the local assembly', and towards an ostensibly more benign, technocratic and enlightened elite rule which could protect property and 'civilisation' from the free speech and rough 'pauper democracy' of the boycott.[13]

What lessons can be learned from reactions to the boycott at the end of the nineteenth century? The first is surely that the question of free speech is inseparable from the possession of political author- ity. Boycotting shows that the right to 'free speech' is not a right to speak, but to act. It is not a question of who can speak, but of who is obeyed. Therefore, the freedom to condemn and to shun, and to encourage others to join in, is not just a democratic right, but is constitutive of democracy itself. Either people are free to persuade and be persuaded, to socially coerce and be coerced as social animals, or they must submit to some other political or economic authority. Relying on shared moral norms and expectations, the power of a boycott stands or falls by popular demand. Unsuccessful boycotts, of which there are many examples today and in the nineteenth cen- tury, highlight this democratic dependence. Authoritarian attempts to restrict the right to boycott, as can be seen in attempts made by the US and Australian governments to proscribe environmental and pro-Palestinian boycotts, remain the principal dangers to free speech and indeed democracy itself.

The second lesson is one of divergence. Having their roots in shared experiences of work and social existence, collective norms and a communal morality are harder to maintain today. Social media is seductively useful for advancing boycotts, but in accelerating and disaggregating the practice into more performative denunciations it actually undermines the very foundations on which they rest. Calls for boycotts or other forms of social ostracism and shaming on social media tend to be atomising rather than bonding; the ferocity of their expression not tempered by face-to-face interaction, nor informed by the necessary trust developed in physical space. It is instructive that the most effective and long-standing boycott is that of *The S*n* newspaper in Liverpool, which is still shunned (primarily) for its coverage of the Hillsborough disaster. Its success relies on a sense of belonging to a political community, which the boycott itself reflexively reinforces. It shows that human interaction on a local scale is the only means by which solidarity can be constructed and truly free speech emerge.

Notes

1 Joanna Walters, 'Trump demands apology from *Hamilton* cast after Mike Pence booed', *The Guardian*, 19 November 2016, https://www.the guardian.com/us-news/2016/nov/19/mike-pence-booed-at-hamilton-performance-then-hears-diversity-plea (accessed 10 July 2020); Froma Harrop, 'Milo Yiannopoulos, Simon & Schuster and the right to boycott books', *Seattle Times*, 19 January 2017, https://www.seattletimes.com/opinion/milo-yiannopoulos-simon-schuster-and-the-right-to-boycott-books/ (accessed 10 July 2020).

2 Charles C. Boycott, letter to *The Times*, 5 November 1880.

3 *Glasgow Herald*, 16 November 1880.

4 Hugh Law, HC Deb, 15 March 1881, vol. 259 cc.1093; Hugh Law, HC Deb, 8 February 1881, vol. 258 c.415; 'State trials', *Freeman's Journal*, 19 January 1881; J. R. McDonnell at Athlone, 7 December 1880, NLI MS 11,289; 'The Dublin trial', *Washington Post*, 3 January 1881.

5 'The Irish conspiracy against property', *Newcastle Courant*, 10 December 1880; *Pall Mall Gazette*, 17 December 1880; 'The doom of the boycott', *New York Times*, 2 May 1886.

6 Donald Jordan, 'The Irish National League and the "unwritten law": rural protest and nation-building in Ireland 1882–1890', *Past and Present*, 158 (1998), pp. 146–71; 'Boycotting', *Freeman's Journal*, 10 December 1880, quoted in Michael A. Gordon, 'The labor boycott in New York City, 1880–1886', *Labor History*, 16.2 (1975), p. 210.

7 'Mr. John Dillon M.P.', *Freeman's Journal*, 28 February 1881; 'The land question', *Freeman's Journal*, 23 November 1880.

8   William Bence Jones, *The Life's Work of a Landlord in Ireland who tried to do his duty* (Dublin, 1880), p. 159; Cork Defence Union, *Boycotting in the County of Cork* (Cork: Purcell & Co., 1886), p. 23.

9   'Conservative meeting in Bristol', *The Scotsman*, 16 November 1881; 'The Gray boycott', *New York Times*, 15 April 1886; Mike Huckabee on Twitter, https://twitter.com/GovMikeHuckabee/status/819946077713534980 (accessed 10 July 2020).

10 'Ireland under coercion', *Edinburgh Review*, 168:344 (1888), p. 571; 'Topics of the week', *The Graphic: An Illustrated Weekly Newspaper*, 27 November 1880.

11 William Graham Sumner, 'Industrial war', *The Forum* (September 1886), p. 5; William Graham Sumner, 'State interference', *North American Review*, 145:369 (August 1887), p. 109.

12 Samuel Laing, *Boycotting* (London: National Press Agency, 1888), p. 8; Thomas Burt, *The Government and the Land League* (Birmingham: National Liberal Foundation, 1881), p. 9.

13 'In re DEBS', in Henry Budd and Ardemus Stewart (eds), *American and English Decisions in Equity: Being Select Cases decided in the appellate courts of America and England*, vol 2 (Philadelphia: M. Murphy, 1896), p. 399; Woodrow Wilson, 'A lecture on democracy', in Arthur S. Link (ed.), *The Papers of Woodrow Wilson*, vol. 7 (Princeton, NJ: Princeton University Press, 1968), p. 347.

Free speech as a weapon

7

When is free speech not about freedom? When it's about racism

Omar Khan

Enoch Powell's 'Rivers of Blood' speech was delivered as a rejection of the 1968 Race Relations Act, which extended the 1965 Race Relations Act, making it impermissible, for the first time, to discriminate on grounds of race in housing or employment. The violent imagery, the back-to-front moral inversion of racism in claiming that 'in 15–20 years' time [i.e. 1983–88], the black man will have the whip hand over the white man', attracts the most comment and condemnation.

However, it's worth reflecting on a less observed aspect of Powell's argument in this volume on free speech, and how that value interacts with racial discrimination. In addition to the empirical or consequentialist argument that more 'coloured' people would inevitably lead to more conflict, violence, and ultimately the overthrowing of the racial order, there was also a principled argument about freedom. However ugly the consequences, Powell argued, the English principle of freedom entailed the right to discriminate, to treat people differently because of their race.

In the post-war story of Britain, Powell's speech is told as a straightforward morality tale in which the Labour government, but also the Conservative opposition, particularly leader Edward Heath, led a wider establishment rejection of racism in British policymaking and public discourse. But the record is a bit more patchy, both then and now. Heath allowed the Conservative Party a free vote on the Race Relations Act that Powell spoke out against, and in the end it passed easily with only 44 votes against. But many Conservatives were deeply opposed to the Bill, with the Home Affairs spokesperson (and 'wet' Tory) Reginald Maudling, for example, offering a version of Powell's argument that freedom required discrimination: 'we believe that it definitely encroaches on individual freedom and individual liberty'.[1]

The argument that freedom requires discrimination is still affirmed, more frequently in the case of gay rights than in the case of racial discrimination, which publicly at least has few defenders.[2] But why speak of freedom to discriminate in a volume about freedom of speech? After all, words are one thing, and deeds another. For critics of hate speech legislation, this is precisely the point on which they object. It might be terrible to say racist things, but that can and must be distinguished from the doing of racist things.

This is a distinction that most anti-racists also affirm, if for a slightly different reason. Anti-racists are less focused on what a neighbour might privately think about a black neighbour, and more concerned that that neighbour might report the black neighbour to the police on frivolous, racially motivated grounds. What matters is that racism harms; it damages people's lives, and picks the people out for that harm because of their race. For anti-racists, furthermore, the fundamental mistake of the free speech debates is a deeper error about the nature of racism. Racism isn't about the naughty speech of a particular wordsmith, but rather about the structures and institutions that reproduce and justify racial inequalities in the world. Individual speech acts are rarely creative or come from nowhere, but instead tap into a deep wellspring of racist ideology that, even in 2020, is marshalled to justify ongoing racial injustice in our society.

For defenders of racist speech, by contrast, the structural or historical weaving of racism into our thinking and culture is not a relevant question, if they even apprehend it. Instead, the point is that even if someone says something racist, that doesn't actually or at least necessarily harm people. Or so the argument goes. When pushed, there is often an equivocation between two different claims or arguments. The first, ultra-libertarian claim is that all racist speech, and indeed all speech, however awful, must be allowed. This position has some, though not very many, real-world defenders, as few would countenance certain kinds of cartoons or arguments being published, whether in terms of racism or, say, child pornography.

Instead, most of those who purport to be defending free speech as a matter of principle are defending a second, different assertion: that a particular speech act is *not* in fact racist. This is, or should be, viewed as an empirical dispute. Opponents of a particular speech act often defend a more general claim that not all speech should be allowed, and that free speech is not an unassailable principle but can instead be trumped by other considerations (such as decency or harm). That is a fairly standard and in my view correct argument, but it sometimes mistakes the relevant terrain of dispute: many defenders of a particular speech act should instead be viewed as *denying* that the speech act in question is in fact racist.

This is because most if not all participants in the endless free speech debates do in fact think that some speech acts are indefensible, or racist to the point of inciting harm. An argument in favour of eugenics might not pass this threshold, but one advocating genocide probably would, for the vast majority of voices in this loud debate. It's possible, though highly doubtful, that some publishers might first ask: well, which group are you suggesting should be rounded up and killed?

Two less provocative points follow. First, that we should usually focus more on the empirical content of a particular speech or speech act, explaining if and why it is racist. In some instances there will be genuine and legitimate disagreement, and there are matters of degree when it comes to identifying racism. But often the problem instead stems from a failure to understand what racism *is*. In a sense the error here is not really or fundamentally about free speech as such, but rather a wider mistake in thinking that racism is merely about individual intent, or about whether a particular person or speech act is racist.

We cannot delve into people's private motivations, but it is striking just how predictable and consistent the actual must-be-spoken racist stereotypes are, and how consistent the social attitudes that allow those stereotypes not just to persist as *opinions*, but to drive *outcomes*, for people of colour in the real world. If I told that you a politician was accused of a racist speech against a young black man, or that a football crowd harassed a black player, you and I would know exactly what stereotypes were involved. In many such real-world instances, the racist speaker might not even be consciously aware of the racism – which is not to say that the racism wasn't wrong or pernicious, but rather to say that the racism has deep, widespread roots in our society that no particular individual is responsible for reproducing. And it's not just football fans or politicians: our art, music, novels, architecture, philosophical texts and of course our economy have been strongly marked by these racist attitudes and stereotypes for centuries, attitudes that have been invoked precisely to justify racist *actions*. One might say, based on historical and recent evidence, that certain views, especially racist views, are murderous in their intent and effects.

What the free speech libertarian is asking us to do is to imagine a case where a new racist speech act *doesn't* have outcomes in the world. A new, creative form of racism that doesn't tap into old stereotypes that were developed to justify – and continue to justify – actions and outcomes in the world that leave the targets of those stereotypes worse off. It is, I suppose, possible to imagine racist comments that are unconnected to the justification of injustice, or at least racist speech acts that don't result in harm for those targeted. The most plausible cases are where a disadvantaged group gently mocks an advantaged group for its advantage, and its ignorance of that advantage (say, by calling white middle-class women 'Karen').

Of course in the real world of the free speech debates, the shoe is on precisely the other foot. The racist speech acts that must be defended as a point of principle are almost always those that depict long-standing disadvantaged groups in precisely the same stereotypical ways that racists have always depicted those groups over the centuries. What we're being asked to countenance is: what if the racists of the eighteenth, nineteenth and twentieth centuries were right?

There is no easy distinction, then, between racist speech acts and racist actions in the world. This is not because there's no distinction between speech and action – of course there is. It's rather because of the meaning of *racism*. Racism is an ideology that justifies racist *actions* and *outcomes*. (The degree to which that justification will be successful in leading to the incitement of actions and outcomes will vary according to the effectiveness of the speaker or platform, and the likelihood that racist speech will lead to racist acts should therefore be judged on past, as well as present, evidence.) The conclusion here also extends to other forms of injustice, such as sexism and disablism, and also indicates the dishonesty of many who frame their arguments in favour of racism in terms of 'free speech'. Their first-order principle is the ongoing justification of a system of injustice, and they are scrambling around for more elevated ideas to obscure those prior commitments.

It's not just the meaning of the concept of racism that exposes the dishonesty of many (though not all) libertarian free speech defenders. Consider John Stuart Mill, usually cited as the best principled defence of free speech. Mill made (at least) two assumptions. First, that the interlocutors in an argument or dispute were committed to truth. He rightly saw that conventional opinion might be wrong or fallible (as Isaiah Berlin put it), and so viewed free speech as necessary for shining a light on consensus viewpoints that were in the end incorrect. It's very hard to describe some purported free-speech-requires-racist-speech advocates, say those who defend eugenics or Donald Trump's walls and bans as not racist, as committed to truth or evidence.

Second, and relatedly, Mill was a 'perfectionist' about human nature. He argued that human beings would and should strive to improve themselves, intellectually and morally. One of the reasons to defend free speech is to test our existing beliefs and ways of thinking, and to adapt our world view and actions in the face of better arguments and evidence. Here too, it's far from obvious that contrarian controversialists who just want to be allowed to say stereotypical things about Muslim women are interested in personal betterment, for themselves or others. This is not to say that we should ban such speech. Instead, we should query whether those insisting on the right to say racist things that have racist consequences in the world are really principally motivated by free speech.

An important consequence of the preceding analysis is that anti-racists should be, in principle, defenders of free speech. This is for two reasons. First, because many purported ultra-libertarians are not in fact motivated by the most morally serious or urgent infringements on free speech or liberty generally. Among those who are most keen to defend racist speech, their aim is instead to re-prosecute racist arguments that we have heard for centuries. Their insincerity means that anti-racists should look again at the principle of free speech, and recognise that it poses little threat to anti-racism, when racism – and free speech – is honestly and properly understood. If we choose to engage in such a debate, we should highlight that its terrain is not 'Is free speech under threat?' but 'Is racism really wrong?', and that this is not just a debate but a question of policies.

Second, providing the state or other institutions with the power to censor speech is unlikely to benefit minorities, particularly unjustly disadvantaged minorities. In general, 'minority' viewpoints are much more vulnerable to censorship than majority ones, and disadvantaged minority viewpoints more vulnerable still. It is much more likely that limitations on free speech will hit those arguing clearly and loudly against existing injustices than that it will constrain the voices of those who seek to defend and justify those injustices.

Just because many participants in free speech debates aren't much interested in ideas, evidence, ethics or truth doesn't mean that anti-racists should follow their lead. Millian defences of free speech are or should be compatible with an anti-racist position, and instead of arguing against free speech, the focus should be on naming and arguing against the racism many are calling for.

It is important to recognise that some free speech libertarians are indeed just that: libertarians. They should not be viewed as seeking to defend historically racist viewpoints, but many can still be challenged on their understanding of racism. Racism isn't just like any other view, and as a view it developed to justify *injustice in the world*. Racism is an argument for *action*. Mill was right that we should challenge convention, but unfortunately in 2020 there's still nothing unconventional about racism or injustice. The sooner we accept the extent and persistence of racism and its consequences, the sooner we can appreciate the value of free speech both as a principle and as a means to challenge falsehoods and injustice, rather than as a way to obscure truth and racism.

Notes

1   HC Deb, 23 April 1968, vol. 763 cc. 53–198; Maudling at col. 154, https://api.parliament.uk/historic-hansard/commons/1968/apr/23/race-relations-bill (accessed 10 July 2020).
2   See, for example, Katy Steinmetz, 'Why federal laws don't explicitly ban discrimination against LGBT Americans', *Time*, 21 March 2019, https://time.com/5554531/equality-act-lgbt-rights-trump/ (accessed 10 July 2020).

8

Drinking the hemlock:
Socrates and free speech

Neville Morley

One recurring motif in recent claims about the illiberal cultures of universities has been the deployment of the figure of Socrates, the fifth-century BCE Athenian philosopher. 'From Socrates to Salman Rushdie, heretical figures have been persecuted by powerful authorities, whether by the church or the state', proclaimed the blurb for a discussion of 'The Dangerous Rise of Academic Mobbing', featuring Professor Nigel Biggar, as part of a UK Battle of Ideas Festival in October 2019. In his account of 'academic mobbing', including his own experience, the sociologist Noah Carl offered a similar view:

> Persecution of intellectual dissidents is not a new phenomenon. In 399 BC, Socrates was tried and put to death, based on the charge that 'he busies himself studying things in the sky and below the earth', which it was claimed would 'corrupt the youth'. In 1633, Galileo ...[1]

'Socrates would be aghast at how few of us are willing to stand up for academic freedom if it risks arousing an angry mob', commented Jonathan Haidt in an email to the writer of a profile of Jordan Peterson.[2] And within an hour of the news that Peterson had been denied a visiting fellowship at Cambridge in 2018, one of his admirers had tweeted: 'Since when did the pursuit of knowledge and intellectual enlightenment have to conform to the latest fad or zeitgeist orthodoxy of the student body? You have become Athenian jurors to @jordanbpeterson's Socrates: you should drink the hemlock yourselves.'[3]

While such references are incidental to the substantive arguments about free speech and its allegedly endangered status, I want to argue here that they are central to the rhetorical presentation of the wider ideological project. In this regard they serve two main functions. First, Socrates has long been seen as the great martyr for secular truth, a man of unimpeachable virtue willing to die rather than disown his beliefs or agree to be silent. Implicitly or directly ('Jordan Peterson is one of the few fearless professors', Haidt's email continued), the comparison with Socrates heroises figures such as Biggar, Carl and Peterson as martyrs in the same tradition. It bestows on them the same aura of courage, integrity and nobility, equates their loss of a platform or receipt of criticism to a formal death sentence, and puts their critics into the role of the ignorant, irrational Athenian mob, enemies of reason and science. It seeks to present the debate about their views as one in which no right-thinking person would ever choose to be on the other side.

Secondly, above all in the United States, Socrates is understood as a model teacher, representing the true essence of education, and especially university education, which is now being attacked or desecrated.

There's a saying common in education circles: Don't teach students what to think; teach them how to think. The idea goes back at least as far as Socrates. Today, what we call the Socratic method is a way of teaching that fosters critical thinking, in part by encouraging students to question their own unexamined beliefs, as well as the received wisdom of those around them. Such questioning sometimes leads to discomfort, and even to anger, on the way to understanding.[4]

This too builds on a long tradition; the 'Socratic method' of education – based, according to Plato, on Socrates' belief that he was wise because he *knew* he knew nothing – was how John Stuart Mill was taught by his father, and was adopted as a method of training in critical thought at Harvard Law School in the late nineteenth century. The essential Socratic spirit of the university was already identified as under threat from relativism and postmodernism in Allan Bloom's 1987 *The Closing of the American Mind*, a title that is deliberately evoked by Lukianoff and Haidt; their book is simply a continuation of that culture war.[5] But there has also been a subtle shift in emphasis, from the need for students to be helped to think critically and ask questions themselves, to the idea that deluded students must be confronted with the harsh but necessary truths possessed by the all-knowing professor, and with people and views they might find objectionable. The modern Socrates is wise because he knows the truth, especially that of science, and knows that his students are trying to hide from it with their talk of safe spaces and micro-aggressions.

> The notion that a university should protect all of its students from ideas that some of them find offensive is a repudiation of the legacy of Socrates, who described himself as the 'gadfly' of the Athenian people. He thought it was his job to sting, to disturb, to question, and thereby to provoke his fellow Athenians to think through their current beliefs, and change the ones they could not defend.[6]

The great advantage of taking Socrates as a totemic figure is that there is relatively little historical data to get in the way of the mythologising. He wrote nothing – all we know about his thinking comes from the accounts of others – and so there are no misjudged remarks or failed jokes to be dug up and quoted against him. Claims

97

attributed to him by hostile sources, such as the comic playwright Aristophanes, are easily dismissed; but so too are ideas which his pupils put into his mouth, if they prove inconvenient, such as the notorious argument in Plato's *Republic* (401b-c) in favour of the censorship of art and literature to make his ideal city a safe space. For Plato's Socrates, as for his modern disciples, freedom of speech meant freedom for *his* speech – but the idealised Socrates is innocent of such fragility and bad ideas.

This uncertainty extends to the reason why, after he had been annoying his fellow citizens with awkward questions for half a century, Socrates was suddenly brought to trial in 399 BCE on a charge of impiety and corrupting the youth. Partly it's a matter of the surviving evidence. Athenian laws were notoriously, deliberately vague; the law established that impiety was a crime, but left it to the citizens in the courtroom – 501 of them in Socrates' case – to decide, on the basis of the prosecution and defence speeches, whether the alleged behaviour was impious.[7] Further, we have only the defence speech, which naturally presented the charges in a manner intended to minimise their plausibility – and not even the speech as actually delivered, but later reconstructions or fictions by Socrates' students and admirers. So, we have to guess at how the prosecution would have made its case, but on the basis of the written record it can be hard to understand why Socrates was accused, or why a majority found him guilty. He presents himself as someone who seeks knowledge and understanding through talking to others, who has loyally served the community, and who follows his conscience even when this might bring him trouble. He does indeed appear as the spokesman for individual conscience and freedom of expression.[8]

Classical Athens prided itself on *isonomia*, equality of speech, the fact that every citizen could contribute to debates in the assembly and so help guide the whole community; every assembly meeting opened with the words 'Who wishes to speak?'[9] Socrates preferred to talk to people in the marketplace and on the street and in private homes, but surely these conversations, making his fellow Athenians think about things more carefully, were just as valuable as those public debates? It's clear from Aristophanes' comic play *The Clouds*, performed in 423 BCE, that there might be grounds for doubt; Socrates appeared there (unfairly, in Plato's view) as an example of the 'sophists', whose clever arguments and manipulative rhetoric could teach people to 'make the worse argument appear better', undermining tradition and the basis of democratic deliberation. But still the majority of citizens were clearly willing to tolerate him for most of his long life.

In 404 BCE, however, Athens was utterly defeated at the end of its long war against Sparta; the democratic constitution was replaced by the brutal oligarchic dictatorship of the Thirty, said to have executed without trial more than 1500 citizens, nearly 10 per cent of the total population, in trying to consolidate its power. One of Socrates' most famous admirers, Alcibiades, had played an ignominious role in the latter part of the war, at one point switching sides to Sparta, and then agitating for a coup against the democracy. Another former student, Critias, was the ruthless leader of the Thirty. These were the most prominent 'youths' whom Socrates was thought to have corrupted; and the corrupting ideas were not, as Carl implies, his proto-scientific researches, but his questioning of the founding idea of the democracy: that ordinary citizens could make a full contribution to ruling the community. In the view of the aristocratic circle around Socrates and his students, ruling required expertise, which only men like them possessed.[10]

In other words, prominent among the beliefs of the Athenians that Socrates thought should be abandoned, because they could not, in his view, adequately defend them, was democracy. The immediate aftermath of a period of violent anti-democratic rule was not a good time to hold such a view. But even this, it is argued, would not have condemned him, not least because crimes related to the rule of the Thirty were now covered by an amnesty; it was rather his refusal to take any responsibility for his words. The counterweight to Athenian freedom of speech was the possibility of being held to account for its consequences: the charge of *graphē paranómōn*, of persuading the assembly to make an illegal decision (which was, incidentally, abolished briefly by a short-lived oligarchic regime in 411 BCE, on the grounds that it would inhibit people from speaking honestly). In his defence speech, however, Socrates denied any responsibility for the actions of Alcibiades or Critias, and flatly refused to offer any undertaking to change his ways or modify his speech in future.

Whether this was enough to find him guilty divided the Athenians – there were, according to Plato, just thirty votes in it, out of the 501 – as it has divided modern commentators. This is why the case of Socrates should be at the heart of debates around free speech and its limits; not because either he or the Athenians were clearly right or wrong, but precisely because it tests the boundaries of different positions, and what happens when they come into conflict. Before the nineteenth century, of course, there was no such problem: democracy was known to be mob rule, with Socrates its blameless victim. But as members of more democratic societies, we might now be wary of the political implications of some of his (or Plato's) arguments, and more conscious of the case that a community might legitimately set limits on an individual right, such as free speech, in the interests of its members.

The problem with evocations of Socrates in the current debate is that they ignore – and work rhetorically to obscure – the possibility that there is anything to be debated. They are profoundly, if not necessarily consciously, anti-democratic, simply assuming the superiority of an enlightened thinker over ignorant students who must be directed and discomfited, and who certainly are not qualified to judge them or their ideas. Now, as then, the concern of Socrates' admirers is to privilege the speech solely of those who supposedly possess superior understanding – themselves – and to reject any responsibility for the possible consequences, whether it serves to legitimise inequality and discrimination, or inspires others to act violently against their society.

Notes

1 Noah Carl, '"Academic mobbing" undermines open enquiry and destroys the soul of universities', *The Economist*, 23 July 19, https://www.economist.com/open-future/2019/07/23/academic-mobbing-undermines-open-inquiry-and-destroys-the-soul-of-universities (accessed 10 July 2020).

2 Quoted in Tom Bartlett, 'What's so dangerous about Jordan Peterson?', *Chronicle of Higher Education*, 17 January 2018, https://www.chronicle.com/article/What-s-So-Dangerous-About/242256 (accessed 10 July 2020).

3 https://twitter.com/adrian_hilton/status/1108383844087025664?s=21 (now deleted).

4 Greg Lukianoff and Jonathan Haidt, 'The coddling of the American mind', *The Atlantic*, September 2015, pp. 42–52 (p. 45). Their 2018 book of the same title (New York: Random House) places still more emphasis on the theme by contrasting such critical rigour – the truths of ancient wisdom (p. 4) – with the lessons of an imaginary visit to another Greek oracle, who of course, unlike noble Socrates, charges for teaching. See also Paul Corey, 'The Socratic method in today's university', in Lee Trepanier (ed.), *The Socratic Method Today: Student-centered and Transformative Teaching in Political Science* (New York: Routledge, 2018).

5 Allan Bloom, *The Closing of the American Mind* (New York: Simon and Schuster, 1987); similarly, Dinesh D'Souza, *Illiberal Education: The Politics of Race and Sex on Campus* (New York: The Free Press, 1991), pp. 189–90.

6 Lukianoff and Haidt, *Coddling*, p. 49.

7 See Josiah Ober, 'Socrates and democratic Athens', in Donald R. Morrison (ed.), *The Cambridge Companion to Socrates* (Cambridge: Cambridge University Press, 2010), pp. 138–78.

8 See James A. Colaiaco, *Socrates Against Athens: Philosophy on Trial* (New York: Routledge, 2001).

9 See Ineke Sluiter and Ralph Rosen (eds), *Free Speech in Classical Antiquity* (Leiden: Brill, 2004), especially the chapters by D. M. Carter and Robert W. Wallace.

10 See Jennifer Tolbert Roberts, *Athens on Trial: The Antidemocratic Tradition in Western Thought* (Princeton, NJ: Princeton University Press, 1994).

9

Secularism, Islamophobia and free speech in France

Imen Neffati

On 7 January 2015 the *Charlie Hebdo* offices in Paris were attacked during the magazine's weekly editorial meeting, leading to the deaths of twelve of its staff. The attack sparked an unprecedented debate about freedom of speech both internationally and in France, and about the Republican values of *laïcité* (French secularism) that *Charlie Hebdo* has been portrayed as representing. The literature that emerged immediately in the aftermath of the attack centred around several dramatic moments such as the 'Je Suis Charlie' slogan, the Republican marches of 10–11 January 2015, *Charlie Hebdo*'s survivors' issue published on 14 January 2015, and the question of free speech. The attack represented a transformative moment in the public debate in France and internationally, centred around a re-evaluation of free speech and France's Republican universalist identity.

The initial media response to the *Charlie Hebdo* attack was framed in terms of an absolutist (though not without inconsistencies) liberal interpretation of free speech perceived as an end in itself: sacred, undivided, uncompromised and based on a problematic binary opposition between free speech and censorship, which often ignores context. However, *Charlie Hebdo* itself does not subscribe to an idea of absolute freedom of expression. In fact, in response to accusations of causing offence to Muslims, Philippe Val (editor of *Charlie Hebdo* from 1992 to 2009 and responsible in 2006 for the publication of the Muhammad caricatures) had argued:

> We never pretended to fight for a freedom of expression that is not restricted by the freedom of others: we acknowledge the necessity of the boundaries that French laws pose, such as the prohibition of incitement to hatred, and defamation.[1]

For Val, freedom of speech is synonymous with democracy, achieved thanks to the joint efforts of civil society in overthrowing blasphemy laws. Caroline Fourest, a *Charlie Hebdo* journalist and a close ally of Val, posits that the absence of blasphemy laws in France enables debate about religion, and maintains that in a secular society all beliefs are equal, or in other words that there is no one religion or faith more sacred than another. *Laïcité*, the conception of secularism as a constitutional principle as detailed by the 42 articles of the 1905 Law on the Separation of the Churches and State in France, in this sense establishes a certain equality of treatment that is overseen by the Republic. Also, *Charlie Hebdo*'s official editorial line does not claim to be politically incorrect, despite the fact that most of the magazine's partisans defend its offensive humour in the name of 'political correctness gone mad'. From the early 2000s, *Charlie Hebdo* had become predominantly focused on Islam and Muslims, especially Muslim women. The magazine's provocative humour about religion in general and Islam in particular was based on a certain understanding of the concept of political correctness. Charb (*Charlie Hebdo*'s chief editor 2009–15) argued that the political right and reactionaries used the accusation of political correctness to silence their opponents, and by using such a qualifier, the proponent of political incorrectness implies that the politically correct is simply conformist and coy. Charb firmly underlined this point when he stated that 'the politically incorrect crook does not overturn the established order; he incarnates the established order'.[2]

The question of Islamophobia in *Charlie Hebdo*'s representations of Muslims, particularly veiled Muslim women, is instead intricately and deceptively linked to the issue of *laïcité*. Deceptively, because *Charlie Hebdo* weaponised and constrained *laïcité*, while itself becoming a tool for free speech absolutists. The editorial of Gérard Biard, editor-in-chief, published in the *Charlie Hebdo* survivors' issue (the first issue after the attack), further stressed the theme of *laïcité* as both the magazine's *raison d'être* and its most commendable value, which guarantees the functioning of France's institutions and laws:

> We hope that starting from 7 January 2015, a firm defence of *laïcité* will be granted for everyone. That we will finally cease, out of posturing, out of electoral calculations, or out of cowardice, to legitimise or even merely to tolerate communitarianism and cultural relativism, which opens the way to only one thing: religious totalitarianism. Yes, the Israeli-Palestinian conflict is a reality; yes, international geopolitics is a succession of manœuvres and dirty tricks; yes, the social condition of what we call 'communities of Muslim origin' in France is profoundly unjust; yes, racism and discriminations should be fought relentlessly. Fortunately, there exist several tools to try and resolve these serious problems, but they are all inoperable if one thing is missing: *laïcité*.[3]

Biard's message aimed to redefine *laïcité* as a sanctified value, and the foundation of the Republic itself. I believe that any analysis of *Charlie Hebdo*'s anti-Islam discourse must include a re-examination of the French Republic's secular traditions, its emphasis on both freedom of expression and a 'neutral' and secular public space grounded on a certain understanding of universalism. Therefore, to understand the rapport between the concepts of free speech and *laïcité*, and how both became entangled with the rise of Islamophobia in France, an explanation of Republican universalism is important in order to recognise the context which led to free speech being defended in absolutist terms and as a fundamental component of secular France.

Universalism is by far the most defining characteristic of the French Republic. It is also its most abiding and protected principle, uniting succeeding French republics since 1792, and the principle by which the Republic and its values – liberty, equality and fraternity – are defined. According to Joan Wallach Scott, 'universalism is a serious (if disputed) philosophical concept and a mythologised restatement of the principles of 1789'.[4] The nation, in a universalist political philosophy, is the articulation of the will of the people, or as Rousseau put it, the 'general will', which – as stated in Article 6 of the Declaration of the Rights of Man and the Citizen – is the same for all; that is, the nation as an abstract notion is taken to represent everyone. Within the nation, individuals do not represent existing and/or competing entities; they rather represent through their actions a singular body of a nation that is one and indivisible. Maurice Samuels adds:

> Whereas in other countries, universalism connotes one law applying to all people equally, in France, universalism has also come to mean that the state accords rights only to individuals, not ethnic or religious groups, and that the individual must be shorn of all particularities in order to access those rights. It is this divorcing of the citizen from group affiliations that defines the singularity of the French case, the 'exception française' to the liberal pluralism that prevails in the Anglo-American context.[5]

The nation's abstract individuals are equal and interchangeable, joined together by a common understanding of rationality that defines political life. The nation they form is therefore equally abstract. Universalism in this sense is secular. What is perceived as one of the main assets of this conception of the nation is that any and all individuals within it are regarded and treated as equal citizens – theoretically.

But critics of an assimilationist universalism that is inimical to difference ask whether there can be limits to abstraction, in the light of the different ways in which Republican universalism has used narratives of equality and freedom to hide colonialist and neo-colonialist ways of thinking and of exerting power.[6] The vehement reassertion of Republican universalist values that we have seen in the aftermath of the *Charlie Hebdo* attack has focused almost exclusively on the value of liberty. If universalism is now framed in terms of an antagonism with Islam and Muslim identity, this was already evident in the 1980s, articulated in racism against immigrants. The immigration question intensified with the rise of the ultra-nationalist Front National in 1983, and its steadily increasing popularity in the presidential elections, which manifested in 14 per cent of the votes in 1988, 17 per cent in 2002, and 33.9 per cent in 2017. This intersected with a surge of identity-based politics in the 1990s, while policies proposed to end years of racism and sexism rejected any understanding of diversity and multiculturalism, both of which were framed as incompatible with Republican universalism. Public debate – led and framed by mainstream media – thus particularly hindered any policies in favour of minorities. The consideration of individuals as members of groups was censored and denied repeatedly, and the Constitution of 1958 and Article 6 of the Declaration of the Rights of Man and the Citizen are usually cited as ample protection against all forms of discrimination.[7]

The rise of anti-Muslim rhetoric, first at the extremes (the Front National) and more recently in the mainstream, occurred through a reframing of the narrative on *laïcité* which is channelled through the practice of free speech. By invoking *laïcité*, race- and religious-equality agendas have been intentionally separated, and this separation has spilled into the debate on *Charlie Hebdo*'s anti-Muslim rhetoric. As a consequence, it became easy and legitimate to speak about religion without referring to race and vice versa. This process helped remove Muslims in France from the broader struggle for equality. The debate is thus formulated in terms of 'Islam de France' because religion provides 'a convenient cover for those wishing to argue that they are attacking a belief and not people, and in a context where racism is allegedly unacceptable, wriggle out of or deflect such charges'.[8] Speaking of *laïcité* as a fundamental pillar of universalism adds legitimacy to criticism of Muslims, but more specifically it is the evolution of the very definition of *laïcité* which led to the perception of free speech as an absolutist cherished value. In fact, throughout its history, the term that *Charlie Hebdo* used to justify its anti-Muslim rhetoric has not been free speech but rather the defence of the Republican idea of *laïcité*.

Charlie Hebdo's criticism of Islam is another way of claiming guardianship over *laïcité* (and free speech). The Baby Loup affair in 2008, for instance, sparked a national debate when Fatima Atif was fired from her job at the Baby Loup nursery in Paris because she refused to submit to her employer's order to remove the veil during working hours. With the support of HALDE, Atif decided to sue her boss Natalia Baleato for racial discrimination.[9] The trial, which took over two years, acquitted the employer. *Charlie Hebdo*'s journalist Silvia Coma dedicated a long interview to celebrating Baleato's victory for *laïcité*, and the cartoonist Catherine offered a strip depicting seven ways in which the burqa is dangerous to wear near babies. In fact, Atif did not wear the burqa, simply a headscarf, while Catherine's cartoon used the blue Afghan-style full-body veil. Needless to say, the plaintiff was not interviewed by *Charlie*

Hebdo – or any other prominent newspaper – which suggests that the terms of public debate around the veil in France silence Muslim women's voices, and some have argued that this has been the case since the Islamic scarf controversies in 1989, 2004 and 2010.[10]

Baleato opined about the increasing numbers of women wearing the veil in her neighbourhood and the reasons they wore it in the past: 'The meaning of the veil has changed. It is no longer a symbol of allegiance, but a sign of protest.'[11] Baleato also tried to stigmatise veiled women working in her institution when she complained that they posed a hygiene risk when they refused to roll up their sleeves and wash their hands properly. She stated: 'some women pretended they were on their periods so that they didn't have to uncover their bodies and go in the swimming pool with the children'. The article also included clichéd claims about veiled women interrupting the children's classes by wanting to take them to prayer. Much of the interview was a campaign against the veil centred on Baleato's biography and her fight for freedom and *laïcité*.

Laïcité has been frequently invoked by members of the public and wider society in a way that suggests that the word itself means the same thing for everyone, that it is a value that should be defended more than explained, and that the biggest threat to it comes from Muslims. It is important to note that in the Republican mindset, the concept of *laïcité* is internally consistent, complete and does not need interpretation. Criticism of the concept, particularly in times of national crisis, is tantamount to betraying France itself, and very few scholars were able to present a nuanced study of the concept's limitations. Jean Baubérot, an expert on the subject, speaks of historical *laïcité* and of a new *laïcité*. The latter designates a politically conservative (right-wing/far-right) interpretation of the term and manifests itself in the creation of a certain inequality between religions and religious people. Most importantly, Baubérot notes a shift from a historical universalist *laïcité* to a 'new franco-French and identity-based *laïcité*'.[12] Evidently, most attempts at defining the idea of *laïcité* in France are framed in terms of the separation of the Church and state as per the 1905 law, especially after its 2005 centenary. Prior to that, the French Revolution used to be the referent. *Laïcité* is, then, in the Republican narrative, an element of progress in the process of society's rupture with the *Ancien Régime*.[13] *Laïcité* is supposed to guarantee religious freedom, that is, equality of respect and freedom of conscience.

But there has been a Republican obsession with the concept of *laïcité*, which has shifted its invocation to become a means to differentiate between 'good French citizens' who live by the Republic's values, and 'others' who do not. Philippe Marlière argues that in contrast to the acceptance of Catholicism in the French secular space, as well as the toleration of Judaism and Protestantism, Islam remains an antagonised body within the French nation.[14] While *laïcité* is meant to facilitate communication between different people on the basis of their citizenship, the new *laïcité* prevents the combination of universalism with difference, rendering *laïcité* incapable of answering the contemporary exigencies of equality.[15] In a way, the contemporary interpretation of *laïcité*, like universalism, is based on a strong sense of assimilation, where the 'other' is accepted as similar to, or the same as, oneself only by making difference an abstraction, especially when this difference is religious.

When it comes to public debate, Baubérot argues that the law is more famous than it is understood: many who invoke it are not fully aware of the content of its 44 articles (which have also been modified, most notably in January 1907). The historian notes many errors in the way *laïcité* is invoked. Many aspects of the law show that it is politically liberal and religiously accommodating.[16] In the process of its issuing in 1905, an amendment aimed at removing religious references from certain holidays was rejected by 466 votes to 60. An amendment to prevent churches from acquiring civil status and acting in the law courts, including against the state, was rejected by 425 votes to 155. This was very important because it shows that religious organisations belong to civil society and have rights before the state.

It follows that most arguments which stipulate that the 1905 law establishes neutrality in public space, or that the same law relegates religion to the private sphere, are erroneous. In fact, it was President Jacques Chirac who, in a speech preceding the vote on the legislation outlawing all overt religious signs from French public schools in 2004, introduced the notion of neutrality. Speaking on 17 December 2003, he emphasised the spatial dimension of the word when he described the Republic as 'the privileged site for meetings and exchanges, where everyone can give of their best to the national community. It is the neutrality of the public arena which permits the various religions to coexist harmoniously.' It can clearly be demonstrated therefore that the restrictive measures of what Baubérot calls the new *laïcité*, which are generally assumed to be in harmony with the 1905 law, are in fact more modern inventions.

Using the example of the cassock, Baubérot refers back to the circumstances of its interdiction during the French Revolution and under Bonaparte in 1802, and its reappearance in the nineteenth century. For many anti-clerical members of the assembly, the cassock constituted a provocation, so during the parliamentary debates on the 1905 law some wanted it banned on the grounds that it is not a religious obligation, it is more clerical than religious, it is an act of proselytism, it is a sign of oppression and, finally, that many priests would want a law that would 'liberate' them from this oppressive clothing – astonishingly, similar arguments were used in favour of the banning of the veil in 2004 and the burqa in 2010. Those advocating for the banning of the cassock wanted to help the progressive cause. This Baubérot describes as a process of relative secularisation in the name of *laïcité*, while *laïcité* is and should be more tolerant, less invasive, more pluralist and less political than secularism, which illustrates a division between a liberal, separatist *laïcité* and a gallic, authoritarian *laïcité*. The amendment to ban the cassock was rejected by 391 votes to 184. Baubérot concludes that within the logic of the 1905 law, the laic change is essentially political: it is to replace the system of religious authority with a system of liberty: public space is pluralist without drama nor violation of the Republic. Everyone dresses as they want and differences in clothing are no longer important: every particular dress becomes like any other dress. *Laïcité* should not imply the secularisation of individuals, it should rather constitute the political regulation of individuals who entertain different relationships to secularisation. However, the ban on the headscarf in public schools in 2004 and the burqa in 2010, along with the recurrent veil affairs which have resurfaced repeatedly ever since, have favoured the gallic, authoritarian *laïcité*, and *Charlie Hebdo*, despite its satirical, anti-establishment self-identity, did not challenge this.

Since the Muhammad caricatures controversy in 2006, *Charlie Hebdo* has been categorised as a media outlet at the forefront of a global movement to defend the right to vilify others in the name of free speech. Proponents of such views have acquired, and sometimes been handed, the most vocal platforms and media privileges to disseminate their dangerous ideas. In 2019 Zineb el Rhazoui, a former prominent *Charlie Hebdo* journalist, successfully established her own brand outside of the newspaper, recycling the same old ideas about the peril of Islam, and being granted legitimacy by many TV channels on the right and the left – always being introduced to the public as the former *Charlie Hebdo* journalist. She benefited from a context derived from the aftermath of the January 2015 attack, when *Charlie Hebdo* became a useful global symbol in the wider conflict over free speech – a symbol exploited by those who are not familiar with the magazine's style, humour, motivation and long history of building its argument on the threat of Islam using a problematic definition of *laïcité*.

Notes

1 Philippe Val, *Reviens Voltaire, Ils sont devenus fous* (Paris: Grasset, 2008).

2 *Charlie Hebdo*, 22 February 2012.

3 *Charlie Hebdo*, 14 January 2015.

4 Joan Wallach Scott, 'French universalism in the nineties', *Differences*, 15.2 (2004), pp. 32–53 (p. 33).

5 Maurice Samuels, *The Right to Difference, French Universalism and the Jews* (Chicago: University of Chicago Press, 2016), p. 3.

6 See Joan Wallach Scott, *Parité! Sexual Equality and the Crisis of French Universalism* (Chicago: University of Chicago Press, 2005); Wendy Brown, *Regulating Aversion: Tolerance in the Age of Identity and Empire* (Princeton, NJ: Princeton University Press, 2006); and Étienne Balibar, 'Y a-t-il un "néo-racisme"?', in Étienne Balibar and Immanuel Wallerstein, *Race, nation, classe: Les identités ambiguës* (Paris: La Découverte, 1997), pp. 36–7. Some, however, argue that French universalism could manifest itself in discriminatory behaviours, not to say that universalism is inherently racist, but to advance a historicised notion of universalism in order to showcase its various pluralist articulations and to highlight the ideal of justice at its heart. For this, see Jean-François Chanet, *L'école républicaine et les petites patries* (Paris: Aubier, 1996); and Mona Ozouf, *Composition française: Retour sur une enfance bretonne* (Paris: Gallimard, 2009).

7 Article 6 reads, 'All citizens are equal before the law and are equally admissible to all offices, places and public employments, according to their capacity and without other distinction than that of their virtues and talents.' Women's equality calls were also ignored on the same basis and a decision by the Constitutional Council in 1982 ruled out special

treatment of women as a way of correcting discrimination against them. See Scott, 'French universalism in the nineties'.

8   Aurelien Mondon and Aaron Winter, 'Articulations of Islamophobia: from the extreme to the mainstream?', *Ethnic and Racial Studies*, 40.13 (2017), pp. 2151–79 (p. 2156).

9   HALDE is the French Equal Opportunities and Anti-Discrimination Commission. In October 2010 the new president of HALDE, Jeannette Bougrab, invoked her fight for *laïcité*, withdrew the organisation's support for Atif and asked for a re-examination of the case. She was a very close friend of President Nicolas Sarkozy, and the alleged partner of Charb. She is the author of *Lettre aux femmes voilées et à ceux qui les soutiennent* (Paris: Les éditions du Cerf, 2019).

10 See Pierre Tevanian, *La Mécanique raciste* (Paris: La Découverte, 2008), which dissects the racist phenomenon in France as a concept, a perception and an affect. Pierre Tevanian, Ismahane Chouder and Malika Latrèche, *Les Filles voilées parlent* (Paris: La Fabrique, 2008), contains interviews with veiled Muslim women in France and recounts their experiences in school, work and society as a whole.

11 *Charlie Hebdo*, 22 December 2010.

12 Jean Baubérot, *La Laïcité falsifiée* (Paris: La Découverte, 2012), p. 85.

13 See Alain Renaut and Alain Tourraine, *Un Débat sur la laïcité* (Paris: Editions Stock, 2005).

14 Philippe Marlière, 'The meaning of "Charlie"', in Gavan Titley, Des Freedman, Gholan Khibany and Aurelien Mondon (eds), *After Charlie Hebdo: Terror, Racism and Free Speech* (London: Zed Books, 2017), p. 52.

15 Renaut and Tourraine, *Un Débat sur la laïcité*.

16 Renaut and Tourraine, *Un Débat sur la laïcité*.

10

The logic of nonsense

Nina Lyon

'Yes or no? Straight answer'

In the British political comedy *Yes Minister*, a naive incoming MP, Jim Hacker, begins each episode with a proposition whose inevitable frustration at the hands of his departmental civil servant, Sir Humphrey Appleby, forms the plot. *Yes Minister*'s success was pervasive because it identified two truths about the nature of governance that transcended political tribes. One of these was the perceived intransigence of civil servants – a group with which factions of Boris Johnson's government, shortly before the time of writing, were openly at war. The other was a truth about truth, namely that politicians will do whatever they can to avoid telling it.

The corollary of the free speech trope of speaking truth to power is that power tends to avoid speaking truth. This chapter will look at some of the tactics deployed to this end, from minimisation to self-contradiction, irony and nonsense, along with their consequences for public discourse.

What do we mean by truth, though? In the interest of avoiding lengthy digressions, it might be better to say that the aim is to avoid making any straightforward, positive statement that can be easily tested and verified. If you make a claim whose veracity can be tested, you make yourself vulnerable: you will be accused of having lied. If you make a claim about a future action – I will slim down the wasteful and inefficient Civil Service – and it is not carried out, you will be accused either of incompetence or insincerity in that claim. Future claims will not be seen as offering an indication of corresponding real-life action; they become empty of denoted content. Making any positive statement, therefore, carries a political risk.

In *Yes Minister*, the information minimisation strategy that Sir Humphrey schools Hacker in is premised on the assumption that the public is unreasonable, emotive and incapable of understanding compromise. The complexity of governance demands compromise, of which the ideal form, so far as Sir Humphrey is concerned, is doing nothing. A figure such as Sir Humphrey might be thought of as the ultimate serious technocrat, as attested by his illustrious Oxford education, knighthood and status as senior civil servant in the Department for Administrative Affairs. The joke is not only that the technocrats do not, in fact, carry out much in the way of technocratic governance, but that Sir Humphrey, for all his outward gravitas, is ultimately nonsensical.

> **Jim Hacker**: When you give your evidence to the Think Tank, are you going to support my view that the Civil Service is over-manned and feather-bedded, or not? Yes or no? Straight answer.

> **Sir Humphrey**: Well Minister, if you ask me for a straight answer, then I shall say that, as far as we can see, looking at it by and large, taking one thing with another in terms of the average of departments, then in the final analysis it is probably true to say that, at the end of the day, in general terms, you would probably find that, not to put too fine a point

on it, there probably wasn't very much in it one way or the other. As far as one can see, at this stage.[1]

The premise here is that the Civil Service is over-staffed and wasteful, and Sir Humphrey knows it. He is tasked by the Civil Service with protecting its interests, but cannot be outwardly seen to be doing so when the institution is under scrutiny; he is also tasked with providing correct information to his minister. Sir Humphrey is in a double bind, of the sort he usually generates for Hacker in order to prevent ministerial ambitions from getting in the way of doing nothing – he cannot state what he knows to be the case, but he cannot deny it either, and is therefore forced to say nothing in comically elaborate form. Sir Humphrey layers phrase after phrase of managerial jargon into a stream of qualifiers that leads us to anticipate something controversial – instead, he concludes that the 'straight answer' is inconclusive, and throws in a further set of qualifications. In seeking to avoid making a statement that will later be proven false, placing him at risk of being considered someone whose statements cannot be taken as meaning what they say, he makes a statement without meaning.

The true meaning of 'covfefe'

The serious technocrat era of carefully qualified information minimisation gave way to more interesting times. The public, wise to the old Sir Humphrey tactics of qualification, equivocation and fudging, or perhaps simply bored of them, began to warm to straight talk: Make America Great Again, Take Back Control, Build the Wall, Get Brexit Done – short, grammatically simple and apparently straightforward assertions.

The leftist writer Amber A'Lee Frost argued in a 2016 essay, 'The Necessity of Political Vulgarity', that

> Trump's vulgarity is appealing precisely because it exposes political truths. As others have noted, Trump's policies (wildly inconsistent though they may be) are actually no more extreme than those of other Republicans; Trump is just willing to strip away the pretense. Other candidates may say 'national security is a fundamental priority', whereas Trump will opt for 'ban all the Muslims'.[2]

Wild inconsistencies proved to be a feature, not a bug. The most generous interpretation was that Trump's straight-talk banter might at first have helped disguise contradictions in his positioning: he was at odds with the Republican establishment on a host of foreign policy issues, leaving a trail of conflicting statements. However, the Pulitzer Prize winning fact-checking website Politifact rates 71 per cent of his statements as either partially, completely or outrageously false, with 15 per cent in the highest 'Pants on Fire' category.[3] The lies and contradictions ceased to provoke outrage and became a source of entertainment: if you cannot work out what speech implies, it has no further meaning, and might as well be treated as a game.

Just after midnight on 31 May 2017, @realDonaldTrump tweeted, 'Despite the widespread negative press covfefe' – the text ended there.[4] Although it was contextually obvious that 'covfefe' meant 'coverage', the opportunity for ironic speculation took 'covfefe' viral, dominating not only Twitter but mainstream media as Trump withdrew from the Paris Climate Accord. Trump, apparently out of bed again early the next morning, played the game, adding 'Who can figure out the true meaning of "covfefe"??? Enjoy!'[5]

When, a year later, an ambiguous recording of a name that sounded either like Yanny or Laurel went viral, Trump released a White House video sharing the opinions of his senior colleagues and announced that he heard it as 'covfefe'. 'It's Laurel', said Kellyanne Conway, counsellor to the president, 'but I could deflect and divert to Yanny if you need me to.' 'Clearly you're getting your information from CNN because that's fake news', added Sarah Huckabee Sanders, the White House press secretary, self-referentially invoking the administration's own reputation for mendacity as part of the joke.[6] Acknowledging one's own habit of lying creates a version of the Liar Paradox – the sentence 'I am lying', if true, means that I am lying, and is therefore simultaneously false. Paradox and self-reference distort the ordinary rules of true and false, and create a layer of ironic distance from reality, making it harder to ascertain.

What seemed a throwaway choice of meme for the White House to inveigh on probably wasn't. The virality of memes such as Yanny and Laurel, or the dress that, depending on the observer, was obviously either blue and black or white and silver, tells us something about the perverse appeal of contradictions. They make the apparent obviousness of perception just as obviously subjective, forcing us to doubt the veracity of what we heard or saw. But that uncertainty is not always uncomfortable, and it has advantages. When speech becomes devoid of meaning, we can project our own.

The satirist Stephen Colbert's concept of 'truthiness', an appeal to direct emotion unencumbered by concerns about denotational accuracy, was first aired in 2005 to describe the American right's tendency to make impassioned, factually misleading statements. 'The truthiness is', Colbert intoned in his professorial on-air persona, 'anyone can read the news to you. I promise to *feel* the news *at* you.'[7] Colbert later added that 'We're not talking about truth, we're talking about something that seems like truth – the truth we want to exist.'[8] It didn't really matter if the facts – at that time concerning the invasion of Iraq – failed to match the narrative; the emotive impact of the narrative was more important. If you could speak to people with conviction, what the speech denoted mattered less.

The embrace of contradiction added another layer of obfuscation to straight-talking truthiness. If you provide a series of contradictory assertions, it provides cover. Nobody expects to hold you to account. You get to speak to lots of different people, forming coalitions with competing interests, each of whom find something in the stream of consciousness that appeals to their own fears and ambitions. In character alignment terms, the rhetoric moved from lawful to chaotic, and people did not mind if it contained elements of evil because it provided plausible deniability: he doesn't really mean that, we could argue; it's a game, or merely rhetoric.

Boris Johnson's landslide victory in 2019 consolidated the era of the out-and-proud political trickster. His policy platform had all the trappings of the serially unfashionable Blue Labour movement: big-state fixes for regional economic inequality with socially conservative leanings. Blue Labour, a bastion of earnestness, had failed to get traction on the left, but Johnson framed the same ideas within jovial *noblesse oblige*, as acts of patriotic generosity to the people. It was a distinctive turn from the Thatcherism that motivated most of his party's activists, raising the question of how he would align their interests, shared by influential party donors, with his election promises to the regions.

But self-contradiction, once again, had not yet proven problematic. Lists of contradictory statements regarding Johnson's position on the Brexit withdrawal arrangements can be found on Remain-backed websites.[9] When pushed, Johnson would typically assert straightforward statements, answering yes/no queries truthily and without qualification. Another member of the government would then set out a new and contrary position. It was the material of *Yes Minister* plot nightmares, but interpreted instead as strategy.

The logic of nonsense

Rather than retreating to Sir Humphreyisms, the populist communication tactic when faced with a double bind was to continue to make apparently straightforward but contextually conflicting statements.

Johnson's joker persona, first as naughty journalist concocting EU banana outrages to disgust Tunbridge Wells, and then as comic London mayor dangling from ropes as entertainment, meant that drafting two entirely contradictory positions on the Brexit referendum could be taken as on-brand. The press behaved like soothsayers, interpreting chosen comments from the haze in order to illuminate what Johnson was and meant: nativist and racist, liberal internationalist, true-blue Tory or champion of downtrodden towns.

The ambiguity of meaning is fostered by appeals to irony: if you joke, as Johnson did in a 2018 article,[10] that a woman in a burqa looks like a letterbox in a way calculated to provoke ridicule and outrage, the joke still contains the statement that a woman in a burqa looks like a postbox, but you can argue that the meaning of that statement is altered by the tone in which it is said, and provide two simultaneous claims on tone: that the ridicule and outrage it provokes argues for its context as a joke, or that it's a common-sense appraisal of a garment that should itself be thought ridiculous. In the heat of subsequent outrage at Johnson's comments, it was often forgotten that they formed part of an argument for the right of Muslim women to wear the burqa. By provoking liberal sensibilities with an inflammatory aside, he was able to argue a liberal case to a right-wing audience. Tone was key: the letterbox comment's boorishness appeased his intended interlocutors, while retaining only-joking as ironic retreat. He could simultaneously assert and deny the validity of wearing a burqa.

Irony arises when we say something in a tone that indicates that we don't fully mean it, or that what we mean is contradictory to what is said. Humour, similarly, arises from inversions of logic, such as misfits with common sense or self-contradictory, paradoxical statements. Both are palatable versions of nonsense, obscuring meaning and leaving the trickster free to say and not-say things that are downright false or supposedly off-limits, so that outrage merely boosts the signal.

The Sir Humphrey era, with its laboured Serious Technocrat rhetoric and barrage of qualifications, had taken a simulacrum of earnest speech to an impossible extreme so that it, and they, no longer felt like something worth taking seriously. The public, as Michael Gove stated in response to the economic forecasts of the Remain campaign, had 'had enough of experts';[11] that Gove was probably the most wonkish, expert-informed politician of his cohort did not matter either. He was playing into the same embrace of contradiction in a post-serious public discourse.

'I must level with you'

The tone of Johnson's messaging and its appetite for experts took an unexpected turn as the inevitability of the Covid-19 pandemic emerged in Britain. Johnson took to the lectern at the first of what would become daily press briefings flanked by experts. With the Chief Medical Officer and the Chief Scientific Advisor beside him, he bluntly set out grim news: 'I must level with you – level with the British public – more families, many more families, are going to lose loved ones before their time.' When setting out forthcoming measures, Johnson opened statements with 'The scientific advice is…' so that the government response was then framed as secondary to it. 'At all times we are guided by the science', he continued in the passive mood.[12] Scientific advisors had more airtime than Johnson himself, setting out the plans and the principles behind them.

Ten days later, in the face of increased hostility to the government's relaxed restrictions compared to other European countries, combined with the release of a conflicting scientific model arguing that significantly more deaths were likely on current measures, the government rapidly changed tack and announced a lockdown. For as long as public opinion trusted 'the scientific advice', it remained at the fore. But social media had allowed a multiplicity of scientists and models offering alternative accounts to reach journalists and gain rapid traction, and influential voices outside the government soon gained airtime too, much of it critical of the government's decision making.

Johnson's ensuing lockdown message did not dwell on 'the science': instead, it shifted focus on to the public to play its part, using 'we' to voice instructions so that the actions to be taken and, by implication, responsibility for the situation, lay with the public. 'We will beat the coronavirus and we will beat it together', Johnson concluded. 'And therefore I urge you at this moment of national emergency to stay at home, protect our NHS, and save lives.'[13] The message deployed the same style of short, verb-driven statement that had won Brexit and the election. The NHS was 'our NHS'; executive decisions taken by the government were eclipsed by a call to collective responsibility and action.

The beneficent wartime paternalism announcing increased NHS capacity and financial assistance programmes and stressing the importance of everyone doing their bit in the national effort was sustained, until Johnson fell ill with the virus. His ministers were largely unable to maintain the same emotive rhetoric and lacked the grammatical sleight of hand that Johnson, as a career writer, excelled in, and soon resorted to the avoidance and obfuscation techniques made famous by *Yes Minister*, assisted by their newfound ability to deflect more thorny questions to the scientific experts on press duty that day. Experts were back in vogue, and so, for the time being, was the politician's art of saying nothing.

Of all the resurgent Sir Humphrey tendencies in handling public affairs, the most notable, in the face of persistent requests for information on an exit strategy, was the repeated assertion that it would not be possible to discuss this publicly because to do so would detract from the importance of the message to stay at home. Sir Humphrey was traditionally upfront with his ministers on the necessity to keep information safe from the general public and, under no circumstances, to level with them, but he did it from behind closed doors; now, the government maintained the assertion within the public domain too, reiterating its simplified instructions for the people – stay home, protect the NHS, save lives.

'It used to be, everyone was entitled to their own opinion, but not their own facts. But that's not the case anymore.'[14]

The term 'post-truth' found widespread use in 2016 to describe the fragmented online ecosystems that fed mutually contradictory world views across social and political divides. A problem for the existence of truth in a big and complex world is that information can be cherry-picked to support a baffling variety of stories. Conflicting world views coexist, each fed by their own sources. If social media helped drive a deeper rift between political tribes, allowing a feed of information targeted to individual prejudices, Colbert had made the same points about selective facts a decade previously: even then the epistemic worlds of the *Guardian* and *Daily Mail* were rarely in alignment.

Cynicism from decades of carefully managed information minimisation and diverging online worlds helped to gestate nonsense politics. When you don't believe that you're being given information in good faith, and when both information and the style in which it is communicated is contested and politicised, you might as well follow what feels satisfying. Nonsense, in turn, gestates solipsistic credulity. Colbert said, of truthiness, 'It's not only that I *feel* it to be true, but that *I* feel it to be true. There's not only an emotional quality, but there's a selfish quality.'[15]

The Covid-19 crisis shows that even science is not resistant to epistemic cherry-picking: Johnson's rhetorical recourse to 'the science', as a singular governing entity, was temporarily eroded when multiple conflicting scientific models became public. Science seeks to map, test and model aspects of the world, but it does that infinitely complex task imperfectly. It also takes time to reach consensus – the closest approximation to a scientific truth. 'The science' was intended to mean a consensus that, in the case of Covid-19, did not yet exist.

Even with respected institutions publishing their models in good faith, differences exist and can become politicised: economic libertarians were quickest to cite models arguing for greater spread and lower rates of fatality than those used to justify the lockdown. When there is influence or reward to be gained from skewing supposedly objective interpretation for a chosen audience, science can be corrupted too, as recent replication crises in psychology[16] and decades of pharma scandals[17] have shown. Areas of fraudulent misrepresentation undermine the unitary authority with which 'the science' is perceived, making it easier for entirely unscientific claims to reach audiences rendered both more cynical and more credulous by abuses of information. As ministers deferred on air to science, 5G towers burned elsewhere.

Across the Atlantic, Trump's handling of the crisis was less deferential to both science and experts, at one point retweeting a call to sack his leading scientific advisor.[18] Asked if he was worried about the pandemic spreading in the US with the first patient confirmed in Washington state, Trump replied, 'No. Not at all ... we have it totally under control.'[19] As the stock market fell precipitously, Trump tweeted that 'The Coronavirus is very much under control in the USA ... Stock Market starting to look very good to me!'[20] Asked about his change in opinion on the severity of the situation after announcing a two-week lockdown, he replied, 'I've always known this is a real, this is a pandemic. I've felt it was a pandemic long before it was called a pandemic.'[21]

While many of his assertions were, as ever, untrue, Trump's strained relationship with reality came under renewed scrutiny in a way that suggested that his habit of contradicting both himself and outside facts might not always be as simple as a lie. In a press briefing where the efficacy of sunlight and disinfectant in deactivating the virus had been discussed, he set out a syntactically and scientifically confused train of thought that appeared to confuse environmental protections against the virus with internal medicine:

> And then I see the disinfectant where it knocks it out in a minute. One minute! And is there a way we can do something, by an injection inside or almost a cleaning? Because you see it gets in the lungs and it does a tremendous number on the lungs, so it'd be interesting to check that. So, that you're going to have to use medical doctors with, but it sounds interesting to me.[22]

It was nonsense of a kind that could not be described as a lie, because a lie demands knowledge that a situation is other than the way it is portrayed, and Trump appeared knowledge-free, speaking in a speculative tone and looking anxiously at his bemused adviser. An article from the satirical news site *The Onion* entitled 'Man Just

Buying One of any Cleaning Product in Case Trump Announces It's Coronavirus Cure', dating back a month previously, was hailed online as prophetic.[23] Nonsense has its value beyond making people laugh: within hours, Trump-friendly media outlets were ready to explain how the principles that he had touched upon were, in fact, legitimate, if clumsily expressed,[24] aided in their attempt at divining some grain of meaning from his comments by the deranged lack of clarity with which they were expressed.

We are meaning-seeking animals, and when faced with no coherent story we can work with, our inclination is to make one up. The pathological form of this tendency to find patterns where there are none is sometimes known as apophenia. The churn of political and cultural commentary in recent years has sometimes looked like apophenia – mind-reading chosen meanings out of noise offering little in the way of denotation. The disinfectant claims had pushed this to its limits. Once even Fox News had shifted from a position of support to denouncing the comments as dangerous,[25] Trump changed tack and argued, vainly, that they had been intended as sarcastic.[26] It was then reported that plans were in place for Trump to cut back the daily briefings as a damage limitation exercise.[27]

Some critics of 'postmodernism' have argued that the 'post-truth' world is fed by a contagious public mood of nihilistic relativism. However, faced with a devastating medical and social crisis, public faith in factual discourse underpinned by scientific process as the best tool that we have to map reality seemed to be edging into favour. The post-expert Brexiteers were back in need of experts; even the American hard right had come round to the benefits of not ingesting bleach. Perhaps Johnson's move to front press conferences with scientists was a sign of a reversion to a more serious world of facts, and of a public appetite for facts to be made public. Facts sometimes arrived as evidence presented for evaluation, and might not be final or perfect, requiring revision, but they offered hope for progress. Johnson, whose success might best be attributed to a shapeshifting talent for reading and responding to the public mood, returned from convalescence sombre, stressing scientific caution. It was as if the virus had successfully deactivated a joker.

Soon enough, however, public affairs returned to their new normal of misrule: a market town in County Durham became metonymous for eye tests in the wake of memes mocking Johnson's advisor Dominic Cummings's improbable account of his trip there during lockdown; culture wars erupted over face masks; statues were toppled; and ahead of the US election, the streets broiled with unrest. In the trickster discourse, all things, from the trivial to the existentially grave, can look like omens.

Notes

1 Antony Jay and Jonathan Lynn, 'The Writing on the Wall', *Yes Minister*, 1980.
2 Amber A'Lee Frost, 'The necessity of political vulgarity', *Current Affairs*, 25 August 2016, https://www.currentaffairs.org/2016/05/the-necessity-of-political-vulgarity (accessed 4 August 2020).
3 Politifact, http://www.politifact.com/personalities/donald-trump/ (accessed 29 January 2020).
4 Matt Flegenheimer, 'What's a "covfefe"? Trump tweet unites a bewildered nation', *New York Times*, 31 May 2017, https://www.nytimes.com/2017/05/31/us/politics/covfefe-trump-twitter.html (accessed 4 August 2020).
5 @realDonaldTrump, 31 May 2017, http://twitter.com/realdonaldtrump/status/869858333477523458?lang=en (accessed 29 January 2020).
6 Jacey Fortin, 'Yanny or Laurel? Trump says something else', *New York Times*, 17 May 2018, https://www.nytimes.com/2018/05/17/us/laurel-yanny-white-house-trump.html (accessed 4 August 2020).
7 Stephen Colbert, *The Colbert Report*, 17 October 2005.
8 Adam Sternbergh, 'Stephen Colbert has America by the ballots', *New York Magazine*, 16 October 2006, http://nymag.com/news/politics/22322/ (accessed 4 August 2020).

9   People's Vote UK, 'Boris Johnson's tangled web of contradictory prom-
     ises is unravelling, showing why he cannot be trusted to solve the Brexit
     crisis', 22 October 2019, http://www.peoples-vote.uk/boris_johnson_
     s_tangled_web_of_contradictory_promises_is_unravelling_showing_
     why_he_cannot_be_trusted_to_solve_the_brexit_crisis (accessed 29
     January 2020).

10   Boris Johnson, 'Denmark has got it wrong. Yes, the burka is oppressive
     and ridiculous – but that's still no reason to ban it', *The Daily Telegraph*,
     5 August 2018, https://www.telegraph.co.uk/news/2018/08/05/den
     mark-has-got-wrong-yes-burka-oppressive-ridiculous-still/ (accessed
     4 August 2020).

11   Michael Gove, interview with Faisal Islam, Sky News, 3 June 2016.

12   Rt Hon Boris Johnson MP, 'PM statement on coronavirus', 12 March
     2020, archived at https://www.gov.uk/government/speeches/pm-state
     ment-on-coronavirus-12-march-2020 (accessed 10 July 2020).

13   Rt Hon Boris Johnson MP, 'PM address to the nation on coronavirus:
     23 March 2020', archived at https://www.gov.uk/government/speeches/
     pm-address-to-the-nation-on-coronavirus-23-march-2020 (accessed 10
     July 2020).

14   Nathan Rabin, 'Interview: Stephen Colbert', *AV Club*, 25 January 2006,
     https://tv.avclub.com/stephen-colbert-1798208958 (accessed 4 August
     2020).

15   Rabin, 'Interview: Stephen Colbert'.

16   Tobias Wingen, Jana B. Berkessel and Birte Englich, 'No replication,
     no trust? How low replicability influences trust in psychology', *Social
     Psychological and Personality Science*, 11.4 (2020), pp. 454–63.

17   Alltrials, 'Why this matters', http://policyaudit.alltrials.net/why-this-
     matters/ (accessed 24 April 2020).

18   @realDonaldTrump, 12 April 2020, https://twitter.com/realDonald
     Trump/status/1249470237726081030?s=20 (accessed 24 April 2020).

19   CNBC transcript: 'President Donald Trump sits down with CNBC's
     Joe Kernen', https://www.cnbc.com/2020/01/22/cnbc-transcript-pre
     sident-donald-trump-sits-down-with-cnbcs-joe-kernen-at-the-world-
     economic-forum-in-davos-switzerland.html (accessed 24 April 2020).

20   @realDonaldTrump, 24 February 2020, https://twitter.com/realDon
     aldTrump/status/1232058127740174339?ref_src=twsrc%5Etfw (accessed
     24 April 2020).

21   Transcript: 'Donald Trump joins the daily coronavirus pandemic
     briefing', *Factbase*, https://factba.se/transcript/donald-trump-press-

conference-coronavirus-briefing-march-17–2020 (accessed 24 April 2020).

22 Remarks by President Trump, Vice President Pence and members of the Coronavirus Task Force in Press Briefing, 23 April 2020, https://www.whitehouse.gov/briefings-statements/remarks-president-trump-vice-president-pence-members-coronavirus-task-force-press-briefing-31/ (accessed 24 April 2020).

23 'Man just buying one of any cleaning product in case Trump announces it's coronavirus cure', *The Onion*, 25 March 2020, https://local.theonion.com/man-just-buying-one-of-every-cleaning-product-in-case-t-1842493766 (accessed 27 April 2020).

24 Joel B. Pollak, 'Fact check: No, Trump didn't propose injecting people with disinfectant', Breitbart, https://www.breitbart.com/the-media/2020/04/23/fact-check-no-trump-didnt-propose-injecting-peo ple-with-disinfectant/ (accessed 24 April 2020); Tyler Olsen, 'Media erupt over Trump comments on disinfectant and sunlight to cure coronavirus: here's what he said', Fox News, 25 April 2020, https://www.foxnews.com/politics/media-erupt-over-trump-comments-on-disinfect ant-heres-what-he-said (accessed 27 April 2020).

25 David Bauder, 'Fox didn't immediately challenge Trump's disinfectant remark', Associated Press, 25 April 2020, https://apnews.com/4199ef60 2eee20d327417781469fd8d9 (accessed 27 April 2020).

26 Brett Samuels, 'Trump says remarks about heat, light and disinfectant were sarcastic', *The Hill*, 24 April 2020, https://thehill.com/homenews/administration/494519-trump-says-remarks-about-heat-light-disinfect ant-were-sarcastic (accessed 27 April 2020).

27 Jonathan Swan, 'Trump plans to cut daily coronavirus briefings', *Axios*, 24 April 2020, https://www.axios.com/trump-daily-coronavirus-brief ings-809becf3-9913-4b71-9f92-1930ad1d29b0.html (accessed 27 April 2020).

11

Weaponised Swissness

Janna Kraus

Unlike many other European countries, Switzerland has managed to fly under the radar when it comes to critical discussions of free speech. Heralded by many (not least its own media and political apparatus) as the epitome of democracy, liberty and neutrality, Switzerland's dominating right-wing parties, questionable policies, feeble efforts in the area of equality and sinking journalistic standards rarely figure in the broader international discourse. This chapter aims to illustrate what lies behind the national myths, how free speech arguments are weaponised against dissenting voices, and what is being done to counteract these reactionary tendencies.

Controlling the narrative

Switzerland has its own Rupert Murdoch in Christoph Blocher, the billionaire who helmed the rise of the right-wing Swiss People's Party (SVP) in the 1990s and controls a substantial share of Swiss media outlets. The polarising figure known for his populist oratory skills and isolationist politics is still seen as a plebeian tribune by his followers, in spite of his immense wealth and his doctorate in law. However, Blocher's influence is not the only thing haunting the Swiss media landscape. Next to its steady descent into oligopoly, the immense popularity and success of decidedly right-wing outlets such as the *Weltwoche* or the *Basler Zeitung* (*BAZ*) has led to those outlets creating coordinated smear campaigns and routinely targeting opposing voices.

One of the targets of such a campaign was the gender studies researcher Franziska Schutzbach. In 2017 the *Weltwoche* and the *BAZ* published a series of articles calling Schutzbach an enemy of free speech who should be fired from her position at the University of Basel because of her feminist, left-wing background and alleged disdain for democracy.[1] The arguments used against her sound familiar: Schutzbach's arguments in favour of boycotting right-wing events and practising civil disobedience (off-handedly mentioned on her private blog in 2016) were likened to the boycott of Jewish businesses in Nazi Germany. Schutzbach's suggestion was made out to be an impediment to free speech, democracy and tolerance. Such ideas coming from a person teaching at a Swiss university, according to the dramatic conclusion reached by *Weltwoche* and *BAZ*, could only lead to a new era of book burnings.[2]

One part of addressing attacks like this is to study and analyse them. Being unable to recognise the functionality and underlying similarities of the rhetoric that furthers the right-wing agenda means being incapable of resisting it effectively. Schutzbach created a viable starting point with her 2018 book *Die Rhetorik der Rechten* (*The Rhetoric of the Right*).[3] In it, she not only describes the rise and enduring success of the SVP and other right-wing parties across Europe, but also provides an overview of their most essential discursive strategies, outlining logical fallacies and verbal trickeries. Among other things, Schutzbach explains how changing the cultural landscape is at the centre of right-wing efforts. Joining, founding or buying up media institutions, publishing houses, magazines and so on helps them to shape the discourse.[4] A closer look at the targets of these right-wing campaigns serves to illustrate this principle.

In 2012 the *Weltwoche* published a list of professors it considered detrimental or dangerous to society, urging readers to be wary of them.[5] Among the named – and pictured – professors accused of spreading heresy (*Irrlehre*) were a gender researcher, several historians and, almost ironically, Kurt Imhof, at the time the head of fög, a research centre assessing the quality of Swiss journalism. These openly anti-intellectual and anti-feminist campaigns might be manageable if they were limited to a few extreme outlets, no matter their popularity. However, other major newspapers such as the time-honoured *NZZ* (*Neue Zürcher Zeitung*) also regularly join in on the defamation and disparaging of gender studies, academics, foreign professors, women in politics, and so on. This became more pronounced after the *NZZ*'s change in editorship in 2015, which has been called a shift to the right (*Rechtsrutsch*); the *NZZ* disagrees with this assessment.[6] The prevalence of these narratives in mainstream media shows that scepticism towards so-called elites or academics is a strong theme in Swiss discourse, not an extreme position held by some outliers.

Furthering isolation

The Swiss pride themselves on being a grounded people, down-to-earth, anti-aristocratic and wary of elites. This can be seen in many areas of life, such as their relationship with language. Switzerland has four national languages: German, French, Italian and Romansh (a Romance language predominantly used in the Canton Grisons). German is by far the dominant language, spoken by 63 per cent of the population.[7] While the written language taught in schools is standardised, differing from the German or Austrian equivalent as much as American English differs from British English, the language used in everyday life is not German but Swiss German (*Schweizerdeutsch*): a diverse array of dialects, differing from standard German (and from each other) in pronunciation, vocabulary and grammar.

Swiss children learn the standard language in school, starting at age 6, since many regions have outlawed the use of standard German in kindergartens – one of the SVP's pet projects – citing knowledge of Swiss German as the main instrument of integration and patriotism.[8] Most daily interactions, professional or private, are conducted in Swiss German. It is not unusual even for university classes to be taught in Swiss German, thereby making it more difficult for international students and Swiss students from non-German-speaking parts of the country to participate. Many programmes on national television and most radio programmes are also delivered in Swiss German.

Predominantly using the dialect has none of the connotations of lower class, lower level of education or rural upbringing that it might have elsewhere. On the contrary, speaking standard German without noticeable accent is often not considered desirable; news anchors and politicians get negative reactions for speaking the language 'too well'.[9] While the Swiss have no problem understanding standard German, it is seen as too fast, too direct, too pretentious to use in everyday life; an assessment that also extends to its speakers. Anti-German and anti-academic resentment therefore often go hand in hand. The last few years have seen many articles decrying the threat of German invaders, mainly medical staff and academics, taking over Swiss positions and edging out the Swiss competition. The fact that just as many Swiss professors work in German universities as the other way around[10] and that Switzerland cannot itself provide the medical personnel it requires[11] rarely factors into those discussions.

Lean in or stay out

The scorn of the general populace does not limit itself to academics, foreign or domestic. Politicians, particularly young, left-leaning, female ones, serve as a lightning rod for all sorts of abuse. In Switzerland, women are still on an unequal footing when it comes to taking up public space, especially in politics. Having only gained the vote in 1971, with some parts of the country not introducing it fully until 1990, Swiss women find themselves at the tail-end of Europe's path to gender equality. This becomes exceedingly clear in the job market. Swiss women are much more likely than most other European women to work part time, are in danger of losing their jobs as a result of motherhood, have to manage with the insufficient supply of childcare, and come in at the very end of the Glass Ceiling Index that measures the treatment of female workers, one place ahead of Turkey.[12]

Several prominent female politicians have been the object of prolonged and intense surges of hatred, including threats of bodily harm, making it even more difficult to weather the already hostile waters. In 2014 Jolanda Spiess-Hegglin, a young local politician for the Green Party, found herself hounded by the Swiss media and public after private medical information about a hospital visit was leaked to the press alongside rumours that she had been sexually assaulted by a fellow politician. The media jumped on the story, not letting up for months, harassing her and accusing her of troublemaking, of falsely accusing an innocent man and of generally seeking the spotlight, even though Spiess-Hegglin had not made any accusations public and suffered greatly from the ongoing torment.

In spite of all this, Spiess-Hegglin managed to hold many of the parties involved accountable, taking a number of media outlets to court.[13]

In 2016 Spiess-Hegglin co-founded *Netzcourage* (web courage), a project she refers to as the 'hate speech ambulance'. *Netzcourage* provides emergency aid for those caught up in shitstorms, for victims of doxxing, and for those confronted with digital violence.[14] Her experience in weathering attacks by mainstream and social media as well as dealing with aggressive individuals has provided her with essential insights into how to address this mass phenomenon. She provides de-escalation services on social media, offers workshops and training for institutions and groups, helps bring perpetrators to court, attends mediations, and personally meets with those attacking and defaming her to reach an agreement and show them the consequences of their behaviour.[15] Since taking up her work, Spiess-Hegglin and the women she supports have been widely criticised, attacked and mocked for supposedly infringing on free speech by reporting comments, posts and profiles on internet platforms, filing police reports and taking people to court.[16]

Not so progressive

In addition to rampant misogyny, Switzerland does not fare too well in terms of LGBTI+ rights, ranking 27th in Europe. The main reasons for this are the lack of protection for intersex people (genital mutilation for intersex children is still routine) and the absence of comprehensive measures to protect people against hate crimes and hate speech.[17] The latter, however, has been partially rectified. On 9 February 2020 Swiss voters decided to add sexual orientation to the list of factors constituting protected groups. Currently, this law (Article 261bis of the Criminal Code) covers racial, ethnic and religious discrimination. The original suggestion of the initiators was to include both sexual orientation and gender identity. However, the latter was rejected by the upper house, the Council of States (*Ständerat*), and was therefore removed from the proposition that was voted on. To pass, the thus limited proposal required only a simple majority of the voting populace.[18]

The campaign opposing the bill, which referred to it as 'that censorship bill', employed the well-tried argument that hate speech is the simple expression of an opinion, and fighting or outlawing it equals censorship. They argued simultaneously that there is no discrimination against the LGBTI+ community and that even suggesting this law was an insult to the tolerant and open Swiss society, while also claiming that scientific, religious, academic, comedic and social expression would be stunted through not being able to tell gay jokes or spread objections to homosexuals as individuals or as a group.[19]

Demystifying direct democracy

Switzerland's democracy is hailed by many as the fairest and most democratic form of government in the world. In reality, things are not quite as simple. In cases such as the aforementioned hate crime protection, a simple majority is enough to decide on the fate of a proposal. If 51 per cent of all voters decide on an issue, while 49 per cent disagree, it can hardly be said that by implementing it one simply follows the will of the people. In addition, voter turnout in Switzerland is notoriously low. The twentieth century saw a sharp decline in the participation rate in federal elections, with recorded lows of around 27 per cent in the 1990s. While the twenty-first century has not quite followed this alarming trend, the numbers still rarely exceed the 50 per cent mark. It also has to be added that the return to a higher voter turnout has been in part due to the populist strategies of the aforementioned right-wing SVP, which managed to mobilise masses of former non-voters for its cause.[20]

There is also the issue of who does not get to vote. Switzerland, with 8.5 million inhabitants, is home to over 2 million non-citizens, which amounts to over 25 per cent of the overall population. This large group of people is not eligible to vote, with the exception of some communities that allow non-citizens to vote on some local issues. Around 44 per cent of these non-citizens live in Switzerland permanently; agreements with the European Union have made it possible for EU citizens to work and live in the country with relatively little effort.[21]

Why, then, do these people, who have made Switzerland their home, not become citizens? It turns out that the road to citizenship is steep and rather thorny. Besides the prohibitive costs of the process (around 3,000 CHF [c. £2,500] for adults), the procedure is often intimidating and unappealing in nature. In many places, applicants not only have to have spent more than ten years in the country, but also a certain number of years in the same canton (with differing requirements for spouses of citizens and young people and children). They can also be subjected to written and oral tests and interviews to demonstrate knowledge about the country, language and customs, required to give proof of integration, or suffer unannounced house calls. Furthermore, many – especially more rural – communes require applicants to be individually 'voted on' at an assembly, where they retain the right to reject candidates for all kinds of colourful reasons, including frequenting Aldi, wearing sweatpants in public, a lack of recycling expertise and championing animal rights.[22] In January 2020 an Italian man, who had spent over thirty years living and working in Switzerland, managed to overturn his rejection, which had been based on him not being familiar with the details of the wolf compound at a nearby zoo.[23]

With around a quarter of the resident population politically disenfranchised, misogynist campaigns and workplace discrimination preventing women from taking an equal part in public life, minority protections ranking low in international comparison, and the habitual weaponisation of free speech arguments to silence dissenters, the results of over twenty years of right-wing domination are dire.

Conclusion

Few are aware of the repressive and reactionary dynamics at play in Switzerland. This is partially due to asynchronous political and historical developments, as well as the country's relatively low importance as a global player, but it is mostly due to the unrelenting and very successful instrumentalisation of and appeals to national myths such as autonomy, liberty, neutrality and direct democracy abroad and at home.

What is to be done about this proliferation of hate, hiding (rather poorly) behind the curtain of freedom of expression? The three examples – Schutzbach's manual for identifying and understanding right-wing rhetoric, Spiess-Hegglin's NGO to help victims of hate speech, and the political initiative to give additional protection against hate crimes based on sexual orientation – are pillars that can serve as a foundation to built a long-lasting movement of resistance and counteraction.

First, we need to study and understand the phenomena in their historical and geographical specificities, as well as the similarities shared across countries and continents. Why is this happening here in this way? What does it look like elsewhere? What patterns do we have to recognise?

Secondly, we have to provide concrete and immediate relief to those crushed under the onslaught of the hate speech machinery, while making full use of existing structures and regulations. Ideally, this service would not have to be provided by a privately run NGO, but would be incorporated into institutions and receive state funding. Ways to combat and deal with hate speech should be included in school curricula and professional training.

Thirdly, we need to work on introducing legislation that will alleviate, if not immediately do away with, the precarious situations that vulnerable groups find themselves in. This would not only have to include the protection of queer people, but also involve easier paths to citizenship and/or extending the vote to the resident population.

Taking a detailed, critical look at the discrepancy between the image and the actual policies of so-called liberal countries is essential to furthering the ongoing struggle for equality, even if some might see it as counterproductive or nit-picking to focus on what remains to be done. We cannot afford to become complacent because of relative progressiveness, or be blinded by false narratives constructed by reactionary actors trying to profit from perceived liberalism.

Notes

1 Gabriel Brönnimann, 'Die Schutzbachkritiker entlarven sich bloss selbst', *TagesWoche*, 16 November 2017, https://tageswoche.ch/gesells chaft/die-schutzbach-kritiker-entlarven-sich-bloss-selbst (accessed 10 July 2020).
2 Ibid.
3 Franziska Schutzbach, *Die Rhetorik der Rechten. Rechtspopulistische Diskursstrategien im Überblick* (Zürich/München: Xanthippe Verlag, 2018).
4 Schutzbach, *Rhetorik der Rechten*, pp. 77–80.
5 Philipp Gut, 'Vor diesen Professoren wird gewarnt', *Weltwoche*, 40 (2012), pp. 28–32.
6 Rafael von Matt, 'Von einem Rechtsrutsch ist nichts zu spüren', *SRF*, 18 July 2019, https://www.srf.ch/news/schweiz/deutschland-strategie-

der-nzz-von-einem-rechtsrutsch-ist-nichts-zu-spueren# (accessed 10 July 2020).

7   'Sprachen', Bundesamt für Statistik (BFS), 2019, https://www.bfs. admin.ch/bfs/de/home/statistiken/bevoelkerung/sprachen-religionen/ sprachen.html (accessed 10 July 2020).

8   S. Ulrich, 'Verschwindet die Mundart aus dem Chindsgi?', *20Min*, 26 December 2018, https://www.20min.ch/schweiz/bern/story/Hochdeut sch-im-Kindergarten-16816990 (accessed 10 July 2020).

9   Roger Blum, 'Verwendung des Schweizer Hochdeutschen im Fernsehen SRF beanstandet', *Ombudsstelle SRG*, 27 August 2019, https://www. srgd.ch/de/aktuelles/news/2019/08/27/verwendung-des-schweizer-hoc hdeutschen-im-fernsehen-srf-beanstandet/ (accessed 10 July 2020).

10 Lena Langbein, 'Schweizer Professoren überschreiten die Grenzen', *Swissinfo*, 20 December 2010, https://www.swissinfo.ch/ger/schweizer-professoren-ueberschreiten-die-grenzen/29056736 (accessed 10 July 2020).

11 'Was, wenn die Deutschen wirklich gehen?', *SRF*, 14 January 2019, https://www.srf.ch/news/schweiz/aerztemangel-in-der-schweiz-was-we nn-die-deutschen-wirklich-gehen (accessed 10 July 2020).

12 Charlotte Theile, 'Die Schweiz, eine Gleichstellungswüste', *Tagesanzeiger*, 23 February 2019, https://www.tagesanzeiger.ch/zuerich/ stadt/die-schweiz-eine-gleichstellungswueste/story/14354380 (accessed 10 July 2020).

13 Raphael Prinz, 'Jolanda Spiess-Hegglin gewinnt gegen den Blick', *SRF*, 10 May 2019, https://www.srf.ch/news/schweiz/ein-meilenstein-jolanda-spiess-hegglin-gewinnt-gegen-den-blick (accessed 10 July 2020).

14 Doxxing is the practice of publishing private personal information about individuals on the internet with malicious intent.

15 Jolanda Spiess-Hegglin, 'Mit Herz gegen Hass im Netz' (Zürich, 2018), http://www.guidle.com/files/attachments/20189222317165980.80338973 8190901.pdf (accessed 10 July 2020).

16 B. Zanni and Q. Llugiqi, 'Wir haben bis jetzt über 7000 Beiträge gemel-det', *20Min*, 8 September 2018, https://www.20min.ch/schweiz/news/ story/-Facebook-koennte-User-zu-Unrecht-aussperren-20611883 (acc-essed 10 July 2020).

17 LGBT-Rechte, 'Schweiz fällt von Platz 22 auf 27', Transgender Network Switzerland, 14 May 2019, https://www.tgns.ch/de/2019/05/lgbti-rechte-schweiz-faellt-von-platz-22-auf-27/ (accessed 10 July 2020).

18 Tobias Kuhnert, 'Diskriminierungsschutz leider nicht für alle', Queeramnesty, 23 April 2019, https://queeramnesty.ch/diskrimini erungsschutz-leider-nicht-fuer-alle/ (accessed 10 July 2020).

19 https://zensurgesetz-nein.ch/argumente/ (accessed 10 July 2020).

20 'Stimmbeteiligung', Bundesamt für Statistik (BFS), 2019, https://www.bfs. admin.ch/bfs/de/home/statistiken/politik/abstimmungen/stimmbeteili gung.html (accessed 10 July 2020).

21 'Ausländische Bevölkerung', Bundesamt für Statistik (BFS), 2019, https:// www.bfs.admin.ch/bfs/de/home/statistiken/bevoelkerung/migration-in tegration/auslaendische-bevoelkerung.html (accessed 10 July 2020).

22 Dominic Knobelt, 'Frittieröl, Aldi, Hornussen: Der Fall Yilmaz schlägt Wellen bis nach China', *Aargauerzeitung*, 20 July 2017, https://www. aargauerzeitung.ch/ausland/frittieroel-aldi-hornussen-der-fall-yilmaz-schlaegt-wellen-bis-nach-china-131540435 (accessed 10 July 2020); Sibilla Bondolfi, 'Kein Schweizer Pass für Tierschützerin', *Swissinfo*, 12 January 2017, https://www.swissinfo.ch/ger/direktedemokratie/ein buergerung-an-gemeindeversammlung_kein-schweizer-pass-fuer-tiers chuetzerin/42820972 (accessed 10 July 2020).

23 'Einbürgerungsbehörde von Arth kassiert Rüffel vom Bundesgericht', *Tages-Anzeiger*, 27 January 2020, https://www.tagesanzeiger.ch/sch weiz/standard/einbuergerungsbehoerde-von-arth-kassiert-rueffel-vom-bundesgericht/story/24657952 (accessed 10 July 2020).

12

Free speech and the British press

Aaron Ackerley

The notion of 'freedom' has been central to how much of the British press has presented itself from the nineteenth century until the present day. This has included freedom from government control and interference, and, as a linked concern, the safeguarding of 'free speech'. However, the manner in which these ideas and terms have been defined and utilised has shifted as the media industry and broader cultural debates and trends have changed. This chapter will provide a brief overview of how the British press has used the concepts of freedom and free speech to boost the industry's reputation and justify its activities. There is a long history of newspapers and journalists employing the rhetoric of free speech and freedom to justify unethical and morally dubious practices within the industry and to thwart efforts at regulation. The emergence of a mass popular daily press at the end of the nineteenth century was a pivotal moment, and the popular press – which evolved into the distinctive tabloid format that endures until today – is the main focus of this chapter. The 1960s was another key moment. Before this, debates about free speech and the press tended to focus on notions of morality, respectability and obscenity, and the tone and intensity of newspapers' critiques of authority figures. After the 1960s, such debates tended to centre on the press's representation of less powerful groups and identities, whether this concerned stereotyping and discrimination or privacy and intrusion into the personal sphere.

The long-standing concern of newspapers to defend and promote their own practices and interests via appeals to the notion of freedom, alongside the conservative and populist political character of much of the press in twentieth-century Britain, meant that newspapers were receptive to the rhetoric of the late twentieth-century 'culture war'. This struggle, between groups championing conservative and traditionalist values and those championing liberal and progressive values, coalesced due to long-term cultural and demographic changes as well as political strategies in the US, but spread to many other nations, including Britain.[1]

A notable feature of the late nineteenth- and early twentieth-century media was the widespread interaction between the US and UK newspaper industries, with ideas, styles and personnel travelling in both directions across the Atlantic. The 1880s witnessed the emergence in Britain of what was termed the 'New Journalism', a forerunner of the tabloid style. Innovations from US newspapers were incorporated by British journalists such as W. T. Stead. There had been a period in the mid-nineteenth century when radical newspapers had reached large audiences in Britain, until the repeal of the so-called 'taxes on knowledge' allowed 'respectable' newspapers to emerge victorious. Once various taxes on newspaper production – which the radical press had evaded paying – were removed, 'respectable' newspapers such as *The Times* were able to utilise expensive new printing technologies, backed by both advertising revenue and political patronage that radical newspapers lacked, to out-compete the radical publications. Reflecting the limited franchise and the fact that most newspapers only reached relatively small, literate sections of the population, the political and commercial pressures placed on newspapers meant that daily newspapers confined themselves to respectable topics and presented news and opinion in a rigid, serious manner. This model was to be later seen as a golden age of journalism in Britain, though, as we will see, it was largely mythologised for strategic reasons. The Sunday press was also already presenting more populist and 'lowbrow' fare at this time, focused on scandal rather than the realm of high politics.

The New Journalism introduced changes to the layout and visuals of newspapers to make them more appealing, as well as a new populist language and sensationalist style of crusading journalism. Famously, Stead was imprisoned for three months for his exposé of the existence of modern white slavery and of children in London's sex trade, published in a series of *Pall Mall Gazette* articles entitled 'The Maiden Tribute of Modern Babylon'. Stead's sensationalist style received widespread criticism, though he was not imprisoned because of what he was saying or how he said it, but because he had purchased a young girl named Eliza Armstrong while undercover.

By the end of the nineteenth century a new popular daily press had emerged, with the first runaway success being Lord Northcliffe's launch of the *Daily Mail* in 1896. Newspapers such as the *Mail*, the *Daily Express* and the *Daily Mirror* further refined the methods of Stead and the Sunday press, placing ever more emphasis on eye-catching aesthetics, brevity and emotive language. This was accompanied by an increased focus on matters beyond the sphere of 'respectable' high politics and business. Lifestyle features, celebrity and crime proliferated. These changes steadily altered the character of elite titles as well, and the tabloid style came to influence the broader media landscape.[2] Press historian Mark Hampton argues there was a shift from an 'Educational Ideal' to a 'Representative Ideal' at this time. Many proprietors and journalists no longer saw themselves as providing reasoned debate to smaller, elite readerships. Those in charge of the press argued they were giving the masses what they wanted, and had few qualms about utilising whatever strategies were necessary to expand their readerships.[3] Although mainly focused on notions of market demand, overstepping traditional boundaries was also justified on the grounds of press freedom and democracy.

The new popular newspapers were a key part of the rise of mass (or popular) culture, backed by ubiquitous advertising. Those running popular newspapers were important architects of this new culture, and key figures such as the press lords Northcliffe (1865–1922), his brother Rothermere (1868–1940), and the Canadian Beaverbrook (1879–1964) shared important beliefs. Although defending and promoting many socially conservative values and being steadfast champions of nationalism and imperialism, the three press lords also adhered to a largely *laissez faire* view of how the economy and social life should function and, unsurprisingly, argued that the promotion of business interests and consumerism would benefit the nation. This economic liberalism and opposition to government regulation and intervention was to be important for later debates about freedom of expression. The jingoistic and consumerist nature of the popular press was also perpetuated by titles that leaned more to the left politically, such as the *Daily Mirror* and the *Daily Herald*; the tabloid style crossed political boundaries.

At the beginning of the twentieth century, those who controlled the popular press presented themselves as radical figures who channelled the voices of their readers to challenge the establishment. While many prominent press men (they were, at the time, all male) came from relatively humble backgrounds, they were quick to accept political honours and enjoyed close relationships with many elite figures in the worlds of business and politics – even if the attempts of the press lords to amass personal political power led to fractious relationships with the main political parties, including the Conservatives.

One early example of the popular press's challenge to the traditional powerholders came during the First World War. As the conflict expanded in scope, a host of new policies and laws were introduced, from central planning of the war economy to draconian suppression of critical and subversive voices. The latter included the Defence of the Realm Act, passed only four days after Britain declared war, which mandated that 'No person shall by word of mouth or in writing spread reports likely to cause disaffection or alarm among any of His Majesty's forces or among the civilian population.'[4] Nevertheless, the popular press launched blistering attacks on the performance of the government. One major example was the *Daily Mail*'s coverage of the shell crisis in May 1915, which ultimately played an important role in Herbert Asquith being replaced as prime minister by David Lloyd George.

However, the record of the British press during the war was hardly one of consistent resistance to state censorship. In 1914 journalists were officially barred from being present at or reporting on the front lines. The *Daily Chronicle*'s Philip Gibbs and the *Daily Mail*'s Basil Clarke both disregarded the policy. Gibbs was arrested, and after being warned that he would be shot if he was caught doing the same thing again, he returned to England. Clarke also returned after receiving an official warning.[5] From then on, British war correspondents stayed away from the front and relied on official communications to inform the reports they sent back to their newspapers. Their coverage was sanitised, clashing with the experiences of soldiers on the front lines. In the years after the war, the British press faced widespread condemnation for the manner in which it had bowed to government censorship.[6]

The critiques that popular newspapers offered of the government during the conflict had often been on militaristic and imperialist grounds – such as calls for conscription. The conservative character of much of the press continued into the interwar period. However, newspapers also gave space to some surprisingly progressive material, with Adrian Bingham having documented the surprising array of content about gender and sexuality that challenged traditionalist views.[7] In some cases this content appeared in specific sections of the newspaper such as the women's pages, which were often overlooked by proprietors who focused on topics that were perceived to be more important, such as politics and the economy.

Moving into the post-Second World War period, newspapers such as the *Daily Mirror* played an important role in the emergence by the late 1950s of the so-called permissive society, which saw a comparative relaxation of traditional conservative social and cultural values and the rise of new forms of consumerism and popular culture. By focusing on new youth cultures and celebrities, and by showcasing different modes of behaviour in lifestyle features, newspapers exposed readers to stories of people transgressing traditional social boundaries. Agony aunts provided space for ever greater discussion of topics such as sexuality. Newspapers persisted with such content in the face of condemnation for a variety of reasons, including the importance of advertising revenue, the need to appeal to younger readers, and the popularity of content that lay outside the traditional scope of the news. Freedom of expression provided a handy defence.

However, the relationship of the press to the new permissive culture remained ambivalent. More oppressive and traditional values – which have persisted to the present – remained apparent across the press, especially in titles such as the popular *Daily Mail* and the upmarket *Daily Telegraph*. This included the persistence of jingoism, the scapegoating of minorities, and the enforcing of conservative moral codes, particularly concerning women.

The new 'permissive' culture also led to gender roles being recon-figured in new ways, with titillation being increasingly prioritised, resulting in the inclusion of soft-core pornography. Following the tradition of featuring pin-up girls, topless women were first pub-lished in the 1930s in the *Daily Mirror* and the *Sunday Pictorial*,[8] while Rupert Murdoch's *Sun* introduced 'Page 3' – a photograph of a topless woman – in 1970 and made it a daily feature by the mid-1970s. The *Daily Star*, launched soon after, followed suit, as later did the *Sunday* and *Daily Sport*. Titillation was also provided by ever greater focus on people's private lives, particularly if it involved sex and scandal. A notable early example was the *Daily Mirror*'s exposé of the Profumo affair in 1963. The scandal centred on John Profumo's relationship with Christine Keeler, a 19-year-old aspiring model who was immediately catapulted into the limelight. The Profumo affair was legitimately of public interest as it concerned the misdeeds of the Minister of War and the possibility of information related to national security being compromised, of particular concern given that Keeler had also been in a relationship with a Soviet naval attaché, Yevgeny Ivanov. Most other cases of the press prying into people's private lives had no such public-interest justification.

Such stories gained greater prominence in the pages of the tabloid press over the subsequent decades, accompanied by paparazzi photos showing celebrities in compromising or embarrassing situations and poses – such as the incredibly creepy practice of taking photos up women's skirts. Despite conflicting with the right to privacy and dig-nity of those being harassed and targeted in such a manner, such fare became a fixture of the tabloids and remained vital after newspapers moved online. The *MailOnline*'s 'side-bar of shame' ensured that this kind of material remained ever present on the right-hand side of its website, contributing to it becoming the most viewed newspaper website in the world by January 2012. Satisfying their readers' desires and hazy claims about free speech remained key to the tabloids' justifications for behaving in such a manner.

Journalists' snooping also veered into outright illegality. While the early 1990s saw controversy arise over the press's harassment of Princess Diana (which ultimately ended with her death in a car accident as she fled the paparazzi), Britain's most popular title, the Sunday paper the *News of the World*, was secretly utilising a variety of underhand and criminal means to secure stories. These included hiring private detectives to stalk targets, bribing police for information, and entrapment. For example, the 'Fake Sheikh' Mazher Mahmood would often dress up in robes and stage elaborate scenarios that were secretly filmed to secure incriminating footage of high-profile figures agreeing to partake in criminal activity. Mahmood was rewarded for his dubious behaviour with a number of journalistic awards, but in October 2016 he was found guilty of attempting to pervert the course of justice and sentenced to 15 months in jail.

The most notorious practice concerned figures working for the *News of the World* hacking people's phones to gain access to their voicemails, a practice that was probably also utilised at other newspapers.[9] They targeted not just celebrities, but also ordinary members of the public who had been thrust into the public eye, such as the parents of the murdered child Milly Dowler and various parents of soldiers who had been killed in action. Former *News of the World* and long-time tabloid journalist Paul McMullan encapsulated the prevailing attitude of those perpetrating such crimes, telling the Leveson Inquiry that was set up to investigate phone hacking that 'Privacy is for paedos.'[10]

Leveson was merely the latest in a long line of intense debates about the activities of the press. The aforementioned failures of the press during the First World War occasioned one such response. Three Royal Commissions on the Press were held 1947–49, 1961–62 and 1974–77. The first led to the formation of the General Council in 1953, later renamed the Press Council, a voluntary organisation with a non-binding regulatory framework that throughout most of its history was funded by newspaper proprietors. At each Commission representatives of the press wheeled out the same arguments, stressing the vital necessity to democracy of press freedom and free speech. While these concerns are of course extremely important, the rhetoric was cynically used to undermine calls for independent regulation of the industry. Instead, even when the Press Council was replaced by the Press Complaints Commission (PCC), and when this was in turn replaced by the Independent Press Standards Organisation (IPSO), oversight remained the purview of the press itself – regardless of how often this has been shown as inadequate in holding the press to account and minimising unethical and destructive practices.

Those defending self-regulation drew on idea of the 'Fourth Estate', which presented the press as an independent actor which holds power to account, a role that is commonly held to have materialised in the mid-to-late nineteenth century. However, this is largely a myth.[11] As previously noted, even during the supposed golden age of the British press, newspapers were reliant on advertising revenue and entangled with and financed by political groups, which undermined their freedom. Regardless, despite warnings that the British press has been at various points 'in the last chance saloon', appeals to the ideals of free speech and the Fourth Estate – alongside acquiescence and in some cases ideological support from Conservative politicians, and intimidation of would-be reformers – have allowed the industry to escape being held to account. Indeed, although the phone-hacking scandal led to the closure of the *News of the World* and brief jail sentences for a small number of perpetrators such as Andy Coulson, most of those involved escaped censure. The *Sun on Sunday* was quickly launched by Rupert Murdoch's News UK to replace the *News of the World*. Most damningly, IPSO was again set up as a vehicle of self-regulation – and has been chaired by figures from News UK such as the former political editor of the *Sun*, Trevor Kavanagh.

Murdoch has been central to another core factor behind the rise to prominence of 'free speech' in the British press. As already noted, from its beginning the British popular press promoted an economically liberal and socially conservative world view that has resonance with the culture war that has arisen in the US in recent decades. Murdoch's media organisations straddle both sides of the Atlantic (and far beyond). Much as Fox News has hosted reactionaries who utilise notionally liberal values such as freedom and free speech to provide cover for their regressive and discriminatory views and activities, so too have Murdoch's newspapers in the UK, the *Sun* and even what was the traditionally Britain's paper of record, *The Times* (as well as the *Sunday Times*). This is part of a broader press environment in which culture war rhetoric has flourished, with constant alarmist articles about 'snowflakes' and PC culture suppressing free speech, attacks on free speech on university campuses, and disingenuous claims that calling out racism, misogyny and homophobia is now the real bigotry and a threat to freedom.

A host of opinion columnists such as Rod Liddle and Richard Littlejohn in popular papers such as the *Mail* and *Express*, upmarket titles such as the *Daily Telegraph*, and the weekly *Spectator* push such rhetoric to extremes. The so-called 'quality' newspapers now host similarly shallow, incendiary fare and use much the same language as can be found in the *Sun* and the *Mail*, and contributors flit between different types of publication as long as they promote the narrative.

Indeed, unsavoury outfits indulging in the kind of behaviour that would have once been too extreme even for the tabloid press provide a well-trodden path into the traditional media. Most notably, the right-wing, smear-mongering website Guido Fawkes and the former revolutionary-communists turned Koch-brothers' financed contrarians of Spiked Online have both been zealous promoters of the culture war discourse, and have been two of the most ardent promoters of the reactionary case for free speech. Their contributors are now ever-present across the media.

Newspapers have long used the rhetoric of free speech and freedom to justify their morally dubious practices, bolster the industry's status and stave off proposed regulation. Recent high-profile issues such as phone hacking and greater condemnation of discriminatory content (aided by social media) has put the press on the defensive. Combined with the enduring conservative character of much of the British media, many journalists have eagerly assumed positions as self-styled guardians of free speech, appropriating terminology from the current culture war. The history of the British press across the last century and a half has exemplified a broader societal shift from popular culture to culture war – and although the manner in which the notions of freedom and free speech have been utilised has changed, they remain potent rhetorical tools.

Free speech is a vitally important issue, especially at a time when authoritarianism is rising around the world. The press is home to a diverse range of voices, including on the issue of free speech. But the appeals to free speech offered by the press in Britain need to be treated with suspicion given the industry's long history of hypocrisy over the issue and the various ways it has sought to weaponise the concept to justify its commercial imperatives and unethical behaviour.

Notes

1 The modern use of the term 'culture war' was popularised by J. D. Hunter, *Culture Wars: The Struggle to Define America* (New York: Basic Books, 1991).

2 A. Bingham and M. Conboy, *Tabloid Century: The Popular Press in Britain, 1896 to the Present* (Oxford: Oxford University Press, 2015).

3 M. Hampton, *Visions of the Press in Britain, 1850–1950* (Urbana, IL: University of Illinois Press, 2004).

4 R. Greenslade, 'First World War: how state and press kept truth off the front page', *The Guardian*, 27 July 2014, https://www.theguardian.com/media/2014/jul/27/first-world-war-state-press-reporting (accessed 10 July 2020).

5 R. Greenslade, 'All the news they saw fit to print', *British Journalism Review*, 25.2 (2014), p. 54.

6 Sarah Lonsdale, *The Journalist in British Fiction and Film: Guarding the Guardians from 1900 to the Present* (London: Bloomsbury, 2016), ch. 2.

7 A. Bingham, *Family Newspapers? Sex, Private Life, and the British Popular Press, 1918–1978* (Oxford: Oxford University Press, 2009).

8 Ibid., p. 208.

9 N. Davies, *Hack Attack: How the Truth Caught Up with Rupert Murdoch* (London: Vintage, 2014).

10 D. Sabbagh, 'Paul McMullan lays bare newspaper dark arts at Leveson inquiry', *The Guardian*, 29 November 2011, https://www.theguardian.com/media/2011/nov/29/paul-mcmullan-leveson-inquiry-phone-hacking (accessed 10 July 2020).

11 G. Boyce, 'The Fourth Estate: the reappraisal of a concept', in G. Boyce, J. Curran and P. Wingate (eds), *Newspaper History from the Seventeenth Century to the Present Day* (London: Constable, 1978), pp. 19–40.

Free speech on campus

13

Free speech and preventing radicalisation in higher education

Shaun McDaid and Catherine McGlynn

This chapter explores the potential impact of UK counter-radicalisation initiatives on free speech in the university classroom and argues for a considerable overhaul of such policies. Since 2015, universities, and other educational institutions and public bodies, have been under a legal duty to have due regard to stop people being drawn into terrorism – known as the Prevent duty.[1] This has required the implementation of a range of policies and procedures, from measures to improve information technology security to the monitoring of external speakers.

Universities are already key sites of contestation in the contemporary culture wars and have faced robust critique from both the left and right, with (often unsubstantiated) allegations that those with whom certain student groups disagree have been 'no platformed', or of 'safe spaces' being provided where undergraduates can seek refuge from discussing controversial topics. The Prevent duty was therefore destined to become intertwined with anxieties about who gets to speak on campus and what they get to say. However, we argue here that the fear that the duty would have a 'chilling effect' on free speech has not come to pass. Nevertheless, the policy should be abolished because it is ineffective to the point of being counter-productive, and is built on poor foundations in terms of evidence. The key threat to the dynamics of contemporary higher education comes not from language that the Prevent duty has the potential to suppress but from the lexicon of safeguarding and vulnerability that has been developed to ease counter-radicalisation into public spaces.

Prevent, radicalisation and terrorism

Prevent is a key plank of the UK's counter-terrorism strategy, CONTEST. Prevent's focus is counter-radicalisation, or preventing violent extremism: in other words, stopping people becoming involved in terrorism before they start. While preventing violence and terrorism is a laudable goal, counter-radicalisation is by no means an unproblematic notion. Counter-radicalisation policies work on the assumption that people who engage in terrorism first undergo a process of ideational and behavioural change, known as 'radicalisation'. The UK's Prevent strategy (in common with similar approaches in Belgium and the Netherlands) reflects an acceptance of radicalisation as the cause of engagement in terrorism. Prevent first emerged in 2003, and has been through several revisions. Originally it had a rather crude focus on Muslim communities, or communities where Muslims were more numerous, but more recently it has also focused on the increasing challenge posed by the far right.[2] As mentioned, Prevent is part of the UK government's counter-terrorism strategy, but there is also a separate counter-extremism strategy, the chief concern of which is the prevention of radicalisation and the curbing of extremist views, even of the non-violent variety.

The concept of radicalisation has been developed by policymakers with reference to academic research on the topic, which has been notable for the method of modelling a journey by different people into political violence. Metaphors of pathways, pyramids and staircases have been used to conceptualise how a sense of grievance (often legitimate) leads towards acceptance of and, if the full journey is completed, engagement in violence as a means of addressing that grievance.[3] A crucial step in many of these models is interaction with groups that are looking to recruit the disaffected and coax or cajole them towards violent acts. For UK policymakers this general academic approach has been tailored into a model known as Extremism Risk Guidance 22+ (ERG22+), which identifies twenty-two risk factors, including the need for excitement, comradeship and adventure, over-identification with a group or cause, dehumanising the enemy, and relevant skills and access to criminal networks. At the heart of ERG22+ is the idea that people, or perhaps more accurately certain people or groups, are 'vulnerable' to radicalisation, and that such radicalisation, where it occurs, can be prevented or potentially reversed with the correct intervention. According to government policy, university students constitute one such vulnerable group.

Academic researchers have by no means universally embraced the concept of radicalisation. It has been critiqued for many reasons, ranging from a lack of empirical data to support the theory to concerns that it has focused too much on Islamist extremism. Further, several studies have shown little evidence that those who disengage from violence have become less radical, which further poses questions about the relationship between ideas and violent acts. Additionally, critics highlight the convenience of radicalisation as an explanation for political violence, in that it ignores other social and political factors that might be attributed to state policy and actions. In the UK context, citizens are already obliged to report potential terrorist threats. Furthermore, although Northern Ireland related terrorism is a recognised threat, and one that predates the

Islamist attacks in Europe of the last two decades, Prevent policies have never been applied to Northern Ireland.

The Prevent duty and higher education

In February 2015 the Counter-Terrorism and Security Act (CTSA) received Royal Assent. The Act imposed a new duty on a range of institutions, including universities, to have 'due regard to the need to prevent people from being drawn into terrorism'. Training packages for staff draw heavily on the above-mentioned ERG22+, with students framed as a vulnerable group who might be seduced into violence by a nefarious recruiter, echoing earlier academic models of radicalisation. This was part of a longer-term anxiety in government circles about the potential for universities be sites of potential radicalisation.[4] Such anxiety was not, entirely, unfounded. University campuses had, for decades, been places where radical politics were fomented. During the 1980s and 1990s Islamist movements such as Hizb-ut-Tahrir used universities as recruiting grounds, and a number of current or former UK students had been involved in high-profile terror plots over the previous fifteen years. One of the most notorious was the British graduate-cum-terrorist Islamic State executioner, Mohammed 'Jihadi John' Emwazi.[5]

The rollout of the Prevent duty was, understandably, divisive. The potential intrusion of the state security apparatus into the classroom, and the conflation of extremism and violence which lay at the heart of government policy, did not sit well, for many, with other statutory duties of universities: upholding academic freedom and freedom of expression. Critics of the policy argued that it would lead to a 'chilling effect' on free speech. For some, this chilling effect would be most pronounced among Muslim students whom they viewed as unfairly targeted by Prevent more generally. These concerns prompted the NUS to launch its 'Students Not Suspects' campaign, with the backing of the main lecturers' union the UCU. Incidents that had occurred before the duty was imposed had already raised concerns.[6] One such incident was the flagging of Staffordshire University postgraduate Mohammed Umar Farooq as a potential security risk after he was seen reading a textbook about terrorism in the library in preparation for the MA he was studying. Since the Prevent duty was imposed the University of Reading has come under scrutiny for guidance issued to students to be careful reading an essay on the ethics of socialist revolution by leftist scholar Norman Geras, lest they fall foul of a Prevent intervention.

Advocates for the Prevent duty would respond, with justification, that cases such as that relating to Geras's article are based on a misunderstanding of the guidance, and are not intrinsic to it.[7] Supporters would also add that it is needed to keep people safe from what is a statistically small, but nevertheless very real, security threat and that campuses have been demonstrated to be sites for agitation and recruitment into activities that could lead to violence. Opposition and support for the Prevent duty generally breaks down across a conservative/liberal axis. Interestingly, it is often more right-of-centre figures or groups such as the Henry Jackson Society who have criticised student activists for opposing Prevent, while also criticising universities for shirking their duty to facilitate free speech.[8] In addition, Conservative universities ministers such as Jo Johnson and Sam Gyimah upheld the Prevent duty while pushing the idea that universities were trapped by what Gyimah in an interview with *The Times* called a 'culture of censorship' (although he has never supplied the details of the university he claimed to have visited where it took students twenty minutes to read the safe space policy).[9]

The Prevent duty in action

What effect, in practice, has the Prevent duty had on the everyday experiences of staff and students in universities? To ascertain this, we conducted a range of focus groups with current staff and students in universities in England and analysed policy documents and guidance issued by 106 English higher education institutions. Our choice of England rather than the UK reflects the actual geographical focus of Prevent. The results of both our documentary analysis and the focus group data do not suggest that the Prevent duty has, so far, led to a chilling effect on free speech within universities.[10]

In terms of university policy, what we found was that the general approach taken by the institutions is one of compliance with the letter of the law, while also taking seriously their legal obligations to ensure freedom of speech and expression. By way of example, institutions are proactive in following bureaucratic procedures concerning issues such as external speakers. Speakers are logged, and staff are either asked to confirm that they are not known to espouse views that might be illegal, or to provide a justification for their inclusion and ensure balance in the panel if they are known to have expressed views that could fall under Prevent's scope.

Our focus groups offered no compelling evidence that students were shying away from discussing controversial topics. We did, however, see evidence that students, from a range of backgrounds, do tread carefully when discussing controversial topics, particularly concerning race, religion and ethnicity. Participants explained that this was not motivated by a fear of legal interventions, but for the rather more prosaic reason of not wishing to cause undue, or unintentional, offence to their peers. But students were, on the whole, very clear that they regarded the need for debate about difficult, and indeed controversial, topics as an essential part of the student experience, and that it was crucial to the development of the critical thinking that they undertook their chosen courses to develop.

For lecturers, the experiences of, and interactions with, the Prevent duty varied across sector and type of institution. None of the staff interviewed reported that they felt the Prevent duty was having a particular impact on their day-to-day activities. Indeed, some participants acknowledged that the Prevent duty was far more onerous for teachers in the school sector, where training programmes were delivered in person and required compliance, or formed part of the overall quality control assessments for those sectors that are regulated by the Office for Standards in Education. Some participants felt that the Prevent duty was rather vague where it applied to higher education, and saw it as another box to tick rather than a serious intrusion into their professional lives. Where staff did see problematic issues was with the utility of the underlying concept of radicalisation and of the safeguarding approach to counter-radicalisation, and it is to this issue that we will now turn.

Safeguarding and vulnerability

Advocates for the Prevent duty claim that it is a form of safeguarding. In this conception, university students constitute a vulnerable group, at risk of brainwashing by terrorist ideologues, with the ultimate aim of recruiting them into terrorism. In framing everyone as having that vulnerability, it could be argued that one of the original criticisms of Prevent, an unfair focus on Muslim communities, no longer applied.[11] If everyone was vulnerable, then it would be difficult to claim that the policy was targeting a particular demographic or demographics – something that the original iteration of Prevent did quite explicitly.

Universities have largely accepted the message of vulnerability and taken the safeguarding route when adhering to the duty. The idea that radicalisation can strike anyone allows higher education institutions to feel that it can be implemented without undermining commitments to diversity and equality. It also cuts down on labour, in that universities already have policies for dealing with safeguarding and vulnerability (albeit initially designed to support students as trainee professionals dealing with external clients and patients) and that training packages offered to staff can be adapted or imported directly from material designed for statutory education and under-18s. Finally, it fits with a broader trend of what the researcher Kathryn Ecclestone calls 'vulnerability creep', where students' well-being becomes more and more the responsibility of universities.[12]

So why is this a problem? Despite the lack of evidence to support the figure of the vulnerable young person lured into violence, these policies have become unduly dominant in the counter-terrorism field, and the lack of critical reflection in adopting the language of safeguarding means that universities are not challenging the safeguarding route for what it is: an attempt to detoxify a policy that has little credibility among the communities it seeks to protect. Accepting the discourse of vulnerability also intensifies the passivity and lack of agency among students that began with the shift towards consumerist understandings of university–student relations as fees were introduced. This does students a disservice. Such policies are unlikely to shield universities from criticism if future attacks are undertaken by current or former students. Indeed, the revelation that any issues with these students were treated as a matter of well-being and care for vulnerability might provoke a great deal of anger. Finally, it has to be acknowledged that despite its claims to universality, Prevent is focused on Islamist and far-right violence, and universities need to be a lot less blasé about the impact of the policy on Muslim students and those from what is termed the white working class, groups that are already under-represented in higher education.[13]

Chill out? The future of the Prevent duty

Our research to date suggests that the Prevent duty has not (or at least not yet) led to a 'Big Brother' situation in universities, but this does not mean that its critics should be more accepting of the policy. While we did not find, and do not foresee, the worst fears of critics of the Prevent duty coming to pass in universities, we see no reason to persevere with a programme that doesn't seem to work as the safeguarding policy it purports to be or the security policy it actually is. The assumptions about radicalisation, and the supposed causal relationship between radicalisation and terrorism, do not seem to us sufficiently grounded in evidence to provide the basis for an almost ubiquitous and nationwide policy. The ERG22+ factors are not fit for purpose, and were never designed to be implemented at societal level. Until that is sufficiently recognised then there will always be issues with Prevent more broadly and the Prevent duty in particular.

Looking to the future, one thing to consider is what the impact will be of an increased focus in UK counter-terrorism on the far right. Until recently, groups and individuals associated with this ideology were not given priority within the CONTEST strategy, but they are now seen as a much more pervasive and organised threat. It might be that many critics of Prevent who saw the policy as racist and discriminatory might have greater anxiety about the influence of far-right politics and the threat of violence from that quarter. And for groups who have decried safe spaces while backing Prevent's safeguarding, the long-standing issue of the conflation of extremism with violence might become something that becomes more person-ally resonant as alt-right or established conservative activists come on to the Prevent radar. How they might react to student groups shifting from no-platform tactics to encouraging universities to fulfil their Prevent duty obligations would be very interesting indeed. Either way, at a time when the prospects of extremists, conspiracy theorists or simply self-identifying 'contrarians' have been boosted by a global pandemic, and with the expansion of teaching and learn-ing interactions occurring more frequently in the online space, there will be a lot more to be said about freedom of speech in higher education in the months and years ahead.[14]

Notes

1   HM Government, *Revised Prevent duty guidance: for England and Wales*, https://www.gov.uk/government/publications/prevent-duty-guidance/ revised-prevent-duty-guidance-for-england-and-wales (accessed 10 July 2020).

2   For a history of Prevent, see C. McGlynn and S. McDaid, *Radicalisation and Counter-Radicalisation in Higher Education* (Bingley: Emerald, 2019), pp. 24–37.

3   See, for example, F. M. Moghaddam, 'The staircase to terrorism: a psy-chological exploration', *American Psychologist*, 60.2 (2005), pp. 161–9; M. D. Silber, A. Bhatt and S. I. Analysts, *Radicalisation in the West: The Homegrown Threat* (New York: Police Department, 2007).

4   M. Lloyd and C. Dean, 'The development of structured guidelines for assessing risk in extremist offenders', *Journal of Threat Assessment and Management*, 2.1 (2015), pp. 40–52.

5   See McGlynn and McDaid, *Radicalisation and Counter-Radicalisation*, ch. 2.

6   National Union of Students, *Preventing PREVENT handbook* (2015), https://www.nusconnect.org.uk/resources/preventing-prevent-handbook (accessed 10 July 2020).

7   S. Greer and L. C. Bell, 'Counter-terrorist law in British universities: a review of the "Prevent" debate', *Public Law* (January 2018), pp. 84–104.

8 'Disruption of King's College event shows the growing level of intolerance towards free speech on campus', 6 March 2018, https://henryjacksonsociety.org/media-centre/disruption-of-kings-college-event-shows-the-growing-level-of-intolerance-towards-free-speech-on-campus/ (accessed 10 July 2020); Rupert Sutton, 'Preventing Prevent? Challenges to counter-radicalisation policy on campus', 14 July 2015, https://henryjacksonsociety.org/publications/preventing-prevent-challenges-to-counter-radicalisation-policy-on-campus/ (accessed 10 July 2020).

9 *The Times*, 3 May 2018.

10 McGlynn and McDaid, *Radicalisation and Counter-Radicalisation*.

11 P. Thomas, 'Failed and friendless: the UK's "Preventing Violent Extremism" programme', *The British Journal of Politics and International Relations*, 12.3 (2010), pp. 442–58.

12 K. Ecclestone, 'Changing the subject of education? A critical evaluation of "vulnerability creep" and its implications', *Social Policy and Society*, 16.3 (2017), pp. 443–56.

13 Jacqueline Stevenson, *Muslim Students in UK Higher Education REPORT Issues of Inequality and Inequity* (Bridge Institute Report, 2018); Amy Walker, 'Half of universities in England have fewer than 5% poor white students', *The Guardian*, https://www.theguardian.com/education/2019/feb/14/half-of-universities-england-have-fewer-than-5-poor-white-students (accessed 10 July 2020).

14 Online abuse of a racist or misogynist nature against educators and students has already been reported. See, for example, 'Virtual meeting with black University of Texas students cut short by racist "Zoom bombing"', *The Hill*, https://thehill.com/homenews/state-watch/490402-virtual-meeting-with-black-university-of-texas-students-cut-off-by-racist-zoom (accessed 10 July 2020); David Batty, 'Harassment fears as students post extreme pornography in online lectures', *The Guardian*, https://www.theguardian.com/education/2020/apr/22/students-zoombomb-online-lectures-with-extreme-pornography (accessed 10 July 2020).

14

Anatomy of a 'trigger warning' scandal

Gabriel Moshenska

I teach archaeology at a UK university, and mostly I keep out of trouble. In autumn 2016 I became a symbol of the supposed academic mollycoddling of snowflake students, and came under concerted attack from a bunch of right-wing dullards and sociopathic libertarians. A brief content warning in one of my module handbooks sparked a storm of frothing conservative outrage, part of an attempt to import US-style campus culture wars into the UK. At the core of this and much other 'free speech' activism around UK higher education lies a cult-like coterie of writers centred around *Spiked* magazine. The purpose of this chapter is to examine the methods and manners of the cynical scandal-mongers, most notably their powerful and sadistic hatred of students.

What is a trigger warning and why do they trigger the right?

Trigger warnings were originally a part of treatment for post-traumatic stress disorder (PTSD) and related conditions, based on the recognition that specific 'triggers' such as smells and sounds can induce flashbacks and panic attacks. More recently, the term 'trigger warning' has expanded to encompass what I would call content warnings, such as the bland announcement that 'some viewers may find the following images disturbing' at the start of a news report. In online discourse 'triggered' has come to mean offended or upset, rather than reflecting the often extreme psychological and physiological effects of PTSD. This is the sense in which 'triggering' is most commonly used by the political right and far right.[1]

The debate around trigger warnings has become a common talking point and attack line in the US campus culture wars. This is best exemplified in the *Atlantic* article 'The Coddling of the American Mind', now expanded into an equally vacuous book of the same title, which states that 'trigger warnings are sometimes demanded for a long list of ideas and attitudes that some students find politically offensive'.[2] Lukianoff and Haidt, authors of *The Coddling*, define trigger warnings as 'alerts that professors are expected to issue if something in a course might cause a strong emotional response'. They argue that trauma responses should not be avoided, but rather that university classrooms are an ideal place for PTSD patients to experience Pavlovian 'exposure therapy'. This is clinical, pedagogical, intellectual and ethical garbage. The barely concealed desire to hurt students, and in particular women and minorities, is a surprisingly common theme in conservative commentary on higher education.

The Coddling and similar recent works tend to rest their arguments on the same small set of anecdotal evidence, such as student activism at the famously liberal Oberlin College. One gets the sense that the use of trigger warnings is far less common and controversial than these crusaders might hope.

My content warning

Since 2011 I have taught an MA module called 'Archaeologies of Modern Conflict'. In 2014 I added a note to the course handbook that read:

CONTENT WARNING
At times during this course we will be discussing historical events that may be disturbing, even traumatizing, to some students. If you ever feel the need to step outside during one of these discussions, either for a short time or for the rest of the class, you may always do so without penalty. If you do leave the room for a significant time, please make arrangements to get notes from another student or see me individually. If you ever wish to discuss your personal reactions to this material, either with the class or with me afterwards, I welcome such discussion as an appropriate part of the course.

I did this for two reasons. The first is that each year one or two students arrived on the course with personal experiences of warfare, including armed forces veterans and a few others who had spent time in conflict zones. The second was a set of changes to my syllabus including more readings from forensics and human remains literature, as well as first-person accounts from twentieth-century genocides. Students who might have expected sessions on identifying regimental buttons and measuring musket balls were being shown magnified images of machete wounds and technical drawings of mass graves full of children – and it seemed only fair and reasonable to let them know.

Outrage

Around the start of the 2016–17 academic year there was an abortive attempt by right-wing commentators in the UK to import attack lines from the US campus culture wars, specifically around free speech and trigger warnings. Chris McGovern of the 'Campaign for Real Education' called trigger warnings 'health and safety going mad', and obliging hacks went looking for examples to illustrate this ersatz soundbite. This coincided, perhaps not coincidentally, with a growth in newspaper coverage of poor student mental health.

I was contacted by the *Mail on Sunday* which had found my syllabus and content warning online. I foolishly but truthfully explained that my primary intention was to support ex-servicemen and women among my students. I also noted that, at that point, nobody had ever asked to leave my classroom for reasons of distress. This remains the case today.

The *Mail on Sunday* printed a reasonably fair and accurate account of my explanation, along with the pre-prepared outrage from McGovern (the journalist read me his ravings and asked if I wished to respond. I declined.) A classicist at another university was lambasted in the same article for mentioning to her students that some of Ovid's poems were rather nasty. I got the sense that the hunt for trigger warnings in the UK hadn't yielded as much as hoped.[3]

Coverage and debate

Within the next few days, a number of other articles appeared on the same theme. There was a shorter piece in *The Times* that named me and focused on my course, and a longer and very hostile story in the *Spectator* by Brendan O'Neill, a well-known right-wing journalist and editor of the libertarian-right magazine *Spiked*.[4] Student website *The Tab* published a short article based largely on the original *Mail on Sunday* article. The following day Chris McGovern himself published an article in *Conservative Woman*, and the day after that two very hostile pieces were published on the US-based websites *Reason.com* and, by James Delingpole, at *Breitbart*. Most of these articles named me (some named no other academics) and discussed my course. By this point I had begun to receive abusive emails and messages on social media, some of them explicitly antisemitic.

Over the following two weeks further hostile articles appeared in the *Independent*, two articles in the *Daily Mail* and *Spiked* by UCL student Jacob Furedi, and one in the *Guardian* by his father Frank Furedi. Apart from Jonathan Petre who wrote the first *Mail on Sunday* article, not one of these writers contacted me for comment.

I began to receive a series of invitations to debates. *Russia Today* asked me several times to debate trigger warnings against opponents including retired UCL academic John Sutherland and Derby University professor Dennis Hayes. Later, the scope of my supposed expertise began to expand: the Oxford Union invited me to debate 'safe spaces', and the BBC's *Newsnight* invited me to debate a whole range of topics, including:

> Are people becoming too weak if they are defensive about having their ideas and opinions challenged?
> Is this a generational change?
> Should any discussion regarding trans be treated differently to a debate on a different topic (due to trans relating to someone's sense of self and identity)?

I was reasonably confident that as a junior-ish academic with no public profile, media training or experience, I would have been chum in the water at these discussions – and that this was the point of inviting me. I was particularly irritated by the idea that a cisgender archaeology lecturer had any right or reason to debate trans* rights on television. I turned down every invitation.

'Special Snowflake Safe Space Lunacy': a closer look

After the first wave of unpleasant news coverage and abusive messages I began to collect the texts of articles about me, ignoring those that wholly or partially duplicated earlier pieces. I gathered a set of eleven articles totalling just over 6,000 words, and began to unpick recurring themes in the texts.

Students (bad)

Who are these students who supposedly demand trigger warnings? Apparently they are Janus-faced monsters, 'fragile little petals' swooning at non-politically-correct thought, but also 'snarling baby-faced SJW students'. For some they are 'a small minority of NUS-supporting students' and 'too fragile to be exposed to the rough and tumble of the real world', while for others they are 'jumped-up, right-on, soya-consuming activists' or (a throwback to the 1980s here) 'right-on' and 'indignant'.

Are we meant to sneer at them or fear their power? It's unclear, but whether 'cosseted generation' or 'campus ayatollahs', they obviously induce a splenetic hatred in a certain sort of self-proclaimed rational libertarian adult.

Academics (bad)

Not one of the content warnings uncovered in the UK was the result of demands by imaginary authoritarian leftist students. This was noted with obvious disgust in several of the pieces, which derided academics as 'over protective'. They were equally irritated by the fact that I 'admitted' that nobody had ever walked out of my lessons in fear or disgust:

So far, no student has taken Moshenska up on his safe space offer. Which is a comfort, of sorts. Except, isn't the most worrying part of the story the plain fact that a member of the university faculty considered making that offer in the first place?[5]

I have never used the fire extinguisher in my house or the airbags in my car. I cannot imagine anybody would consider their presence 'worrying', although the libertarian right have always frothed and fretted about seatbelt laws and other impositions of the 'nanny state'.

On a deeper level, this highlights a fundamental and probably wilful misunderstanding of the purpose of content warnings: they are intended as a safeguard against already rare mental health emergencies, and this is how they are mostly understood outside the ranks of the professionally enraged. The fact that no student has walked out of one of my classes (as far as I know) does not mean that the content warning has not been used. The intention of content warnings is to provide enough information to allow students to prepare themselves in whatever way they choose.

American-style anti-intellectualism (good)

Poorly written, contradictory, mean-spirited and desperately short of evidence: what are these articles trying to achieve? One clue is the way they describe trigger warnings: as a 'trend, rampant on American campuses', as a 'practice, more common in America', and in one rather optimistic case as an 'Anglo-American' phenomenon. Universities in the US are a political battleground where the right flings muck and fights dirty. Liberal academics are accused of spreading 'cultural Marxist' propaganda to brainwash naive young students.

Like the imaginary leftist student simultaneously 'triggered' into panic and brutally bullying their conservative peers, the liberal academic of conservative nightmares is both a weakling, cowering in fear of their radical students, and a sinister puppet-master manipulating their innocent, sheep-like charges.

In February 2016 Michael Gove famously declared that 'people in this country have had enough of experts'. Considering the political contexts of late 2016 Britain in the aftermath of the Brexit vote, one can see how conservative and proto-fascist ideologues might have seen a fertile ground for US-style sneering anti-intellectualism, and sought to emulate its most successful attack lines.

Conservative academics (good)

Luckily there are still some 'seasoned academics' who can be found 'down the pub' moaning about 'how students "aren't what they used to be" and "need to start living in the real world"'. The writer of this dross, who paints Amis's *Lucky Jim* as a model of good-old-days un-politically-correct academia, warns that 'for those who are still critical of trigger warnings, taking the piss out of students is not enough'.[6] Presumably these are not the same academics who allegedly live in fear of their students and 'feel they have to mind their words'. There is a deep-seated hatred of students underlying much of this writing, as well as an implicit assumption that this hostility is shared by their readers and by right-thinking academics.

Who are they?

Around half of these attacks can be traced back to a gaggle of professional contrarians often known as the 'LM network' after the magazine *Living Marxism*. The group, including academic Frank Furedi, journalist Mick Hume and Brexit Party MEP Claire Fox, was profiled a decade ago by Jenny Turner in the *London Review of Books*.[7] At that time they clustered around a think tank called the Institute of Ideas, the website *Spiked*, and a series of cover organisations focused on civil liberties, science and education policy.

The LM network's political journey, from Trotskyist roots in the Revolutionary Communist Party to the forefront of the libertarian right, is one of the strangest in British politics. Today the group is notable for their anti-environmentalism, and have received funding from the right-wing Charles Koch Foundation in the US. Some of the themes that Turner noted in her profile of the group can be seen in their furious attacks on trigger warnings. These include a hatred of 'health and safety' in all its forms, free speech absolutism, and an odd rhetorical obsession with being treated as 'grown-ups'. In one article by Jacob Furedi, we are reminded that students 'were actually adults', that universities 'rather than treating students as young adults … treat us like oversized children', and that they 'need to respect the fact that students – adults – are capable of making rational decisions'.[8] As Turner notes, 'If you talk constantly about "grown-ups" it makes you sound like a child.'

Do no harm

Can disturbing texts or images cause harm? This is the crux of the argument. I believe that, *in extremis*, they can. In contrast, the LM network's Frank Furedi, Brendan O'Neill and James Delingpole ground their denunciations of trigger warnings and 'snowflakery' in furious denials of this harm. Delingpole derides as 'psychobabble hokum … the idea that words and ideas can cause actual physical harm, that being exposed to … shocking information is somehow dangerous, and that avoidance coping (staying away from things that upset you) actually works'.[9] Turner argues that this erasure of victimhood and weakness is a common theme:

> The one thing, perhaps, that ultimately holds the LM network together is its members' refusal to countenance the existence of psychic conflict or confusion. People are not 'hapless, fragile victims' ... People run fine on 'democracy, science, reason'. We are, after all, 'grown-ups'.[10]

We can perhaps divide opponents of trigger warnings into two groups: those who relish the thought of harming students, and those who, for ideological reasons, cannot or will not accept the reality of those harms.

Reflections

My favourite piece of hate mail declared me unfit to teach students and suggested a move into a purely research or curatorial role. I briefly considered raising this suggestion with my employer.

I would like to offer a little advice to any academic who finds themselves the subject of right-wing media scorn and the resultant abuse and attacks. First, disabuse yourself of the notion that your employer will support or assist you in any way. Their media, HR and legal teams work to protect the institution, not you. Second, resist all urges and invitations to respond, to comment, or to give 'your side'. Third, take comfort in support and solidarity. Students sent me a care package of biscuits, beer and crisps; former students fought my corner in newspaper comment sections; and senior colleagues wrote in my defence and in support of content warnings.[11]

Around the same time, there was a growth in press coverage of the student mental health crisis in the UK, some of it compassionate but a much of it 'snowflake'-type sneering attacks. The hate mail and abuse I received had an impact on my own mental health and well-being for several months, exacerbating my pre-existing anxiety. Compared to others, my permanent contract, maleness, and other social and professional privileges offered a degree of protection, and the right-wing hate machine soon moved on to other targets.

I remain convinced that content warnings are a moderate means of maintaining an inclusive and respectful learning environment. They are as necessary, unobtrusive and uncontroversial a part of a classroom as fire escapes and wheelchair access, and their absence should be just as unacceptable. I have yet to hear a counter-argument that is not based on disdain (at best) for students, and I reckon that any educator who professes a principled opposition to content warnings is unfit to teach. Fight me.

Notes

1 Lindsay Holmes, 'A quick lesson on what trigger warnings actually do', *Huffpost*, 26 August 2016, https://www.huffingtonpost.co.uk/entry/university-of-chicago-trigger-warning_n_57bf16d9e4b085c1ff28 176d (accessed 15 June 2020).

2 Greg Lukianoff and Jonathan Haidt, 'The coddling of the American mind', *The Atlantic*, September 2015, https://www.theatlantic.com/magazine/archive/2015/09/the-coddling-of-the-american-mind/399356/ (accessed 15 June 2020).

3 Jonathan Petre, 'Warning to archaeology pupils that "bones can be scary" sparks fresh fears over cosseted generation of students', *Mail on Sunday*, 24 September 2016, https://www.dailymail.co.uk/news/article-3805872/Warning-archaeology-pupils-bones-scary-sparks-fresh-fears-cosseted-generation-students.html (accessed 15 June 2020).

4 Brendan O'Neill, 'If archaeology students can't cope with "scary bones", they really are doomed', *The Spectator*, 26 September 2016, https://www.spectator.co.uk/article/if-archaeology-students-can-t-cope-with-scary-bones-they-really-are-doomed (accessed 15 June 2020).

5 James Delingpole, 'Archaeology students given "trigger warning" about disturbing historical events and scary old bones', Breitbart, 28 September 2016, https://www.breitbart.com/europe/2016/09/28/archaeology-students-given-trigger-warning-about-disturbing-historical-events-and-scary-old-bones// (accessed 15 June 2020).

6 Jacob Furedi, 'Spare me the campus ayatollahs ruining my student life:

an undergraduate's fearless broadside against the joyless PC takeover of our universities', *Daily Mail*, 4 October 2016, https://www.dailymail.co.uk/news/article-3820668/Spare-campus-ayatollahs-ruining-student-life-undergraduate-s-fearless-broadside-against-joyless-PC-takeover-universities.html (accessed 15 June 2020).

7   Jenny Turner, 'Who are they?', *London Review of Books*, 8 July 2010, pp. 3–8, https://www.lrb.co.uk/the-paper/v32/n13/jenny-turner/who-are-they (accessed 15 June 2020).

8   Furedi, 'Spare me the campus ayatollahs'.

9   Delingpole, 'Archaeology students given "trigger warning"'.

10 Turner, 'Who are they?'

11 Tony Pollard, 'Trigger warnings about war graves do not mollycoddle archaeology students, they are essential', *The Conversation*, 30 September 2016, https://theconversation.com/trigger-warnings-about-war-graves-do-not-molly-coddle-archaeology-students-they-are-essential-66292 (accessed 15 June 2020).

15

Grad school as conversion therapy: 'free speech' and the rights of trans and non-binary people on university campuses[1]

Grace Lavery

On 21 October 2018 the *New York Times* reported that the Department of Health and Human Services was planning to rewrite Title IX guidelines to define an individual's sex as 'the sex listed on a person's birth certificate'.[2] The purpose, evidently, is to abolish the idea of trans people by executive fiat. The same day, by some coincidence, I found myself looking at a paranoid, joyless manifesto that a colleague (not at Berkeley) had posted on his departmental profile page, in which he claimed that the national 'climate' is at present – the page is marked 'edited and archived, October 2018' – excessively deferential to the whims of trans people.[3] Jesus Christ, I thought. What the fuck do they *want* to do to us, that eradicating our legal existence appears too lenient? The manifesto's answer seemed to be the same as that of the Trump administration: consign us to our old names, strip us of the pronoun changes that we have so peremptorily demanded that the world accommodate, and tell us that they are doing so for the sake of truth and our mental health. Or, as the author, Christopher Reed, puts it, he wants to 'allow for a reasoned variety of pronoun address and citation'. And what, *mes élèves*, could be more liberal than that?

Grad school as conversion therapy

On the evidence of Reed's document, trans and non-binary students do not have either the privileges I enjoy, nor necessarily the
power to assert the privileges to which they are entitled. On the
other hand, I'm wary of supplying this man with the outraged and
angry attention that he has solicited. His manifesto is tiresomely
keen to assert its author's credentials – variously professional
('expertise on sexuality and gender studies'; 'protected by academic
rank'), entitled by seniority ('veterans of gay and lesbian activism')
and, most audaciously of all, by literary style (which like … you
sound nothing like Oscar Wilde, my dude, and *saying* you're invoking the unruly spirit of the trickster is not something a trickster
would do). So there's a strong argument to be made for simply leaving him alone to polish his medals. And there are risks associated
with saying anything – even above the usual risks of a junior scholar
criticising a senior one. Reed flatters himself that he is brave enough
to initiate a debate that others are too cowardly to join, and I am
wary of appearing to validate that fantasy by responding at all. It is
a *remarkably* common fantasy in my profession, and I'm certainly
not immune to it myself. Still, in addition to reviewing the *History of
Sexuality* to which he refers rather casually, he should take another
look at *Fearless Speech*, the late lectures on free speech that Foucault
gave at Berkeley. Foucault is witheringly satirical about the self-
congratulation of the *parrhesiastes*, the relatively privileged man
who takes it upon himself to tell unpopular truths. There's nothing
courageous about trolling.

I'm not responding to this garbage in a spirit of collegial engagement or professional dispute. I respond in order to attempt to
establish a baseline protocol for scholarly discourse with trans and
non-binary students and faculty – both in research and in teaching;
to encourage other faculty to sign on to such a protocol; and to place
Reed's 'axiomatic' solidly on the other side of it. That protocol is: no,

deadnaming and misgendering are not acceptable scholarly practices, and no, despite Reed's claims to 'reasoned variety', they are not
covered by the principle of academic freedom.

Deadnaming and misgendering are not acceptable scholarly
practices, and they are not covered by the principle of academic
freedom!!!

But let's back up here. Why are the fascists so obsessed with trans
people? And why does that obsession seem to affect university professors whose politics seem, in other respects, impeccably liberal?

The answer is not just that fascists rise by stoking the desire to
patrol boundaries and bodies – sexual, reproductive, national and
racial – although certainly it is also that. Instead, and perhaps more
importantly for the overlap between fascism and academic discourse, the answer concerns the figure of the *parrhesiastes* himself:
it concerns free speech. To clarify my position on free speech: I'm
for it. If anyone wants to accuse me of advocating the repression
of free expression, well you've got the wrong tranny. I invoke the
unruly spirit of the trickster, or whatever. But trans people pose
a specific kind of challenge to free speech discourse, and it's kind
of interesting. Because many of us change our names, and because
our changes in sex and gender often place us in new relations to
the gendered pronouns of third-person reference, it therefore falls
to others to make minor adjustments in the way they describe us.
Of course, trans people did not invent, and can hardly be expected
to un-invent, the rather remarkable fact that the English language
requires a speaker to gender every object (even hypothetical ones) to
which she refers. But never mind. It's a simple ask, not much more
complicated than that of someone who gets married and chooses to
change his last name.

Why is Reed not writing manifestos in defence of maiden names?
For the same reason that any bully weaponises referential speech by

making up names, repeating cruel epithets, and so on. Misgendering and deadnaming are modes of abuse, designed to humiliate and hurt trans people. When performed in a workplace, they fall solidly under the definition of sexual harassment constitutive of a hostile work environment. That is, if someone refers to me as a man, even after I've asked them not to, they are treating me disrespectfully *on the basis of their perception of my sex.* If they repeatedly target me on that basis, they are committing an actionable aggression, which can be grounds for disciplinary action against them. It is true that being trans is not a specifically enumerated protection under Title IX, but this is because there is no need to enumerate trans/cis status as a separate category, when *sex* and *gender* are already protected. (Official legal protections vary state to state; California, for example, does have legislation that mentions trans issues specifically.) Accordingly, a Title IX coordinator is – currently, at least – required to ensure that 'transgender students are treated consistent with their gender identity'.

So when Reed writes that 'the new litany of "correctness" is enforced by appeals to authority to suppress alternative ideas', he is using the language of academic intercourse ('ideas') to normalise two types of sex-based harassment that neither are, nor should be, protected by tenure, by the doctrine of academic freedom or by the First Amendment. And when one is being harassed at work, appealing to authority is literally the *exact right thing to do.* Publishing a bullshit defence of your harassment strategies on your faculty profile page does not mitigate a Title IX officer's obligation to investigate the harassment, however clever you think you are. To be clear: I'm not saying the manifesto isn't protected – it certainly is. But it's a defence of two abusive practices that aren't, much like a polemic in defence of arson.

Meanwhile, blurring the line between harassment and hate speech has been one of the signal strategies of the ethnonationalist movement that currently encompasses the federal government, and it is remarkable that so many people in colleges and universities have fallen for it. Because of the distinctiveness of the trans position – the distinctiveness, that is, of entailing a change in *referential pronoun* on the part of a third party – trans people have been made into a convenient scapegoat for the idea that a group (or generation, or class) of people are forcing others to change the way they are speaking. That the phantom authority in question is simply good sense – that it makes sense to refer to trans women as 'she' because, well, we look, speak, act, dress and identify as women, and many of us have estrogen rather than testosterone in our bodies – can be ignored in favour of the paranoid fear that someone else is coming to dispossess us of our language.

And once that fear has been established in relation to trans people, it can be expanded indefinitely: indeed, in our current political climate, an anxiety about trans people serves just that propagandistic purpose. For a clear example of how the victimisation of trans students mutates, through the careful manipulation of conservative media, into a wholly abstract debate about the nature of free speech in which liberal academics rush to wax lyrical about the spirit of liberal tolerance represented by the famous Skokie case, we need look no further than the despicable machinations of Reed's kindred spirit, Milo Yiannopoulos.

In January 2016 a trans woman named Adelaide Kramer, a student at the University of Wisconsin, Milwaukee, was excluded from a locker room, complained, and had her complaint upheld provided that, in future, she concealed her genitals while in the locker rooms. She complained to the UW-Milwaukee equity office, which decided in June 2016 that her rights had not necessarily been infringed, because the US Department of Education had yet to provide clear guidance on Title IX applicability of locker room and bathroom access. Kramer's appeal of that decision was in process when, in early December that year, she talked to a campus newspaper and described her experiences and feelings about the delay.

At an event he held at UW-Milwaukee on 13 December 2016, Yiannopoulos projected a photograph of Kramer against the back wall, without her permission. He jeered at her and encouraged others to do so, and, among a number of other degrading and disturbing attacks, quipped that 'the way that you know he's failing is I'd still almost bang him'. Later that evening, the UW-Milwaukee chancellor Mark Mone wrote publicly: '[I] will not stand silently by when a member of our campus community is personally and wrongly attacked. I am disappointed that this speaker chose to attack a transgender student.' It might be noted that Mone had, precisely, stood silently by while Yiannopoulos did just that.

The same night, 13 December 2016, Kramer wrote to Mone: 'Free speech does not cover harassment, and that's exactly what Milo did to me.' She announced that she would be dropping out of school as a result. There's a legal complication here that is worth observing: Kramer was not, as it happens, correct in the second part of her assessment. Being attacked *once* by a visiting speaker does not constitute, even for a student, an actionable Title IX infringement, which entails not merely targeting on the basis of real or perceived sex/ gender, but also repetition. It was, however, ample grounds for the Berkeley College Republicans to extract from Yiannopoulos a pledge not to target any particular students on his visit to the Berkeley campus – a goal that, in private discussions, they said they shared. When I asked them to do so sometime in January 2017, they said they would. When I followed up on the matter with them a few days later, they admitted that they didn't have a direct phone number for Yiannopoulos and had no way of contacting him. This from the hapless students who had been positioned as the event's organisers, but who were in reality a cipher for Yiannopoulos's real backers, about whose identities we can still only speculate.

On 15 December 2016 *breitbart.com* reported the Milwaukee story, calling Yiannopoulos, with the same self-regarding intellectualism of the Reed manifesto, 'a second-wave feminist hero in the vein of the late Phyllis Schlafly' (I'm not linking that), and framing Kramer's departure from UW-Milwaukee as a victory. The Breitbart article reports Yiannopoulos saying, 'If all it takes are a few strong words from me to make trans people leave women in peace in their bathrooms, I'm definitely going to up the ante.'

As his caravan marched onwards towards Berkeley, the ante was upped. On 20 January 2017 a 34-year-old medic named Joshua Dukes was shot by one of Yiannopoulos's supporters at a protest in Seattle. At a meeting of UC Berkeley English Department faculty and students arranged that week to discuss the escalating crisis, a representative of the College Republicans claimed, instead, and falsely, that the victim was one of Yiannopoulos's supporters. Marc Hokoana, the husband of Dukes's attacker Elizabeth, and who was himself charged with third degree assault, wrote to a friend on Facebook the night before his wife shot Dukes: 'I can't wait for tomorrow. I'm going to the milo event and if the snowflakes get out off hand [*sic*] I'm going to wade through their ranks and start cracking skulls.' When Hokoana was posting that on Facebook, a good number of academics were using the same social media platform to claim that Berkeley students and faculty calling for the cancellation of the event were 'playing into his hands', 'walking into a trap', 'doing just what Bannon wants' or, of course, failing to meet our responsibilities as intellectuals to welcome dissenting ideas. It's worth reflecting that the 'ideas' in question were not of a kind that could be debated in a seminar, but were rather a form of discourse – the misgendering of an individual trans student – that they could get fired for instantiating in their own classrooms.

On 2 February 2017 Milo Yiannopoulos's UC Berkeley talk was eventually called off by local police, after a targeted strike against campus property by anti-fascist activists. *The Daily Cal*, our student newspaper, reported that the cost of the property destruction would amount to about $100,000. When the same protagonists lived through the same scenario the following September, the cost reached $800,000. Somewhat belatedly, campus administrators announced the creation of a committee to determine whether our First Amendment obligations included spending every last cent in the public purse at the mere request of the nearest Proud Boy.

I realise all of this detail is dreary and unpleasant, but it's necessary because academic commentators on both sides of this fiasco generally represented it as a confrontation between two accounts of hate speech, a more liberal approach and a more restrictive approach. (This is what 'both sides' meant in this context: I heard nobody, even the conservative voices on Berkeley's campus – to whom, yes, I went out of my way to listen – defend Yiannopoulos on his merits, though presumably some of them did so in private.) As is clear from these reports from all sides of the Milwaukee confrontation and its aftermath, the initial event had little to do with hate speech. That term describes protected forms of speech expressing ideas and opinions that are racist, transphobic, misogynist, etc. But that is not an especially good description of what Milo Yiannopoulos did to Adelaide Kramer. He singled her out for humiliation and degradation.

The sentence cited in the initial email trying to drum up community support to exclude Yiannopoulos from Berkeley was 'the way that you know he's failing is I'd still almost bang him'. And the most conspicuous features of that sentence are 1) its misgendering of Kramer, and 2) the conflation of that action with a sexual threat. So it was not, as the senior administrative staff at Berkeley, justifying their decision to let Yiannopoulos walk over them, claimed, merely salutary evidence that universities are still 'places where all ideas and views can be expressed, even vile ones'. The liberal Berkeley administration had been manoeuvred into publicly arguing the fascists' own case against the Title IX protection of trans students. The whole debate was deliberately and carefully staged on the wrong terms, and revealed that for some in academia the political personhood of a trans woman is, in fact, unimaginable. Adelaide Kramer's existence is, from that perspective, merely notional, hypothetical, postulated.

Once more, with feeling: deadnaming and misgendering are not acceptable scholarly practices, and they are not covered by the principle of academic freedom.

I have said that I don't want to engage Reed on the substance of his argument. But since his swashbuckling defence of the way he treats his students reveals something of the casual contempt with which trans people (especially those early in transition) are often met, I thought it worth spinning out an analogy that, this weekend, came to my mind. That is: for Christopher Reed, the many-mindedness and capacious intellectual largesse that demonstrates the effective absorption of an education in the liberal arts presents, by that very token, an existential threat to trans people – to be a well-educated queer would have to mean, perforce, that one is an ex-trans person. Because trans people are not merely an obstacle to Reed's complacent self-regard as a senior and well-compensated scholar of gender and sexuality who, it turns out, has nothing but disdain for younger queers. We also appear to him as arrested subjects with infantile attachments to sexed and gendered particularities, to whom our brave teachers are compelled to administer an abrasive but medicinal draught. Reed might seem to be pleading for the rational exchange of secular ideas in the public sphere of academic debate, but his mode of addressing his readers makes him sound like nothing so much as a travelling huckster shopping that good old-time religion.

In short, for Christopher Reed, transness is a phase, and grad school a kind of conversion therapy. Consider these remarks:

3. In a capitalist culture, we are expected to solve our own problems – ideally by buying something. Experiences of identity that involve buying things – including objects and forms of body modification – can be very seductive.

4. A stable gender identity may be like an iPhone X: a lot of people tell you you need to get one – but probably you don't. Put another way, you might be OK just the way you are.

17. Queer Theory emerged as an antidote to essentialist identity politics. Drawing on the forms of play in 'queer' performance practices, Queer Theory contested diagnosticians' claims to 'know' sex – one's own or anyone else's – and resisted campaigns to dictate the nature of our identities and to legislate the forms of language we use to inhabit them. Queer activism picked up much of the social and political power lost by second-wave feminism, sustaining feminist challenges to medical and legal authority.

25. We're all in this together. Instead of imposing ideology, let's try to have conversations that respect everyone's intellect and value a true diversity of experiences and points of view.

What kind of liturgy can he believe might spring up when we have put away our childish things, our iPhones and our hormones, and agreed to follow him on to the path of true queerness? Something like: we hate the sin, but we love the sinner. Before the mystery of our own sex, we are as innocent as lambs. We are all subject to our own particular forms of temptation, and all of us have been individually saved. Professor, make me whole and queer and diverse, and take away from me the particular habits, cathexes, desires and experiences that have kept me isolated for so long. Only by losing myself will I be born again.

This is grad school as a cult. No graduate student should ever be made to drink this hogwash.

One of the things that makes trans people intolerable to the genial liberalism that Reed half-heartedly ascribes to, and that Yiannopoulos gleefully exploits, is that we want no part of the empty type of 'diversity' in which our particular desires have no value other than as tactical proof of a kind of sophisticated, polygendered cultural literacy. We will be men and women and non-binary and gender-fluid people, and we will do so without the permission of our betters. We cannot force Chris Reed to respect us. But we can see, better than he can, the ugly complicity between fascism and the liberal arts that he has taken up the mantle of defending.

In any case, the practical lesson is not his to learn, and it isn't for trans/nb people either. It is a matter for all scholars, both as individuals and institutions. So to end with the only part of all this that really matters: deadnaming and misgendering are not acceptable scholarly practices, and they are not covered by the principle of academic freedom.

Notes

1 An earlier version of this chapter was published on the *LA Review of Books* blog: https://blog.lareviewofbooks.org/essays/grad-school-conversion-therapy/ (accessed 10 July 2020).
2 Title IX is a federal civil rights law, passed as part of the Education Amendments Act of 1972, which forbids institutions that are in receipt of federal funding from discriminating against students on the basis of sex: 'No person in the United States shall, on the basis of sex, be excluded from participation in, be denied the benefits of, or be subjected to discrimination under any education program or activity receiving Federal financial assistance' (Cornell Law School's Legal Information Institute [20 U.S. Code § 1681 – Sex]). The Act has been used to guarantee, for example, that women in higher education institutions have equal access

to and funding for sporting activity as male students; it is also the mechanism by which students are protected against sexual harassment or abuse by other students or faculty members.

3 The manifesto has since been removed from the Penn State University website.

16

Teaching 'freedom of speech' freely

Paul Whickman

This chapter takes a position on the supposed 'free speech crisis' on university campuses from the perspective of someone who actually teaches students. In particular, I suggest that the concept of 'freedom of speech', as well as being wilfully misrepresented by some of its staunchest self-appointed defenders, is itself worth interrogating. To do this, I suggest, is to subject revered 'liberal values' to question and, in turn, ultimately to encourage multiplicity of voices in the classroom.

In January 2015 I began teaching a new final-year module that I had designed for the English course at the University of Derby. Dealing with censorship, offence and 'freedom of speech' in literature from the seventeenth century to the present day, the issues raised by this module seemed particularly timely. A few weeks earlier on 7 January, two heavily armed men, Saïd and Chérif Kouachi, had entered the Paris offices of the satirical French newspaper *Charlie Hebdo*. After the Kouachi brothers opened fire, killing twelve people, a pursuit and standoff resulted in their own deaths later that evening. While there were subsequent attacks by other individuals in

Île-de-France between 7 and 9 January, it is the first and deadliest of these that has received the most media attention and comment.

The Kouachis' motives were soon the subject of speculation. *Charlie Hebdo* had, after all, been struck before. In 2011 its former offices were destroyed in a firebombing attack following the publication of its provocative 3 November edition. Renamed *Charia Hebdo* ('Sharia Hebdo' in English), it had included caricatures of Muhammad while purporting to be guest edited by the prophet. *Charlie Hebdo*'s long-standing irreverence towards political, religious and other cultural figures therefore offered a ready-made explanation for the attack. Indeed, on the day of the 2015 shooting, Prime Minister David Cameron stated in the House of Commons that, 'while details remain[ed] unclear', the attack was nevertheless in opposition to French and British values of 'free speech and democracy'; values that 'these people' could never hope to destroy.[1] The following evening, the BBC's *This Week* opened with a monologue from its presenter and host Andrew Neil who accused 'Fundamental [*sic*] Islam' of lacking a sense of humour: 'it doesn't like to be mocked, ridiculed, belittled or made to look silly. It can't even take a joke and it can't take criticism.'[2]

The idea that the *Charlie Hebdo* attack was an attack on satire or the very concept of 'free speech' gained traction within a post-9/11 climate that asserted Islam's supposed 'intolerance' and incompatibility with 'Western values'. This can be traced at least as far back as the so-called Rushdie Affair of the 1980s and 1990s. The publication of Salman Rushdie's novel *The Satanic Verses* (1988) infamously angered many Muslims and led to organised book burnings, attacks on bookshops, the murder of Rushdie's Japanese translator and the Ayatollah of Iran issuing a *fatwa* against the author's life that forced him into hiding. *Charlie Hebdo*'s own provocations of Islam, on the other hand, aligned with the more recent *Jyllands-Posten* controversy of 2005. The Danish newspaper had similarly published images of the prophet Muhammad in the name of 'free speech', leading to protests across the Muslim world and even sparking a diplomatic crisis. *Charlie Hebdo* itself republished these cartoons in 2009. The notion that Muslims were less inclined or even hostile towards 'free speech' was therefore well established by 2015.

While it perhaps would have been crass of me to have explicitly asked students to reflect upon so recent a tragedy, the implications of *Charlie Hebdo* nevertheless informed my thinking, and that of my students, throughout the new module. I do not wish to imply that the positions I assert in this essay are informed by one iteration of the module in 2015. Instead, my thinking has changed through both my own retrospective thoughts and, more importantly, the experience of engaging with *multiple* cohorts of intelligent, diverse and well-informed people in the classroom.

To be a student on a degree in the Arts and Humanities is to anticipate interrogating pre-conceived ideas. From the perspective of a lecturer, the ideal situation is that your students will end a module thinking rather differently from when they had entered it. While a certain segment of observers might see this as evidence of 'indoctrination', it should instead be seen as an act of liberation; to risk over-inflating what it is that we do, we encourage students *how* rather than *what* to think. As a young academic who had only been in the role for a year in January 2015, I was excited that my new module should do just this. The syllabus was full of provocative and challenging texts, many of which had been historically banned or subject to censorship, which would hopefully encourage students to rethink their attitudes towards, for instance, morality and the representation of sex and violence in literary art. An awareness of history – for instance why, what, when and how texts were censored or deemed offensive in different historical periods – would similarly allow students to comprehend that 'values', including their own, are largely determined by context.

I had not guessed, however, that interrogation of the very notion of 'freedom of speech' itself would prove to be the module's major theme. This was to always form part of the syllabus – incidentally when studying *The Satanic Verses* and the play *Behzti* (2004) by the Sikh playwright Gurpreet Kaur Bhatti – but over the years it has come to inform the module as a whole. This has primarily been due to the influence of students, as I discuss below, but the media response to incidents such as the *Charlie Hebdo* attack as well as more contemporary calls for 'freedom of speech' on university campuses have made such an interrogation all the more urgent. The new Office for Students names 'freedom of speech' on campus as one of their 'public interest governance principles' for instance, while the notorious *Spiked! Online* published a series of 'Free Speech University Rankings' between 2015 and 2018.[3]

Examining the immediate aftermath of *Charlie Hebdo* exposes a contradiction at the heart of 'freedom of speech'. To assert the importance of being able to belittle, critique or ridicule even the most sacred of things is to argue for the primacy of irreverence. It is paradoxical then that this very irreverence becomes itself revered. It is more complex than arguing that the 'sanctity' of a satirical magazine's right to poke fun is weighted equally against the 'sanctity' of an icon revered by a minority group; David Cameron's comments following the *Charlie Hebdo* attack, after all, asserted the predominance of the former. For me to make these remarks is to risk being misunderstood as an apologist for an appalling terrorist attack or, perhaps worse, to intellectualise it. Indeed, I myself unfairly accused friends and colleagues of doing just this in January 2015. Criticism of *Charlie Hebdo* and those who write disparagingly about Islam, for instance, I felt was being used to justify the murder of twelve people. Although I was wrong, the affair does reveal a problem with the conflation of 'freedom of speech' with the victims of terrorism. Not only does the horror of the event itself resist objective reflection – one does not 'speak ill of the dead' after all – there is also the risk that such a narrative turns the victims, ironically, into martyrs. In this way, the irreverent satirists become revered as champions of free speech. Anshuman Mondal's description of free expression 'as a totem of Western culture' is, then, an apt turn of phrase since it emphasises the quasi-religious reverence placed on something that ostensibly stands for the opposite.[4] There is an irony, too, in individuals labelling themselves as 'free speech fundamentalists' on social media platforms. While it is possible that these people are playfully aware of such an obvious contradiction, it nevertheless reveals the paradox at the heart of the supposed 'free speech debate': a dogmatic adherence to something that should be anti-dogma by nature.[5]

What then might be the implications for the study of freedom of speech in the classroom? Certainly, the very notion of freedom of speech itself should be subject to question. Also, that the concept has been weaponised in a manner designed to assert the superiority of 'Western' culture has important ideological implications for teaching. This should be considered a topic for discussion of course – such as on a session covering the consequences of the Rushdie Affair for instance – but it should also inform teaching *practice*. This is not a question of sensitivities; students in my experience are far from censorious and are not the sensitive 'snowflakes' they are so commonly painted as in the media. My students read texts by the Marquis de Sade and engage with his troubling libertine philosophy; they read *Saved* (1965) by the controversial playwright Edward Bond and do not feel compelled to censor it, unlike, allegedly, a *Daily Mail* reviewer of its 2011 production.[6] Similarly, in a diverse class that every year includes at least one Muslim student, we openly discuss Rushdie's *The Satanic Verses.*

Teaching 'freedom of speech' freely

It is this very diversity and the willingness of students to engage thoughtfully with provocative material that has led to a plurality of perspectives and the 'freest' discussion. A self-proclaimed 'free speech fundamentalist' might well agree with me when I suggest that students should be challenged and be expected to reckon with ideas they might personally find distasteful. There is, of course, no expectation that students should somehow endorse the values of the writers they study: if there has been an unusual upsurge of Sadeian perversion in the East Midlands over the last five years, I certainly have not heard about it. Yet I confess that in designing the module in 2014 I had anticipated, or at least hoped, that students would leave the module having internalised the values of 'free speech', whatever I then meant by that. On reflection though, this raises the question as to why students, taught both to be critical and disinterested towards course material, should nevertheless be expected to ultimately adopt a certain set of values. If anything, perhaps the most important experiences that students have on the module are those that shake their pre-existing certainty in free speech; this is not the sort of 'challenging ideas' that a 'free speech fundamentalist' would necessarily have endorsed.

Having students from a wide variety of backgrounds – ethnic, social, economic or religious – has been key to the module's success. Because our students at Derby are not all middle-class people from the Home Counties, dissenting perspectives on some of the major controversies that we engage with on the module are not simply those of an absent 'other'. This is useful in highlighting that 'freedom of speech' is neither neutral nor universal. For a Muslim student to freely discuss *The Satanic Verses*, for instance, is of course important in defying frankly racist stereotypes of supposed Muslim bigotry. At the same time, encouraging the articulation of any offence taken at a work in a supportive classroom environment helps to understand the nature and extent of it. It is surely illiberal to force individual students to 'suck it up' or to marginalise their perspectives. 'Freedom of speech' – if it is anything – should not be monolithic or 'all or nothing'; it is quite possible for an individual to reject literature or art that they find distasteful without them being opposed to a broader abstract concept of free expression.

To teach 'freedom of speech' freely and without restraint, then, is to discourage monopoly of conversation. This requires a respectful and diverse classroom environment that, in encouraging a multiplicity of perspectives, must by its very nature resist the dogmatic. The under-examined notion of 'freedom of speech' can in itself ironically become prescriptive; that the Office for Students is to soon enforce that it be 'upheld' on university campuses makes this clear. If we *truly* stand for free and open discussion in class, we must be willing to entertain critique of the supposed 'liberal values' deemed to make the conversation possible in the first place. In short, to promote 'freedom of speech' in UK higher education should not mean having to ultimately uncritically endorse the supposed 'values' of British 'liberal' democracy.

Notes

1 CBC News, 'British prime minister reacts to *Charlie Hebdo* shooting', 7 January 2015, https://www.youtube.com/watch?v=lGzG_uHlebs&feature=youtu.be, 0:16–0:33 (accessed 16 February 2020).
2 BBC *This Week*, 'Andrew Neil – Islam "squalid death cult"' [uploaded by Elliptical878], 9 January 2015, https://www.youtube.com/watch?v=HFiDR7swINE&feature=youtu.be, 0:20–0:33 (accessed 16 February 2020).
3 Office for Students, 'Freedom of Speech', https://www.officeforstudents.org.uk/advice-and-guidance/student-wellbeing-and-protection/freedom-of-speech/ (accessed 16 February 2020); Tom Slater, 'Free Speech University Rankings', 24 February 2019 https://www.spiked-online.com/free-speech-university-rankings/ (accessed 16 February 2020).

4   Anshuman A. Mondal, 'Revisiting *The Satanic Verses*: the fatwa and its legacies', in Robert Eaglestone and Martin McQuillan (eds), *Salman Rushdie: Contemporary Critical Perspectives* (London: Bloomsbury, 2013), pp. 59–71 (p. 61).
5   The word 'fundamentalist' carries with it a set of associations that in the contemporary world suggest 'free speech fundamentalist' to be a label that is possibly more than just 'playful'; rather, it is potentially provocative.
6   See Dan Rebellato, 'The limits of criticism', http://www.danrebellato. co.uk/spilledink/2013/3/12/the-limits-of-criticism (accessed 16 February 2020).

17

The politicisation of campus free speech in Portugal

Adam Standring and Daniel Cardoso

In February and March 2017 a controversy erupted in the Faculdade de Ciências Sociais e Humanas – Universidade Nova de Lisboa (Faculty of Social and Human Sciences of the New University of Lisbon – FCSH-UNL) when a prominent but controversial historian, Jaime Nogueira Pinto, had his invitation to speak on campus cancelled. This was one of the first and most high-profile cases of 'no-platforming' to occur in Portugal and garnered a great deal of mainstream media attention. Nogueira Pinto, a staunch defender of the former dictator António Salazar, was originally invited by a small right-wing student group, Nova Portugalidade, to speak on the populist wave. The cancellation provoked protests and counter-protests, invited comment from politicians up to the president on the importance and limitations of free speech in a liberal democracy, and was an important moment in what was then still a nascent culture war.

In this chapter, we give an account of these events, witnessed first-hand by each of the authors, and we attempt to place them within their wider social, historical and political context. Since the

Carnation Revolution in 1974, and the transition to democracy, Portugal has been a country that prides itself on its tolerance, social liberalism and peacefulness. It seemed remarkably unaffected by the wave of nationalist populism that enveloped much of Europe after the financial crisis of 2008. Yet, as we will argue, behind the façade lay much more regressive attitudes, deeply embedded in socially unexamined accounts of Portuguese colonial and anti-democratic history. The events of Nogueira Pinto's no-platforming would be exploited and politicised by sympathetic figures in the media and politics and ultimately contribute to the belated arrival of populist discourse in Portugal.

The context

Portugal, at first glance, does not seem the most fertile ground in which to sow the seeds of a culture war, but as will be explored later, many of the factors that seemingly inoculated Portuguese society from populist and reactionary sentiment were built on shallow foundations. The country emerged from the recent financial crisis relatively unscathed in social and political terms – it didn't experience the widespread political protests that countries such as Greece and Spain witnessed, nor did nativist populists gain mainstream media or electoral success.[1] In fact, once again breaking with the European trend, the 2015 elections saw a loose, left-wing, anti-austerity government come to power, led by the Socialist Party (PS) and with the support of the Left Bloc (BE) and Communist Party (PCP).

Despite the relative political stability, global political currents were of great interest in Portugal, both in the public consciousness and in academic circles and particularly in FCSH-UNL. FCSH-UNL is a public university, founded in 1973, the year before the Carnation

Revolution when democracy was restored, which specialises in social sciences and humanities. Given just these facts, this might seem the ideal space to host a lecture entitled 'Populism or Democracy? Brexit, Trump and Le Pen Debated', but to understand why this was considered a provocation we need to know a bit more about who was asked to give the lecture and where it was to be held.

Jaime Nogueira Pinto is a public historian and political commentator. Originally trained in law and political science, he has published a number of books on political and historical subjects. He is most popularly, and controversially, known for hosting an episode of the 2006–07 television series *Os Grandes Portugueses* (*The Greatest Portuguese*) – the programme featured profiles of ten prominent Portuguese historical figures, followed by a public poll – in which he presented the case for the dictator António Salazar. In more recent years, he has added his name to the growing conservative reaction against Islam, publishing a book in 2015 called *O Islão e o Ocidente – A grande discórdia* (*Islam and the West – The Great Discord*), and as such has increased his popularity with the small but growing radical right in Portugal.

Nogueira Pinto's public profile – and increasing prominence in right-wing circles – would have made him a controversial guest in most academic situations, but we can consider his invitation to FCSH-UNL particularly provocative. Unlike many Anglo-American universities, Portuguese universities often have historically established political tendencies, either through direct links between the faculty and political parties or else sympathies that are more implicit but still well known. Additionally, most political parties will have, to a greater or lesser degree, representatives of their youth organisations (*Jotas*) present within the universities. FCSH-UNL has a long history of left-wing activism, with strong links among faculty and students to PS as well as BE and PCP.

Nova Portugalidade at FCSH-UNL

Given the historical political tendencies within FCSH-UNL, any student or student group from outside a broad left tradition would find themselves in a minority. It was within this context that Nova Portugalidade was founded by Rafael Pinto Borges, a Political Science and International Relations undergraduate. Pinto Borges was also an activist for the youth wing of the Centro Democrático e Social – Partido Popular (Democratic and Social Centre-People's Party – CDS-PP), a socially conservative party, often considered the most right-wing of the mainstream parties in Portugal. Nova Portugalidade positions itself as a movement dedicated to promoting the history of Portugal and celebrating virtues such as liberty and democracy. In doing so, it also finds itself providing a revisionist account of the Portuguese dictatorship (1928–74) and celebrating the Portuguese colonial past.

In February 2017 Nova Portugalidade submitted a request to the Student Association of FCSH-UNL – an elected body of student representatives with responsibility for administering student organisations – to book an auditorium for Nogueira Pinto to speak. Despite originally having accepted the request, the Student Association subsequently considered the platform of Nova Portugalidade and the profile of Nogueira Pinto to be against the general principles of inclusivity under which they were elected. The executive of the Student Association put the matter to a vote of the General Assembly of Students which rejected it, removing their acceptance and referring the request to the university administration which had ultimate authority. The request was subsequently denied by the director of FCSH-UNL, Francisco Carmelo,[2] on the grounds that threats of violence had been received and the talk constituted a 'security risk', while the university's commitment to freedom of speech and plurality of opinion was also affirmed.[3] The director also rejected the suggestion that security guards or police should be brought in to guarantee the safety of participants, arguing that this was 'not part of the culture of our institution'.

Meetings between students from different factions and the university administration were tense, culminating in a confrontation on 7 March 2017 when up to forty unidentified far-right activists attempted to remonstrate with representatives of the Student Association and enter their premises. A demonstration against the 'no-platforming' of Nogueria Pinto, billed as a defence of democracy and free speech against 'cultural Marxism', was organised by the neo-fascist Partido Nacional Renovador (National Renovation Party – PNR). These events were met by significant resistance and at the demonstration, on 21 March, the thirty or so protestors from PNR were confronted by many more counter-protesters. The protest ended with the students and staff of FCSH-UNL joining together to sing the classic Portuguese revolutionary song, *Grândola Vila Morena*.

While the protest was ultimately peaceful, it did garner the attention of the media, and political figures jumped into the row, less on the side of FCSH-UNL and more to defend freedom of speech and academic freedom. The president, Marcelo Rebelo de Sousa, called the decision to cancel 'absurd' and 'incomprehensible', going so far as to suggest that the talk be reorganised by the Association of the 25th April – a national organisation designed to promote the memory and values of the democratic revolution.

A history unexamined

The date 25 April plays an extremely important cultural role in Portuguese society, signifying a distinct break from the dictatorship and marking the end of a largely unfree society and the beginning of Portugal's journey to democracy. The immediate post-revolutionary period saw moderate political forces of the centre-left and centre-right join with 'rehabilitated', liberal figures from the Estado Novo such as Francisco de Sá Carneiro, in order to wrest power from the military and radical left figures. This complicated history of revolution and democratisation means that 25 April plays a symbolic role for a variety of political traditions, from far left to far right,[4] and sees it associated with values such as freedom of speech and political liberty.

The Carnation Revolution also marked the beginning of the end of Portugal's colonial ambitions. One of the principal flashpoints of the revolution had been popular exhaustion with an unpopular colonial war. Portugal's African colonies (Angola, Mozambique, Guinea-Bissau, Cape Verde and São Tome & Principe) won their independence in 1975,[5] prompting a wave of immigration into Portugal by white settlers (*retornados*), as well as a large black contingent who tended to settle in distinct areas such as Amadora in Lisbon or across the river Tagus in Almada. The ghettoisation of Portugal's black population combined with the strong cultural embeddedness of the philosophy of luso-tropicalism to produce a relatively unreflexive popular view of the Portuguese Empire. Luso-tropicalism, an idea originally developed by the Brazilian anthropologist Gilberto Freyre but later used and adapted by the Salazar regime to legitimise colonialisation, claimed that Portugal was uniquely unafflicted by racial prejudice, and its colonial exploits (whose early stages are still commonly referred to as *os descobrimentos* ['the discoveries']) were therefore broadly considered by the white population to be benevolent.[6]

The Nova Portugalidade affair came at a time when a wave of critical thought and progressive political movements were challenging many of these historical and cultural legacies. The financial crisis (2010–14) encouraged the flourishing of a number of anti-austerity movements whose organisation and mobilisation was often intersectional with a number of existing and ongoing struggles among marginalised groups, such as those for women's rights, LGBT rights and immigrants' rights.[7] Again, 25 April was of high symbolic value to these groups because, while most participants were too young to have participated directly, it provided a discursive space in which to examine Portuguese history and the gaps and injustices left unaddressed by the revolution.

The fallout: new culture wars in Portugal

One thing learned from the events at FCSH-UNL was that a far-right strategy of intimidation would get a 'fair hearing', or at least be viewed as a legitimate side in a debate, within the Portuguese media. A few months after the FCSH-NOVA controversy, SOS Racism – an anti-racist NGO – organised a protest in front of a recently inaugurated statue in memory of the sixteenth-century missionary priest António Vieira. Vieira was depicted in a gesture of conversion, with three indigenous children at his feet.[8] The NGO protested what they considered to be a celebration of slavery and the Church's role in it. The protest was interrupted by a neo-Nazi group, 'the Hammerskins', who pushed protesters away from the statue. The incident highlighted the difficulties black communities face in having their voices heard in a city seemingly indifferent to their historical suffering.

The question of historical memory was raised again in early 2018, when several Portuguese and foreign academics signed an open letter condemning an electoral pledge by the recently elected mayor of Lisbon to build a museum to celebrate Portugal's maritime expansion. The proposed name and purpose of the museum, either 'The Museum of Discoveries' or 'The Museum of Portuguese Interculturality',[9] prompted an intense debate on social media and in the newspapers. Those against argued that the names whitewashed Portugal's colonialism, portraying it again in a benevolent way. Those in favour claimed that Portuguese history was a matter of national pride and should be celebrated.[10]

The role of academics in contesting or embedding visions of Portugal's history is complex and contested. In 2019 a new controversy arose as Fátima Bonifácio, an academic historian and regular contributor to the national newspaper *Público*, wrote a piece arguing that racial quotas would never work as a mechanism of integration because Africans and Roma people are too different from Europeans. In her own words, neither of these minority groups 'descend from the Universal Human Rights launched by the Great Revolution of 1789'.[11] The piece was condemned as racist by various commentators, forcing the newspaper to justify why they had allowed such a text to be published in the first place – again resting on notions of freedom of speech. Defence of Bonifácio's piece came mostly from columnists writing for a website called Observador. Historians Rui Ramos and Gabriel Mithá Ribeiro, among others, argued that the reaction to Bonifacio's piece was based only on left-wing hypersensitivity.[12] In the more open phase of Portugal's culture war, Observador has become a popular platform for intellectuals to write on identity and Portugal's history from a conservative standpoint.

The debate over race and memory became one of the central issues in Portugal's 2019 parliamentary elections. André Ventura, the founder of far-right populist party Chega! (Enough!), built a national reputation as a football analyst as well as by making inflammatory comments against Roma and other minorities in local election campaigns. In October 2019 he was elected to parliament, meaning that for the first time in recent history the far right was represented. Within parliament Chega! is largely isolated, but Ventura has increased his profile through frequent attacks on Joacine Katar Moreira, a black female academic, born in Guinea-Bissau and elected to represent the left-wing party Livre (Free). The media are frequently more critical of Katar Moreira than they are of those attacking her. In more recent comments, and in response to Katar Moreira's suggestion that items in Portugal's museums, taken under colonial rule, be returned to their countries of origin, Ventura suggested that Katar Moreira should be returned to hers.

Conclusion

The shift within Portugal, from a country in which nationalist populism was largely absent (or at least less visible) to one in which populist sentiments are an increasingly frequent feature of the popular media discourse, might seem sudden, but it's important that this is put into context. The events of 2017 at FCSH-UNL was not the match that sent the whole thing up in flames, but it does point to the underlying tensions within Portuguese society as well as indicating the strategies that populists are likely to embark on to further their cause.

One of the big changes since the incident at FCSH-UNL is how the populist far right has become emboldened in its attacks on anyone voicing a critical reading of Portugal's history, knowing that a more supplicant media will present this as legitimate debate. This works towards a popular desensitisation of hate speech and makes it still more difficult for under-represented minorities to have their voices heard.

Since the episode of 2017 at FCSH-UNL, issues of identity and memory have gained a central place in political debates in social media, traditional media and political campaigns. As Portugal's past becomes increasingly the subject of public analysis and discussion, it is likely that political struggles over culture, identity and memory will become more common and divisive.[13]

Notes

1 S. Salgado, 'Where's populism? Online media and the diffusion of populist discourses and styles in Portugal', *European Political Science*, 18 (2019), pp. 53–65.

2 Although disagreement remains between the two sides on whether the event was officially cancelled or merely postponed.

3 The full text of the director's email to staff and students is available (in Portuguese) here: https://www.tsf.pt/sociedade/educacao/diretor-da-fcsh-voltaria-a-tomar-a-mesma-decisao-ainda-com-mais-conviccao-5722773.html (accessed 10 July 2020).

4 A. Costa Pinto, 'Coping with the double legacy of authoritarianism and revolution in Portuguese democracy', *South European Society and Politics*, 15.3 (2010), pp. 395–412.

5 Portuguese decolonisation would continue with India annexing Goa (1961), Indonesia annexing East Timor (1976) and China annexing Macau (1999).

6 J. Vala, D. Lopes and M. Lima, 'Black immigrants in Portugal: Luso-tropicalism and prejudice', *Journal of Social Issues*, 64 (2008), pp. 287–302.

7 B. Baumgarten, 'The children of the Carnation Revolution? Connections between Portugal's anti-austerity movement and the revolutionary period 1974/1975', *Social Movement Studies*, 16.1 (2017), pp. 51–63.

8 N. Ferreira and M. Louro, 'Estátua do padre António Vieira guardada por "neonazis"', *Público*, 5 October 2017, https://www.publico.pt/2017/10/05/sociedade/noticia/accao-de-protesto-contra-a-estatua-do-padre-antonio-vieira-barrada-por-neonazis-1787874 (accessed 10 July 2020).

9 C. Margato, 'A controvérsia sobre um Museu que ainda não existe. Descobertas ou Expansão?', *Expresso*, 12 April 2018, https://expresso.pt/cultura/2018-04-12-A-controversia-sobre-um-Museu-que-ainda-nao-existe.-Descobertas-ou-Expansao- (accessed 10 July 2020).

10 J. P. Oliveira e Costa, 'A propósito da polémica sobre o Museu das Descobertas. Equívoco, teimosias e hipersensibilidades', *Diário de Notícias*, 12 May 2018, https://www.dn.pt/opiniao/opiniao-dn/convid

ados/a-proposito-da-polemica-sobre-o-museu--das-descobertas--equiv oco-teimosias--e-hipersensibilidades-9332629.html (accessed 10 July 2020).

11   F. Bonifáco, 'Podemos? Não, não podemos', *Público*, 6 July 2019, https://www.publico.pt/2019/07/06/sociedade/opiniao/podemos-nao-nao-podemos-1878726 (accessed 10 July 2020).

12   R. Ramos, 'A máquina de inventar racistas', *Observador*, 9 July 2019, https://observador.pt/opiniao/a-maquina-de-inventar-racistas/ (accessed 10 July 2020).

13   This chapter was written in January 2020, before the global Black Lives Matter protests sparked popular demonstrations in Portugal, in which many of these themes regarding racism and Portugal's memories of its colonial past were present. In opposition, Ventura and Chega! inflamed tensions by holding marches to proclaim that 'Portugal is not a racist country.'

18

Do we need safe spaces?
Waiving the right to free speech
on campus

Marta Santiváñez

On 19 March 2019 a group of thirteen students and one staff member were shocked to discover that their ID cards did not work at the entrance gates to the main King's College London (KCL) buildings. On that day, the Queen and the Duchess of Cambridge were visiting campus for the official opening of its new venue, Bush House. Other than students from King's Business School, nobody had been given notice that there would be limited access to the buildings on the day of the event.[1]

The university claimed that the event 'demanded the highest level of security' and therefore it 'had to minimise movement through buildings for security reasons'.[2] As would come to light in the days and weeks that followed, all the students who raised concerns about this incident put their spare time into the activist campaigns Justice 4 Cleaners and Action Palestine, and had been specifically banned from campus because of their political activity. The university denied having targeted specific students or demographic groups (eight of the students singled out were Muslim). Ilyas Nagdee, the National Union of Students (NUS) Black Students' Officer at the time, highlighted the racialised nature of the ban, which KCL denied in its report on the incident, published four months later.[3]

The evidence gathered in that same report, which includes email communications between the security team and the Metropolitan Police, suggests that limiting movement from students who were politically active was the goal at the core of the operation. KCL's head of security had contacted the Met with 'unconfirmed reporting' of possible protests on that Tuesday. The Met then requested 'reassurance that none of the identified individuals from the groups identified [sic] ... will be allowed access... during the event'. The security team proceeded to forward a list of named activists from groups including KCL Action Palestine, KCL Justice 4 Cleaners and KCL Climate Strike, all identified from previous protests, in some cases using CCTV footage and comparing it with images of the students entering campus with their ID cards. When the Met asked for the students' dates of birth, the security team refused the request because they would need to get the information from student services, which would 'raise flags and cause chatter so would rather not as this is sensitive around student freedosm!!! [sic]'

The boundaries of student freedoms are precisely what stood on the line in this incident. In the overdone debate over free speech at university, 'no platform' and safe space policies have been attacked as challenging academic practice. The focus of this debate mischaracterises the challenges that universities are facing and hinders discussion over the structural struggles that might truly be impeding free speech on campus through policies of securitisation and anti-radicalisation.

According to Evan Smith, a historian of politics and free speech in the UK, the debate over whether there is a 'crisis' over freedom of speech on campus goes back to the late 1960s, when the disruption of speeches by Enoch Powell and Patrick Wall was presented as student hostility towards different ideas. Over the five decades that followed, Smith argues, the free speech crisis 'trope' has returned again and again, to its present point.[4]

This debate revolves around the impact of 'no platform' on campus, broadly understood as a policy that prevents individuals from contributing to a public debate because their ideas are considered unacceptable. The NUS first approved a policy of no platform for racists and fascists in 1974, in an attempt to protect students and 'enfranchise their freedom of speech'.[5] The policy has been voted on by National Conference every year since. To date, it lists just six organisations known to hold racist or fascist views that should not be allowed a space for discussion at any NUS event. Three of these groups promote Islamic extremism, while the other three promote far-right English nationalism and fascism. Despite it being an extremely specific policy that has seen little to no change over its thirty-six years of existence, the past decade has borne witness to a common cry over censorship executed in the name of no-platforming in some of the UK's most renowned academic institutions.

Smith blames the increased currency of the 'free speech "crisis"', particularly since 2015–16, on two events: the rise and 'mainstreaming' of far-right ideologies and the push to 'no platform' alleged transphobes. The former has led to the normalisation of speech that was previously deemed unacceptable, whereas the latter is the result of conceptualising a new position as not up for debate. Smith notes:

> Since the attempt to 'no platform' Germaine Greer at Cardiff University in late 2015, sections of the British media and academia have portrayed the extension of 'no platform' to transphobes as an abrogation of the original intention of the 'no platform' policy, which was to be used only against explicit fascists and racists.[6]

Much of what is seen as censoring free speech has been, in fact, criticism of (usually right-wing) points of view, as commentators such as Nesrine Malik and Dawn Foster have argued.[7] Student unions function as independent entities, so the NUS has no control over their policies of no-platforming. And often what is amplified and criticised as an institutional ban on a speaker turns out to be somebody's decision not to share a stage with somebody else, or the result of the organising group changing its mind about an event – which, although sometimes rude, is not an act of censorship. Germaine Greer did in fact give her talk at Cardiff in 2015; Peter Tatchell, an LGBT activist, also spoke, while his co-panellist refused to partake in the event (exercising her own right to freedom of speech). When Amber Rudd was kept from speaking at an event at the University of Oxford in early March 2020 because the organisers did not want her input any more, she cried no platform to her 119,800 Twitter followers.[8] However renowned these cases of no-platforming might be, there were only twelve institutions that banned controversial speakers or events in the 2014–17 period, according to the free speech absolutists *Spiked Online*.[9] Their analysis assessed a total of 115 higher education institutions across the country.

The framing of the free speech debate as a crisis often pushes aside the structural elements that are inhibiting free speech among certain demographics. For years now universities have implemented policies seemingly at random, preventing and limiting the scope of what students can say and defend. The incident at KCL in March 2019 might be an isolated event, but it remains worrying: it raises questions over undefined boundaries that are imposed arbitrarily, without explicit authority to do so; over the impact of those boundaries on students; and over the securitisation of our own spaces for debate and protest. Over a span of hours, data protection laws were breached and identities were left in the open, against the advice of some members of the university administration.

Without a doubt, the larger question students, academics and the public in general need to ask is when, if at all, these measures are justified. The ban on students during the opening of Bush House was deemed 'a failure to protect the wellbeing and future prospects of King's students'.[10] Uncertainty prevails over when similar systems of surveillance, monitoring and profiling have been implemented in spaces of learning, as well as over what happens to this data as time goes on. Universities are no longer spaces of discovery and political engagement, and the safety of their student bodies comes second to the interests of the institutions themselves.

These forms of profiling had been present on campus long before the Queen visited Bush House. When considering the extent to which there might be a challenge to freedom of speech in the UK, Smith points out without hesitation that 'one thing raised by NGOs,[11] the NUS and the University and College Union (UCU) is the government's Prevent policy, which requires university staff to report students and academics who might be involved in political extremism'.[12]

Prevent is part of the government's strategy against radicalisation, and comprises a system for private citizens and other institutions to denounce people whom they think may be at risk of radicalisation. The government receives referrals made by educational institutions, the police and other outlets and proceeds to investigate the cases in greater depth. Those individuals who are considered at risk by the authorities can then opt-in to Channel, 'a programme which focuses on providing support at an early stage to people who are identified as being vulnerable to being drawn into terrorism'.[13]

The Prevent guidance is built around a definition of extremism as the 'vocal or active opposition to fundamental British values, including democracy, the rule of law, individual liberty and mutual respect and tolerance of different faiths and beliefs'.[14] The specific interpretation of this definition is up for grabs: there are no clear recommendations on how to define British values nor how to draw the boundaries between debate and worrying extremism.

Matthew Nelson, a Reader in Politics at SOAS, where he teaches a course on Islamic and democratic political thought, considers that the guideline lacks 'granularity' in its understanding of religious thought and debate and thus risks engaging 'in the business of stigmatising and [over-generalised] demographic profiling, which is massively counterproductive'. This lack of granularity percolates across civil society, leading not only to the state but also citizens engaging in forms of profiling that are detrimental to the populations they target and the societies in which they live. The small proportion of people referred to Prevent who then raise further concern and continue on to Channel is evidence that the scheme does not have 'a very high hit rate', in Nelson's words.[15] The year ending March 2019 had the highest percentage value of individuals referred to Channel through Prevent, yet just one in ten of these referrals required acute support. During the three years leading up to that point, only 5 per cent of Prevent referrals were adopted as Channel cases.

The effects of this demographic profiling on university students have been studied at length by Alison Scott-Baumann, a Professor of Society and Belief at SOAS researching Islam in Britain. In her work she has found that the non-specific nature of the Prevent guidelines leads to restriction of 'the discussion of interrelated issues about identity, Britishness and the Middle East because expressing interest in such topics, and the speakers of these, can be flagged up as indicating possible extremism'.[16]

The impact of this policy can be seen around campus events. Those that raise flags among university administrators are often allowed to go ahead, but with the imposition of certain rules that 'mitigate the risk' of the event and severely impact its reach. 'The university says they'll let you go ahead with the event, but it will put certain constraints on it: all the attendees will have to come from the university, you need a chair. Essentially, it really limits who you can have participating in the event', says Zuhayr Seedat, a final-year undergraduate at the London School of Economics (LSE) and former president of the Islamic Society at the School.[17] He recalls bringing Abdullah al-Andalusi to give a talk as particularly challenging, as the students' union was prompted to 'prevent the event'. Al-Andalusi is a prominent academic of Islamic political thought, who has previously given talks at the Oxford and Cambridge Unions and Chatham House, and works to demonstrate 'the intellectual proofs for the Islamic belief system'.[18] Al-Andalusi worked for Her Majesty's Inspectorate of Constabulary and has been accused of Islamic extremism.[19]

Seedat understood the uneasiness on the side of the university, but complained about a nonsensical system. In his telling, the students' union researches the speaker before deciding whether to approve them or not, 'but when they say research, they basically just Google the name, and whatever comes up, if it shows red flags, they won't have them. That is quite problematic, too.'[20]

There is a generalised lack of interest in the specifics of Islam, both as a dynamic and internally debated religious tradition and as a political ideology, leading to broad generalisations devoid of meaning and nuance, both on the part of ordinary citizens and on the part of those who work on Prevent. 'They [often] just don't understand the language that they are listening to in a way that would let them hear which things are really concerning', Nelson points out, in reference to those who are working on Prevent.[21] The strategy leaves those minorities who are directly profiled and targeted without support that would protect them from being singled out for no clear reason, and vulnerable to getting caught up in what might be a misunderstanding.

The public and the private aspects of the impact of the Prevent guidance on students come together at this point. While student organisers are forced through bureaucratic hoops in order to bring speakers to campus, they also face the stigmatisation that comes with it. Seedat argues that Prevent has a good reason to exist, but needs to work in tandem with counter-initiatives that support Muslims, target Islamophobia and discourage discrimination. In the absence of a response from the students' union when he sought out support, he attempted to fill the gap by organising seminars on Islamophobia, attending interfaith initiatives and encouraging his brothers and sisters at the Islamic Society to work on better explaining themselves, seeking to end a cycle that, he says, 'polarises Muslims away from the rest of the community'.[22]

It should not fall on individual students to fight stigmatisation and discrimination that should not exist in the first place. Scott-Baumann and her research team have found that these forms of profiling are leading to many Muslim students modifying their behaviour as a result of the Prevent strategy by 'self-censoring or disengaging from campus life and their studies for fear of being stigmatised, labelled an extremist or subjected to discrimination'.[23]

Nelson describes his experience in different terms. He teaches a course on 'Islam and Democracy' or, as he puts it, 'Islamic Law and the politics of Muslim difference or debate' (I was a student in his class a couple of years back). He recalls only a handful of instances when students have actually raised concerns about vulnerabilities related to his class. He cautions, however, that his sample of students is not a good indication, 'because, obviously, the students who are turning up in my class are already prepared to be talking about Islam and politics'.[24]

To him, risks regarding free speech on campus are often linked to international interference. 'What I've seen, in my experience, is that the heavy hammer of Prevent is like a feather compared to what you see from the Chinese, the Turks, the Pakistanis.' He notes that, sometimes, 'an event is held at a university, and an issue of the event concerns the country in question, and its own security apparatus [intervenes indirectly, for example by contacting the family, friends, or contacts of those involved in the event]'.[25] Far beyond the reach of the UK government, let alone its universities, foreign governments pressure their citizens studying abroad to not engage in events and academic practices that contradict their values. According to Nelson, government officials or their agents will request that certain events are cancelled or postponed; they will ask for information on the attendees or send one of their representatives to attend, observe the event and gather intelligence on those involved. The information is used to control citizens abroad, particularly when they have relatives back in their home countries.

Nelson does not recall any instance when he has been personally asked to cancel an event for this reason. International pressures are, nonetheless, undeniable, particularly in a climate of increasingly globalised universities with campuses in more than one country. At the height of the Hong Kong protests in autumn 2019, supporters of the pro-democracy movement complained of being harassed by pro-Beijing students, and linked these counter-demonstrations to organisations backed by the Chinese Communist Party. A report by the Foreign Affairs Select Committee pointed towards 'alarming' Chinese meddling at UK universities in late 2019, which could hinder academic research and practice.[26]

Arguably, there is a limit to the actions that a government might implement to respond to pressures exerted indirectly by international actors, yet universities should continue to abide by their duty to protect their students and present them with a space that allows them to learn, grow and develop, exploring new concepts and ideas without fear of retribution.

The incident at KCL in 2019 was resolved with the recommendation that the university's executive leadership and student union work together to repair the damage in 'a spirit of reconciliation and healing'.[27] Professor Evelyn Welch, the acting principal at the time, issued an apology; the head of security is understood not to be working at the university any more. Remarks about the difficulty of balancing the preservation of a safe campus against the right to freedom of expression were made throughout the report on the incident. The students singled out never came forward with their private stories, but the organisations they supported have continued with their work.

The idea of no-platforming has been corrupted by a segment of the political spectrum and taken to mean something that it was never intended to be. No-platforming remains a policy that aims at opening space for students to actively engage in campus life without fearing for their safety. By keeping ideologues who defend violent principles away from campus, the hope is that the violence that accompanies them will also be left behind, and the groups they are targeting will be protected. While the concept of 'no platform' may not be self-explanatory, the principles behind it are out in the open for anybody who cares to look them up, as activists and student politicians often declare to no avail.

By grounding the debate on freedom of speech around no-platforming, we are distracting from the structural challenges that freedom of speech is indeed facing on our campuses, and missing the failings of a system that is discriminatory and stigmatising. The discourse promoted by the student activists at KCL through their work is one of resilience and respect in the face of injustice, not a call for discrimination or violence against any particular group. The demographic profiling and stigmatisation that result from the Prevent guidelines is closing the space for debate for the Muslim community, challenging processes that build tolerance and integration.

The debate over freedom of speech itself is polarised to the point that we walk with no further guidance on what discourse should, or even could, look like. If we want to do better as a society, we need to do better by the institutions that represent our intellectual endeavours and demand more of them.

Notes

1. Irina Anghel, 'King's students denied access on campus for "security reasons" during Queen's visit', *Roar News*, 19 March 2019, http://roarnews.co.uk/2019/kings-students-denied-access-campus-security-reasons-queens-visit/ (accessed 14 April 2020).
2. Ibid.
3. Laura Gibbs, 'Report of a review of security arrangements for the opening of Bush House, 19th March 2019', June 2019, https://www.kcl.ac.uk/news/statements/bush house-security-report.pdf (accessed 9 April 2020).
4. Evan Smith, *No Platform: A History of Anti-Fascism, Universities and the Limits of Free Speech* (Abingdon: Routledge, 2020).
5. NUS, 'NUS' No Platform Policy', 13 February 2017, https://www.nusconnect.org.uk/resources/nus-no-platform-policy-f22f (accessed 17 March 2020).
6. Personal communication.
7. Nesrine Malik, 'The myth of the free speech crisis', *The Guardian*, 3 September 2019, https://www.theguardian.com/world/2019/sep/03/the-myth-of-the-free-speech-crisis (accessed 14 April 2020); Dawn Foster, 'Free speech works both ways – as Toby Young is finding out', *The Guardian*, 4 January 2018, https://www.theguardian.com/commentisfree/2018/jan/04/free-speech-toby-young-office-for-students (accessed 14 April 2020).

8 Amber Rudd, Twitter post, March 2020, 'Badly judged & rude of some students last night at Oxford to "no platform" me 30 mins before an event I had been invited to for #IWD2020 to encourage young women into politics. They should stop hiding and start engaging #freespeech', https://twitter.com/AmberRuddUK   https://twitter.com/AmberRudd UK/status/1235838618221948928?ref_src=twsrc%5Etfw%7Ctwcamp%5Et weetembed%7Ctwterm%5E1235838618221948928&ref_url=https%3A%2 F%2Fwww.thecanary.co%2Fopinion%2F2020%2F03%2F06%2Foxford-stud ents-were-right-to-no-platform-amber-rudd-and-heres-why%2F (accessed 27 April 2020).

9 'Free speech university rankings 2018 results summary', *Spiked Online*, https://media.spiked-online.com/website/images/2019/02/2115 3835/FSUR-PACK-2018.pdf (accessed 1 April 2020).

10 Gibbs, 'Report of a review of security arrangements'.

11 Richard Adams, 'UK's Prevent strategy "biggest threat to free speech on campus"', *The Guardian*, 26 June 2019, https://www.theguardian. com/uk-news/2019/jun/27/uks-prevent-strategy-biggest-threat-to-free-speech-on-campus (accessed 14 April 2020).

12 Personal communication.

13 Home Office, 'Channel duty guidance', 2012, https://www.gov.uk/gov ernment/publications/channel-guidance (accessed 20 March 2020).

14 Home Office, 'Revised Prevent duty guidance: for England and Wales', 2015, https://www.gov.uk/government/publications/prevent-duty-guid ance/revised-prevent-duty-guidance-for-england-and-wales (accessed 20 March 2020).

15 Personal communication.

16 Alison Scott-Baumann, '"No platform" isn't the real danger to free-dom of speech on campus', *The Guardian*, 25 October 2017, https:// www.theguardian.com/higher-education-network/2017/oct/25/no-plat form-and-safe-spaces-arent-the-real-dangers-to-freedom-of-speech (accessed 1 April 2020).

17 Personal communication.

18 Abdullah Al-Andalusi, 'About', https://abdullahalandalusi.com/about/ (accessed 14 April 2020).

19 'Dangerous ideas can't go unchallenged', *The Telegraph*, 7 December 2015, https://www.telegraph.co.uk/news/uknews/terrorism-in-the-uk/11 733678/Dangerous-ideas-cant-go-unchallenged.html (accessed 20 March 2020).

20 Personal communication.

21 Personal communication.
22 Personal communication.
23 Alison Scott-Baumann, 'Re/Presenting Islam on campus: the larg-est study of Islam and UK higher education', *Inside Government*, 18 March 2019, https://blog.insidegovernment.co.uk/blog/representing islamoncampus (accessed 1 April 2020).
24 Personal communication.
25 Personal communication.
26 Patrick Wintour, '"Alarming" Chinese meddling at UK universities exposed in report', *The Guardian*, 5 November 2019, https://www.the guardian.com/education/2019/nov/05/alarming-chinese-meddling-at-uk-universities-exposed-in-report (accessed 20 March 2020).
27 Gibbs, 'Report of a review of security arrangements'.

The internet:
the Wild West of
free speech

19

A postmodern neo-Marxist's guide to free speech: Jordan Peterson, the alt-right and neo-fascism

Ben Whitham

In recent years, Jordan Peterson, an obscure Canadian academic psychologist and publisher of self-help books, has been elevated to the level of poster boy for the insurgent transnational far-right movement styling itself the 'alt-right'. His refusal to recognise students' non-binary and transgender identities, his patriarchal and misogynist clichés about women and men, his insistence upon the significance of 'Western civilisation' and attacks on Muslims, even his bizarre practice – in the face of rising veganism – of eating *only* meat, have all struck a chord with the various 'incels' and Islamophobes that constitute the movement.

As a key 'culture warrior', much of Peterson's influence is exercised through social media. He has 1.4 million Twitter followers at the time of writing (far more than most of the world's most eminent living academics). It is on Twitter that Peterson claims and defends his right to 'free speech' – a unifying concern of the new far right, from the AfD in Germany and Generation Identity in Italy, to the EDL and the Brexit Party in the UK, and the 'Proud Boys' in the USA. It was also on Twitter that Peterson called Indian novelist and critic Pankaj Mishra a 'racist son of a bitch', in response to a critique of his book *12 Rules for Life*. 'And you call me a fascist?' Peterson went on, in a fit of frothing 'white fragility'.[1] 'You sanctimonious prick. If you were in my room at the moment, I'd slap you happily.'

This chapter uses the figure of Peterson to explore the contemporary politics of 'free speech', the rise of a transnational racist, misogynist, homophobic and transphobic far-right movement that can properly be called neo-fascist, and the inadequacy of liberalism to protect us from it.

Free-speechism and (neo)liberalism in the 'culture wars'

It is no exaggeration to say that lately not a day passes without the phrase 'free speech' appearing, often many times, in Western news media – the concept sits at the heart of the so-called 'culture wars'. The far right discursively situates itself as the guardian of free speech in the face of a totalitarian 'political correctness'. The latter is the preserve of anyone the far right hates: centrist liberals, leftists, feminists, anti-racists and anti-fascists, critics of colonialism, and of course actual ethnic minority people, women, gay and lesbian people, transgender and non-binary people. Peterson's public appearances, writings and social media posts are littered with claims that he and his comrades are standing up for free speech, and he interprets all attempts to 'no-platform' or exclude him from events as attacks on free speech.

But it is not only the far right that has been whipping up the deafening cacophony of free-speechism in recent months. On this issue, neo-fascists find common ground with conservatives and liberals. It has become a social media in-joke that far-right figures describe themselves as 'classical liberals' in their Twitter bio. In 2017 Peterson himself tweeted, in response to an article published on *Inside Higher*

Ed, an American digital media company that focuses on higher education news: 'Inside Higher Ed also insists that I'm "right-leaning." I'm a classic [*sic*] liberal (now known as "far right")'. Other right-wing UK- and US-based self-identifying 'classical liberals', including Niall Ferguson, Toby Young and Maajid Nawaz, have made similar claims. Their view seems to be that recent mainstreaming of anti-racist, feminist and transgender rights movements means that 'core enlightenment values of individual liberty and reason are under threat'.[2]

Self-proclaimed liberals lament the 'conflation of words and violence' by Nazi-punching Antifa activists[3] and black students campaigning to end the celebration at universities of their ancestors' murder and enslavement.[4] The misogyny and racism at work in the ideas of influential 'alt-right' figures such as Peterson or Steve Bannon certainly offends against the liberal conscience but, as Dawn Foster notes, political centrists are convinced that 'a smart liberal with a propensity for misquoting Voltaire can destroy their worldview'.[5] The 'argument for platforming and debating fascists', she suggests, rests upon 'the flawed assumption that, when challenged, their arguments will fall to pieces'. According to the (neo)liberal creed, fascism will be cold product in the 'marketplace of ideas', and so lack of demand will eventually kill off supply.[6] Foster highlights the role of elite educational culture in producing this view: 'When Nick Griffin led the British National Party, university debating societies were champing at the bit to invite him [...] convinced they could crush the BNP with a sharp argument, ignoring the fact that Griffin himself had studied law at Cambridge.'[7]

The persistence of the BNP and the emergence of new, arguably more successful, far-right organisations in the UK – the English Defence League (EDL), Democratic Football Lads Alliance (DFLA), Britain First and the proscribed far-right terrorist group National Action – is evidence of the flawed logic of free-speechism.

But the problem with free speech runs deeper: free speech is a pure abstraction. It does not exist, and has never existed.

Free speech does not exist

When Aristotle described the human condition as that of a 'political animal', he did so specifically by reference to our capacity for speech:

> Nature, as we often say, makes nothing in vain, and man [*sic*] is the only animal whom she [*sic*] has endowed with the gift of speech. And whereas mere voice is but an indication of pleasure or pain, and is therefore found in other animals [...], the power of *speech* is intended to set forth the expedient and the inexpedient, and therefore likewise the just and the unjust.[8]

Yet in Aristotle's ancient Greece, just as in our own time, there were prohibitions – legal, moral and practical – on what could and could not be said, and *by whom*. In Euripedes' *The Phoenician Women*, the characters acknowledge this fact:

IOCASTA: This above all I long to know: What is an exile's life? Is it great misery?

POLYNEICES: The greatest; worse in reality than in report.

IOCASTA: Worse in what way? What chiefly galls an exile's heart?

POLYNEICES: The worst is this: right of free speech does not exist.

IOCASTA: That's a slave's life – to be forbidden to speak one's mind.[9]

A slave's life indeed; but in ancient Athens, Euripedes' home, where tens of thousands were enslaved, not an uncommon one. The 'slave's life' here operates not as the sort of overblown analogy made by liberals and conservatives who accuse leftists of 'Stalinist' political correctness, but rather a literal statement in a context where slavery thrived. The freedom to 'speak one's mind' was limited to those who would say the right sorts of things, and excluded those, like slaves, who might say things that endangered the social order. Only much later, with the 'Enlightenment' and the dawn of liberalism, did it became normal to present rights such as freedom of speech as universals.

While mass, institutionalised slavery no longer persists in Western societies, its legacy in systems of neo-colonialism and racialised citizenship ensures that dangerous, dissenting and minority voices are still suppressed. Today's liberal democratic, rights-based regimes, rooted in Enlightenment universalism, maintain exclusive forms of free speech, and not only with regard to hate crime and speech in support of political violence. When, for example, politically radical women of colour such as Priyamvada Gopal speak publicly about structural inequalities, they are hounded for failing to maintain standards of 'civility' ('uncivilised' is avoided, but implied).[10] Free speech, *in practice*, is not for such people. It remains primarily the right of white men to publicly speak their racism, sexism and all of the other ideas that reinscribe and reproduce their own social supremacy.

In 2018 *The Economist* invited white supremacist and former Trump aide Steve Bannon to speak at its 'Open Festival'. Responding to critics of this decision, 'the most sober, the most rational, the most moderate organ of the industrial Bourgeoisie', as Marx called the magazine,[11] declared that:

> Our premise has been that progress is best achieved when ideas are tested in open debate [...] Mr Bannon stands for a world view that is antithetical to the liberal values *The Economist* has always espoused [...] The future of open societies will [...] be secured [...] by subjecting ideas and individuals from all sides to rigorous questioning and debate. This will expose bigotry and prejudice [...] That is the premise *The Economist* was founded on.[12]

And so the Oxbridge debating club clique hands a megaphone to a crypto-fascist in the name of an abstract ideal. It is hard to recall *The Economist* being so generous to communist or anti-fascist agitators. The political naivety of liberals is apparent to the far right, who delight in having their voices amplified by platforms that think their world view 'antithetical'. Winning over some liberals to some parts of their cause will be necessary for neo-fascists to triumph, whereas the left is irredeemable to them – what today's neo-fascists accurately perceive and exploit is the opposition common to their 'leftist' enemies to abstract universals such as free speech.

Postmodern neo-Marxist anti-racist feminists of the world, unite!

Peterson's bigotry is openly expressed, and his misogynist anti-feminism is a case in point. Peterson makes frequent negative references to feminism and feminists. He sometimes refers angrily to 'leftist feminists', and clearly has a special loathing for Judith Butler, whom he variously regards as a 'queer studies feminist', a 'star among postmodern neomarxists' and 'Jacques Derrida's female doppelganger' (as a woman, of course, Butler's theory can only imitate a man's). Often, his anti-feminism manifests as closely woven into racism. He asks his followers 'Do feminists avoid criticising Islam because they unconsciously long for masculine dominance?', blending misogynist anti-feminism (wherein women, including feminists, 'long for masculine dominance') with a popular trope in Islamophobic racism (wherein 'Islam' denotes an intrinsically sexist endeavour that is always about 'masculine dominance' and female submissiveness; an old orientalist trope).

The nebulous, sometimes contradictory nature of Peterson's 'insights' and terminology are characteristic of the thrust of fascist thought, as I will show later, but for now it is worth focusing on what he *correctly* identifies: a degree of unity among diverse 'critical' and left-wing traditions of theory and activism that otherwise exist in a state of tension with one another. The source of this unity is shared opposition to social orders based on abstract universalism. It is the insistence that how we explain, theorise and change our world should stem from actual social practices. While 'postmodern neo-Marxist' is an ostensibly contradictory far-right construction, it is worth unpacking.

Marx was hostile to the whole notion of 'so-called human rights' for precisely the reason that they are abstract universal principles that treat the human being 'as an isolated monad',[13] and do not reflect the context-bound and inescapably *social* nature of actual human life. True political emancipation was not, for Marx and Engels, to be found in the institutionalisation of rights through 'bourgeois revolutions', but rather in concrete struggles rooted in the material social conditions of labour relations. 'Postmodernism' (or poststructuralism), meanwhile, emerged precisely in critical opposition to Marxism. For poststructuralists taking their cues from Foucault, the Marxist conceptual vocabulary of 'ideology' and 'mystification' is at best problematic and condescending, at worst totalitarian.

Yet poststructuralists, many of whom (Foucault and Derrida included) started out as Marxists, do share with Marxists the philosophical conviction that social theory and ideas are inseparable from social practice. Foucault argued that social thought is not something

> to be sought only in theoretical formulations such as those of philosophy or science; it can and must be analysed in every manner of speaking, doing, or behaving in which the individual appears and acts as subject of learning, as ethical or juridical subject, as subject conscious of himself and others.

The study and theorisation of the social, he infers from this, 'can thus proceed from an analysis of "practices" – discursive or not'.[14] Foucault's practice-focused, 'genealogical' method rests upon an injunction to 'suppose that universals do not exist'.[15]

Similarly, the emphasis on *lived experience* as an engine of theory and practice is central to many varieties of feminism, including the 'standpoint' methodology embraced by radical (but largely 'white') feminisms of the Second Wave, and the black and intersectional feminisms that rose to challenge them.[16] Kimberlé Crenshaw recently noted that '[i]ntersectionality was a lived reality before it became a term',[17] emphasising, as in her earlier work that coined and developed the concept, the centrality of *experience* – in opposition to the abstract or universal principles informing some white, liberal feminism – to the insight that 'the intersection of racism and sexism factors into black women's lives in ways that cannot be captured wholly by looking at the race or gender dimensions of those experiences separately'.[18] Living and knowing intersecting inequalities is, on this view, the basis for theorising and challenging them.

Finally, the 'queer studies feminism' that Peterson identifies with Judith Butler, by which he seemingly means contemporary gender theory itself, is grounded in actual social practice too. Butler's best-known theoretical contribution, that gender is 'performatively produced', rests on a deeper insight that builds on earlier waves of feminist thought: 'If there is something right in Beauvoir's claim that one is not born, but rather becomes a woman, it follows that woman itself is a term in process, a becoming, a constructing […] an ongoing discursive practice […] open to intervention and resignification.'[19] Indeed, a primary contribution of gender theorists has been to undermine essentialist universalism and draw attention to the fact that, *in practice*, gender and sexuality are both culturally (re)produced and exist as *spectrums* rather than conceptually neat but abstract binaries.

Jordan Peterson: postmodern neo-fascist?

Contrary to free-speechists, we must refuse a 'right' to be publicly racist, misogynist, homophobic or transphobic. This is precisely what the current far-right movement – enabled by liberals – seeks to (re)produce. Speech is the currency of politics and, as Aristotle saw, the horizons of political possibility are negotiated through it. Centrist liberals, who pride themselves on their superior reasoning and pragmatic nous, have become the useful idiots of the far right, as the latter strives to redefine social norms in fascistic ways.

Peterson exists as part of a symbolic political network on the new far right, calling itself the 'alt-right'. As an academic, he fulfils a crucial function: validating far-right knowledge of the world, and offering intellectual support for the 'boots on the ground' of street-fighting fascists. In this sense, Peterson fulfils a parallel function to allegedly 'mainstream' right-wing politicians, including Donald Trump and Boris Johnson, who publicly disseminate more-or-less explicit signals of their misogyny, homophobia, Islamophobia and racism to the far right, saying 'we are on your side'. The alt-right accuses its enemies of 'virtue signalling'. What Peterson and other professedly 'liberal' right-wingers do can, conversely, be described as neo-fascist 'hate signalling'. Such signalling is essential to the dynamic of emergent fascism, as one its key architects, Alfredo Rocco, noted in 1926:

> [T]here are many in our ranks [...] who know Fascism as action and feeling but not yet as thought, who therefore have an intuition but no comprehension of it. It is true that Fascism is, above all, action and sentiment and that such it must continue to be [...] Only because it is feeling and sentiment [...] has it the force to stir the soul of the people [...] Only because it is action, and as such actualizes itself in a vast organization and in a huge movement, has it the conditions for determining the historical course of contemporary Italy.

This vision of fascism from its heyday is not an aberration but typical of accounts of those who lived through it. Alberto Moravia's 1951 novel *The Conformist* details the process by which a bullied and disturbed young boy grows up to become a fascist:

> [T]he chain was unbroken, all its links well soldered by his *simpatia*, felt before any reflection, to the knowledge that this feeling was shared by millions of other people in just the same way; from this knowledge to the conviction of being in the right; from the conviction of being in the right to action.[20]

The passage from an intuition arriving as if 'from the air'[21] to a belief in universality, and then an imperative to take (violent) action is a continuum that requires the hate signalling of free-speechists. It is therefore no exaggeration to describe Peterson – or Trump, Johnson and Farage – as leading enablers of a neo-fascist movement.

Conclusion

Liberalism, as I have sought to show here, is fundamentally inadequate to guard against this insurgent fascist tendency. The fascist appropriation of liberal rights-talk on free speech is emblematic of the deep contradictions of liberal ideology; a rights-based politics fails in the face of authoritarianism and hate because rights are universal abstractions that do not, and cannot, exist in practice. The basis for our opposition to Peterson and the crypto-fascist vanguard of the alt-right must be more substantial, more genuinely *political*. We must show that a viable alternative to liberalism is possible, desirable and essential; the gains of democratic socialists in the US and UK in recent years may be the first step to doing so.

Notes

1   Robin DiAngelo, *White Fragility: Why It's So Hard for White People to Talk About Racism* (London: Allen Lane, 2019).

2   William Davies, 'The free speech panic: how the right concocted a crisis', *The Guardian*, 26 July 2018, https://www.theguardian.com/news/2018/jul/26/the-free-speech-panic-censorship-how-the-right-concocted-a-crisis (accessed 16 June 2020).

3   Cathy Young, 'Why you shouldn't punch a Nazi', *Boston Globe*, 23 September 2017, https://www.bostonglobe.com/ideas/2017/09/23/why-you-shouldn-punch-nazi/sjghT8vcvVkpbJWMiOrEqN/story.html (accessed 16 June 2020).

4   Nigel Biggar, 'Rhodes, race, and the abuse of history', *Standpoint Magazine*, 23 February 2016, https://standpointmag.co.uk/issues/march-2016/features-march-2016-nigel-biggar-rhodes-race-history-rhodes-must-fall/ (accessed 16 June 2020).

5   Dawn Foster, 'The fundamental problem with "free speech" & the UK media', *Huck*, 7 August 2018, https://www.huckmag.com/perspectives/opinion-perspectives/the-fundamental-problem-with-free-speech-the-uk-media/ (accessed 16 June 2020).

6   Milton Friedman, *Capitalism and Freedom* (Chicago: University of Chicago Press, 2002), p. 21.

7   Foster, 'The fundamental problem'.

8   Aristotle, *Politics*, in *The Basic Works of Aristotle*, ed. R. McKeon (New York: Random House, 1941), Bk I, ch. 2, 1253a.

9   Euripides, *The Phoenician Women*, in *Orestes and Other Plays* (London: Penguin, 1972), p. 249.

10 Nigel Biggar, 'Vile abuse is now tolerated in our universities', *The Times*, 10 April 2018, https://www.thetimes.co.uk/article/vile-abuse-is-now-tolerated-in-our-universities-xqnbpl7ft (accessed 16 June 2020).

11 Karl Marx, 'Corruption at elections', in *Dispatches From the New York Tribune: Selected Journalism of Karl Marx*, ed. J. Ledbetter (London: Penguin, 2007), p. 105.

12 Zanny Minton Beddoes, 'A statement from our Editor-in-Chief: The Open Future Festival and Steve Bannon, why our invitation to Steve Bannon will stand', *The Economist*, 4 September 2018, https://www.economist.com/open-future/2018/09/04/the-open-future-festival-and-steve-bannon (accessed 16 June 2020).

13 Karl Marx, 'On the Jewish Question', in *Karl Marx: Selected Writings*, ed. David McLellan, 2nd edn (Oxford: Oxford University Press, 2000), pp. 59–60.

14 Michel Foucault, 'Preface to the *History of Sexuality Volume II*', in *The Foucault Reader*, ed. P. Rabinow (London: Penguin, 1991), pp. 334–5.

15 Michel Foucault, *The Birth of Biopolitics: Lectures at the College de France 1978–1979* (Basingstoke: Palgrave, 2008), p. 3.

16 bell hooks, *Feminist Theory: From Margin to Center*, 2nd edn (London: Pluto Press, 2000), p. 16.

17 Kimberlé Crenshaw, 'Why intersectionality can't wait', *The Washington Post*, 24 September 2015, https://www.washingtonpost.com/news/in-theory/wp/2015/09/24/why-intersectionality-cant-wait/ (accessed 16 June 2020).

18 Kimberlé Crenshaw, 'Mapping the margins: intersectionality, identity politics, and violence against women of color', *Stanford Law Review*, 43.6 (1991), pp. 1241–99 (p. 1244).

19 Judith Butler, *Gender Trouble* (London: Routledge, 1990), p. 33.

20 Alberto Moravia, *The Conformist* (Hanover, NH: Zoland Books, 1999), p. 73.

21 Ibid.

Free speech and online masculinity movements

Henry S. Price

The ideology that this chapter examines – the Red Pill (TRP) – is often portrayed as a radical and subversive counter-cultural movement. It has been associated with the successful anti-establishment campaign to elect President Trump, with the resurgence of interest in 'free speech' and with male rights. And yet TRP maintains an air of mystery. It is rarely featured or discussed in the mainstream media, does not get debated by political parties and is commonly presented as an exclusively online phenomenon. I want to begin by clarifying some facts and dispelling others, including the notion that advocates of TRP are seriously engaged in the protection of free speech. Consider the following, fictional but all-too-common kind of comment:

> Free speech is being destroyed. Only certain views are allowed these days: there are more than two genders, we shouldn't have limits on immigration, and Churchill was a war criminal. Political correctness has run amok, and its snowflake acolytes are more interested in signalling their own woke virtue by condemning and excommunicating than they are in seeking the truth. Not only is the truth unsayable, it's

also increasingly uninhabitable: just try being a *real* man or woman
today and see how society treats you!

Even if the reader passionately rejects this world view, it probably
isn't alien to them. Most of us know someone who, to some extent,
perceives society in this way. It's also a reasonable summary of the
Red Pill world view, which describes a binary world where dominant
political correctness (informal guidelines on permissible speech)
battles vulnerable free speech. This is a narrative which provides a
lens to interpret our social environments, and while the term 'Red
Pill' itself might not be well known outside of an online ecosystem,
its narrative is both known and popular. The most obvious illustration of its popularity – the election of politicians who advertise
themselves as rejecting political correctness – is only symptomatic of
an already successful effort to establish it as 'common sense'.[1]

This chapter unpacks the effects that TRP has had on discussions
about gender, and the role that 'free speech' has in those discussions. To do so it focuses on the loosely affiliated network of communities interested in protecting men and masculinity known as the
'Manosphere'. My analysis is based on extensive observations of TRP
and Manosphere forums, blogs and other documents, as well as academic reports on contemporary online misogyny. I am not going to
debunk the claims made in these spaces, but ask of them: what is the
unspeakable truth of gender, the hidden reality that TRP promises to
make visible? Are there fractures between and within these groups
and, ultimately, what is at stake when these groups discuss free speech?

The Red Pill, the Manosphere and the feminist illusion

It can be difficult for the unacquainted to ascertain exactly what is
meant by the Red Pill and Manosphere, terms which carry more

resonance online. What and where are they? The Manosphere con-
sists of several communities of people (largely men)[2] who share a
perception that the reality of gender has been especially obscured by
political correctness. That is partially because of the heightened visibility of feminist ideas, shared by influential celebrity figures such as
Emma Watson and Beyoncé.[3] According to Manosphere groups, this
puts forward an image of gender relations that is not only incorrect,
but that has helped foster a culture broadly sympathetic to women
and derisive of men. The level of support and attention given to
issues which concentrate on the gendered discrimination/abuse
faced by women (for example #MeToo and institutional sexism)
does not reflect the existence of that abuse, but the success and dominance of feminism. The prevailing consensus on these sites is that
the forces of political correctness and feminism have *already won* in
a battle against free speech, by controlling cultural narratives to prevent people speaking the truth, and by using public policy to legally
secure unfair advantages for women.

Underpinning these Manosphere communities is TRP, which refers
to a *process* of enlightenment ('taking the pill' or becoming 'red pilled')
as well as a set of *observations* and *principles* about how the world really
is ('Red Pill philosophy'). Advocates have concluded that political correctness obscures a series of uncomfortable realities, but they are confronted with a world in which most people – including their friends,
families and colleagues – remain duped. These obscured realities are
not just gender-based, but can relate to realities of ethnicity, democracy and nationalism. Free speech is therefore in both cases something
of a red herring. It isn't a value or even a 'debate', but a coded signifier
for unfree speech, the truth that cannot be spoken without incurring
social disapproval and, at times, institutional punishment.

The history of TRP is characterised by the collision of multiple
knowledges (popular, conspiracy and academic) about a variety of

phenomena. This has occurred (and occurs) in numerous arenas including large online platforms such as Reddit, YouTube, Facebook and 4chan, as well as more formal online publications including *Quillette* and *American Mind*. In these discussions many older ideas about gender roles, sexual behaviour and evolutionary psychology are reinterpreted and applied to contemporary events and hot topics. The style of communication is ironic and laden with in-jokes, particularly on those larger platforms which encourage user-generated content. While there is irreverence at play, both TRP and Manosphere sites also seek legitimacy via sometimes misleading appeals to scientific research or data, as well as intellectual figures considered – rightly or wrongly – sympathetic to their perception of embattled free speech.

Without a founding charter or authoritative organisation, it is difficult to know where to begin researching TRP. I consider two early references particularly helpful in introducing its themes, and how TRP understands power and gender. The first of these is the cinematic reference from which TRP takes its name. In *The Matrix* (1999), protagonist Neo (Keanu Reeves) is contacted by freedom fighter Morpheus (Lawrence Fishburne), who tells him that the universe humans accept as reality is in fact an illusion, the product of a robotic attempt to enslave all humanity. Sensory experience, Morpheus explains, has been manipulated by 'the machines' to create a great distraction. Neo is then offered the opportunity to be freed from the prison and confront the terrible reality: 'You take the blue pill, the story ends… You take the red pill, you stay in Wonderland, and I show you how deep the rabbit hole goes.'

The second reference is the first post on the original Red Pill subreddit, which sheds light on how Red Pill ideas have from the beginning been particularly interested in gender relations. Its anonymous author, 'pk_atheist', was later revealed to be former Republican lawmaker Robert Fisher, a sign of the blurring between political process and what was until recently considered 'merely' internet culture:

> we [men] no longer run the show … Feminism is a sexual strategy. It puts women into the best position they can find, to select mates, to determine when they want to switch mates, to locate the best DNA possible, and to garner the most resources they can individually achieve. The Red Pill is men's sexual strategy. Reality is happening, and we need to make sure that we adjust our strategy accordingly. (pk_atheist, 11 August 2012, 'Introduction')

The machines in *The Matrix* rely on their material strength and their control of perception to maintain power over the humans. Likewise, TRP views power as existing in cultural norms and 'extra-political' areas, rather than in simply holding office and wielding the executive power of the state. The values (re)produced in Hollywood films, viral memes and 'influencers' produce the (false) knowledge which sustains the politically correct illusion. In this context the use of 'strategy' and other militaristic language – common on Red Pill sites – points to a *metapolitical* agenda. This is the idea, associated with neo-Marxist writer Antonio Gramsci, that attempts at systemic change have a greater chance of success if they build upon existing cultural sympathies.[4] According to Fisher, feminism has accomplished this expertly. This is also a model, advocated by some identified Red Pill theorists, for collective action: confront popular culture and make it sympathetic to Red Pill ideas. One way of doing this is framing TRP as a response to embattled free speech. As in *The Matrix*, those who have taken the pill are cast as heroic truth-tellers who have chosen to confront harsh reality, and potentially defeat the dominant institutions. This is an important detail that can go under-reported: TRP uses a framing and the language of *emancipation*.

Manosphere groups consider: the reality of gender and how to fight it

There are four main Manosphere groups, differentiated by how they pursue a male 'sexual strategy' and connected by a relative consensus regarding the reality that (heterosexual) men confront today. Bear in mind that in the TRP world view, there is a clear line between those who suppress free speech (feminists, anti-racists, progressives generally and the unthinking 'herd' or NPCs)[5] and those who fight for it.

The core of the Manosphere consensus is that women have been legally, politically and financially empowered at the expense of men since the counterculture movement of the 1960s.[6] Aided by the state and culturally brainwashed men (who 'orbit' women, seeking their approval and sexual gratification), feminists have secured for women the best of both worlds: they can rely on men to go to war, pay the majority of bills, keep in good shape and be chivalrous; they can cry 'sexism' when the same demands are placed on women. Evidence for female dominance usually focuses on the higher risk of male death at work or by suicide, changes in divorce law (especially with regard to child custody), the under-reporting of discrimination/abuse endured by men, the number of women in higher education and the workforce, and a cultural zeitgeist which champions women and disparages men. The freedom to speak this truth has, of course, been lost.

This diagnosis relies on an understanding of empowerment as a zero-sum game between men and women, as well as a firm belief that biologically determined differences explain enduring disparities in outcome. The gender pay-gap, for example, is often dismissed as the result of biological differences between male and female behavioural predisposition, scaled and applied to career choices. Attempts to redress these outcomes are then interpreted as either meddling with nature, or as an attack on men and masculinity. There is an element of backlash to this zero-sum world view. As described by Faludi, backlash emerges acutely during periods of perceived improvement to women's status, which includes cultural expressions of feminist ideas.[7] This is certainly backed up when observing how campaigns to empower women are discussed in Manosphere groups (hint: it's not positive!)

There is also a recurring frustration, at times bordering on paranoia, with the *sexual* power that women have acquired. The autonomy facilitated by dating apps and social media has, it is argued, combined with a culture that champions women's sexual and financial freedom, as well as biological differences between the sexes (for example, male promiscuity and female choosiness). The result is accelerated *hypergamy*. Originally a social science term referring to the phenomenon of marrying someone of a higher social class, Manosphere groups claim that as women are encouraged to have high demands of potential partners, an increasing number of men are being 'locked out' of developing relationships.[8] In the 'sexual marketplace' women play 'on easy mode', while among men it is only the conventionally attractive who enjoy similar choices. Again, 'free speech' functions as something lost and a symbol of male victimisation: not only are men discriminated against in the sexual marketplace, they are denied the agency to communicate their victimisation.

In several senses then – sexually, culturally, politically – men are supposedly at a stark disadvantage compared with women. Each Manosphere group has a response to this unspoken reality.[9] Male Rights Activists (MRAs) focus on organising men to fight changes in the law, to offer support to men who have been discriminated against, and to put pressure on politicians and companies that do not respect the rights of men. MRAs typically have more confidence in political or institutional processes for restoring the balance between men and women, and have engaged in some high-profile campaigns to draw attention to specific issues or cases (for example, male circumcision). Their forums are less likely to concentrate on dating difficulties per se, and more likely to include threads detailing systemic prejudice against men.

Men Going Their Own Way (MGTOWs) argue that men should withdraw and rid themselves of responsibility for women. Their absence will eventually force the world to recognise the good in men and masculinity. Until then, women will continue to exploit them. The extent to which separatism is pursued varies. Some argue that MGTOW should concentrate on full autonomy and zero interaction with women; others acknowledge the implausibility of this isolation but still caution against being emotionally or financially invested in any relationship with a woman.[10] MGTOW forums often feature stories of suffering at the hands of women, tips on avoiding the temptation to be with women, and more esoteric posts on the spiritual side of masculinity, the natural world and solitude.[11]

Pick-Up Artists (PUAs) take a more interventionist approach. While acknowledging that women hold an advantage in today's dating scene, PUAs believe that the best response is to learn seduction skills ('game'). Feminist culture has, many PUAs argue, divorced women from their biologically driven desires to be dominated and to appreciate masculinity. This manifests in the controversial practice of trialling techniques to overcome 'last minute resistance' (LMR) before sleeping with uncertain female partners. PUA websites are a mixture of 'field reports' which describe attempts to have sex with women in a specific city or country, and more general speculation on seduction strategies. In both cases sex is presented as a transactional activity, and there is a shared mantra of personal responsibility to recognise your strengths and invest in your weakness, whether that is gym work or practising 'spontaneous' or 'dominant' behaviour.[12]

Incels argue that accelerated hypergamy has prevented them from engaging in any sexual relationships with women, because they do not score highly in looks, money or status (LMS).[13] This framing of systemic, gendered injustice differentiates incels from people who are merely involuntarily celibate. Their forums are marked by stories of rejection and isolation, examples of how easy it is for women to attract men, and expressions of violence directed either at women, successful/compliant men, or themselves. Attempts to improve the chances of a sexual encounter (e.g. by employing PUA techniques) are often dismissed as wishful thinking. The lack of hope in this world view has led many incels to identify with the 'Black Pill', which shares many of TRP's observations while rejecting the possibility of any resolution to their plight. Some studies have concluded that this hopelessness ('It's Over' in incel parlance) informs the extremist violence that is often fantasised about and on some occasions tragically perpetrated by contributors to this side of the Manosphere.[14]

Conclusion

Even from this very brief dive into Red Pill ideas and Manosphere communities, I can offer considered responses to my initial questions. The role of 'free speech' in Red Pill and Manosphere communities is seldom apolitical or separate from ideology, which posits that free speech has already been suppressed or vanquished. There is therefore little debate over the most effective or ethical lines to draw around free speech rights, and instead TRP focuses on the *loss* of these rights as a way of structuring a binary, conflictual world view. This allows Red Pill and Manosphere communities to symbolically present themselves as fighters for freedom, while simultaneously putting forward arguments that circumscribe all manner of freedoms for those groups deemed the beneficiaries of political correctness and feminism. Free speech is a shibboleth for advocates of TRP to demarcate themselves as on one side of this conflict, with political correctness and feminist ideas the opposition.

Each of the Manosphere groups holds the view that women have been empowered at the expense of men over several generations, and that men today are suffering the consequences. In the words of Robert Fisher, women 'run the show', and the Red Pill was from the beginning conceived of as a tool for discovering this and constructing an opposition. Within Manosphere groups an awareness of male disempowerment is absolutely fundamental to subsequent analyses, jokes, speculation or affirmation.

While these groups share a central diagnosis regarding the adverse conditions facing men today, they differ wildly on how best to develop a male 'sexual strategy'. Indeed, these differences are the basis for vicious antagonism between groups, particularly incels and PUAs. The latter regularly admonish the former for failing to improve their situation and their selves, while posters on incel forums regularly ridicule the naivety of PUAs for thinking that learning seduction techniques can overcome a deficiency in physical appearance. To a lesser extent, there is also disagreement with regard to how TRP should be applied to truths about race/ethnicity, sexuality, age and class. While there is substantial evidence of support for right-wing politicians, there is also a motif of disengagement from the political system altogether.

Finally, while TRP and Manosphere groups are open to ridicule and – understandably – revulsion or fear, together they represent a register in today's culture wars which is highly appealing to a not insignificant number of people. TRP's story of suppressed masculinity, as with embattled free speech, simplifies the complexities of social structures, power and individual experience. In place of this complexity, it offers an alternative, binary vision in which dominant political correctness and feminism are the sworn enemies of rational thought and liberty. In turn, those engaging in a backlash against anti-sexist and anti-racist efforts are framed as brave protectors of the most threatened groups in society, and indeed of enlightened society itself. It would be a mistake to underestimate this appeal or how successful it has been in spreading itself into popular discourses. Of course, when confronted with a group of men bemoaning their lot, there is a temptation to roll our eyes and reply 'welcome to the club!' History teaches us, however, that nothing is more fatal than angry men. My research suggests that tracing the points of contact between TRP and more mainstream 'common sense' is an important aspect of the effort to better understand that anger, to guard against it, and to uncover the ways in which we might be unknowingly affirming its claims.

Notes

1 This includes but is not limited to President Trump, President Bolsonaro and former Deputy Prime Minister Matteo Salvini.

2 It can be difficult to assess the demographics of Manosphere or Red Pill posters, due to the anonymity of most members and challenges in gathering reliable data. Several polls conducted on Manosphere forums visited while researching this chapter pointed to the vast majority of contributors identifying as male.

3 Interestingly the rise in visibility of feminist ideas, in celebrity and consumer culture more generally, has been theorised and critiqued by several scholars of 'postfeminism' such as Rosalind Gill. See R. Gill, 'Postfeminist media culture: elements of a sensibility', *European Journal of Cultural Studies*, 10.2 (2007), pp. 147–66; R. Gill, 'Post-postfeminism? New feminist visibilities in postfeminist times', *Feminist Media Studies*, 16.4 (2016), pp. 610–30.

4 While Gramsci was not mentioned by name during my observations, strategies for best communicating Red Pill ideas in political and pop-culture arenas were widely discussed.

5 'Non-player character' – individuals who repeat cultural scripts (e.g. 'women suffer from a culture which sexualises or ignores them') without critical reflection or objective thinking. This can include right-wing politicians and commentators.

6 On several occasions I observed nostalgia in Manosphere groups for the benefits of an idealised image of 1950s dating etiquette.

7 Susan Faludi, *Backlash: The Undeclared War Against Women* (London: Vintage, 1991), pp. xviii–xiv.

8 These demands include but are not limited to height, bone structure, wealth, being neurotypical and having a dominant persona.

9 To give some indication of popularity, as of March 2019 subreddits on 'MensRights' [*sic*] had over 210,000 subscribers, 'MGTOW' over 96,000 and 'Seduction' ('Primarily for men looking to seduce women in their life. Help with dating, learn to be a pickup artist (PUA), fix your Game') over 315,000. Incel subreddits are regularly banned due to their propensity for violent sexual fantasy, but one of the most notorious incel forums (Incels.co) has over 100,000 members.

10 Still others argue that marriage and procreation is justifiable, so long as your future wife is traditional, uninterested in feminism and innocent of political correctness. The key theme is an aversion to 'decadent' feminist values.

11 There is a clear precedent for this in the mythopoetic men's movement of the 1970s.

12 There is a burgeoning industry in PUA camps and guides. See R. O'Neill, 'Whither critical masculinity studies? Notes on inclusive masculinity theory, postfeminism, and sexual politics', *Men and Masculinities*, 18.1 (2015), pp. 100–20.

13 Incels have arguably developed the most extensive list of acronyms to describe in shorthand their ideas, although many of these are now used across different Red Pill and Manosphere communities. They include LDAR (Lay Down And Rot), AWALT (All Women Are Like That) and SMV (Sexual Market Value).

14 S. J. Baele, L. Brace and T. G. Coan, 'From "incel" to "saint": analyzing the violent worldview behind the 2018 Toronto attack', *Terrorism and Political Violence* (2019), pp. 1–25, doi: 10.1080/09546553.2019.1638256.

21

Choose your fighter: loyalty and fandom in the free speech culture wars

Penny Andrews

This chapter uses fandom as a way of looking at the intense attachment many people have to charismatic figures and exciting campaigns that reflect and feed their views, and how that impacts on the free speech debate – particularly as it plays out through the media and online discussion. People need to pick between untrammelled 'free speech' on one side and a free press and democracy on the other. They can't have both. Broadcasters and event organisers platform fascists in the name of balance and free speech, and then are surprised when they threaten journalists, murder politicians and grow their fanbase all the while.

Life can be difficult, confusing and depressing, and sources of joy can be limiting and limited. Some find their happy place by following musicians, actors, fictional characters, sportspeople and celebrities, as always. Others find a different kind of well-known, sometimes magnetic and often political figures appealing: party politicians and campaigners. Those who have lost faith in the Establishment could be attracted to 'intellectual dark web' figures such as Jordan Peterson, Jonathan Haidt or Sam Harris. For others, it might be

Tommy Robinson,[1] campaigns such as Alfie's Army[2] (a social media and offline community that grew up around the Alfie Evans case of a brain-damaged child, his parents and the doctors treating him) or the Yellow Vests[3] (an imported take on the French *Gilets jaunes* that defends the Brexit vote and attacks communities perceived to be complicit in paedophile grooming and other populist issues) that appeal to their sense of injustice, support for free speech, need for identity and desire for community.

For this last group, in the absence of faith (though they may speak of Christian values) and affordable, live, high-level football, family and flag become the focus. Those strong communitarian values can be exploited for identitarian ends. Radicalisation via YouTube, social media and online forums plays its part, but not everyone turning out for Tommy Robinson is a hardline far-right activist or committed racist. Looking at this phenomenon through the lens of fandom makes it easier to understand why it is so appealing, why the fans are so dedicated and loyal, and why the grifters at the top of parapolitical movements can make so much money from crowdfunding and merchandise. It also rehumanises many of those attracted to the personalities and the campaigns, rather than the ideologies. Dismissing huge swathes of people as stupid racists and deluded fascists does not make the problem go away, and keeping the grifters famous makes it worse.

Parapolitical movements that are not explicitly linked in the UK to the far right (or Islamist extremism, outside the scope of this chapter) do not have such obvious populist and right-wing touch points, but nevertheless are as obsessed with identity and community as their opponents and borrow some of their trappings when it comes to communication with the fanbase, extracting money via donations and T-shirt sales and online behaviour. Examples of this are the anti-trans movement – led by charismatic individuals such as Posie Parker and Julie Bindel, well-supported academics such as Kathleen Stock and

Selina Todd, and groups such as A Woman's Place and LGB Alliance – and those parts of the Eurosceptic movement connected to Nigel Farage's various ventures and the Leave Means Leave organisation.

Fandom in politics and free speech are inextricably linked because the concept of free speech, ambiguously defined, is one of the main weapons that different individuals and groups use against their opponents. It can end up being treated in fan wars as sacrosanct and inviolable, despite there being no equivalent to the United States Constitution's First Amendment in English and Welsh, Scottish or Northern Irish law. Freedom of expression is part of the Human Rights Act (1998) but is subject to multiple restrictions. Other laws such as the Public Order Act (1986), the Terrorism Act (2006) and the Communications Act (2003) can be far more salient, particularly when it comes to the behaviour of fans and the objects of their fandom online. The internet can make everyone act as if the whole world shares the US approach to free speech and copyright exceptions. It does not.

It is important at this point to define fandom, and explain what fans get from being part of it, as so far this chapter has made it sound miserable and obnoxious. A fandom is the community that develops around a cultural property, be that a fictional world, a football team, a musician, a brand or a building. It is intentional – someone chooses to become a part of it – and is distinguished from a fanbase or group of supporters by the sense of identity and community that it brings to its members. Initially, at least, fans get joy and belonging and a pastime from being part of a fandom. Comic Book Guy from *The Simpsons* is a perfect illustration of when the joy goes out of it and yet the fan cannot leave their fandom.

Those who 'get' fandom more generally, perhaps because they used to be really into a band or television programme or are in a sport fandom, can struggle to understand why people become fans

253

of politicians, campaigns and parapolitical actors.[4] In a UK context, it can seem weird or dull or embarrassing – and the same people who are in a fandom can also end up rejecting the idea that they are because of the stigma attached to it and the idea that because fandom requires emotions such as passion and joy, it is irrational. However, it is the same as being a fan of anything else – if you are talking to other people about it a lot, collecting information about it, perhaps buying tote bags or attending events relating to it and/or feel the need to defend it when it is attacked … you are a fan. Owning a shelf of political biographies makes you a fan. A Resist necklace, campaign T-shirt or political badge makes you a fan. If you join in (or lurk in) discussions with other people, online or offline, who are connected to your fandom – you are in the fandom. That is your community, that is part of your identity.

Traditionally we have seen far-right recruiting methods as similar to those of religious sects and cults, with an element of grooming vulnerable people and isolating them from friends and family so they come to rely on the group for all their emotional and spiritual and even physical needs. As Trilling notes, the 1980s far-right splinter group the Official National Front attempted to run housing cooperatives and take recruits for training on private land. However, when fandom is involved, the fans seek out the content, the community, attention from the subject of their fandom.[5] They may end up being radicalised, and their interests may put off people around them, but they are not reluctant participants and can often maintain their regular jobs and relationships. This has been seen in 'Islamic State fanboys' as much as Tommy Robinson supporters, and the focus on individuals or causes draws much bigger crowds to events and larger online support than previous organisation around groups such as the English Defence League.[6] However, what these fandoms do have in common with cults is that people within them can feel that their position is the only justifiable and correct one, and that being part of the fandom community (even if they reject the term) reflects their existing values and core aspects of their identity. It feels personal and morally vital. An attack on the object of their fandom or the group is wounding.

Fans support their favourites through statements of support, sharing content online and offline, financial donations, event attendance, merchandise purchases and petition signing. All campaigns, politicians and parapolitical actors rely heavily on both volunteer and financial support and organic (not paid for) sharing of their messages – as do pop bands. When their favourite or a prominent fan with a lot of support within the community says or does something controversial, they defend them with all their might and will post online, write to various outlets or call in to broadcasters relating to this individual or group's right to free speech, their favourite being morally correct and 'whataboutery' – giving examples of others who have said or done similar things without equivalent censure. They will attack opponents with as much fervour as they love their favourites, on their behalf. Tommy Robinson fans will search for his name on social media and bombard anyone who criticises him with abuse. If this abuse is questioned, they once again mention free speech. The Democratic Football Lads Alliance claims to abhor all forms of extremism and puts out angry slogans and messages to that end, but studies of its networks show strong links to Tommy Robinson and anti-Muslim speakers and groups.[7] Members were recruited via their love of football and the political ideology followed, rather than the past extremist practice of recruiting from within football 'firms' for the politically inclined. People who have long studied extremism, such as Nigel Copsey, have found themselves surprised by the extent to which fans in this space are motivated by love and pride and not merely hate.[8]

Darker than defensive fandom are anti-fans, who are intensely interested in and attack their objects of anti-fandom. Anti-fandom can be paired with a fandom; for example, One Direction fans who despise and attack the part of the fandom called 'Larries' who write fanfiction about Harry and Louis from the band as a romantic couple, or Brexit fans who harass prominent Remainers and become obsessed with them. They believe that these people should not be allowed free speech, because they are wrong, and that as anti-fans they are correct in their behaviour. Comments on online stories about abuse of elected politicians results in these anti-fans restating their right to free speech as legitimate criticism and the key to democracy. Anyone seeking to restrict their speech for legal or other reasons or who calls it 'hate speech', as with the defensive fans, is undemocratic. The legal definitions of free speech, terms such as 'fascist' and 'hate' can seem very important to them, even if they do not know the relevant laws, if they exist, in detail themselves.

A decade ago, the popular perception of UK politicians was that they are all the same and quite distant and technocratic. The effect of social media, rolling news, highly emotional politics around Brexit and demographic changes has resulted in some humanising of politicians, parapolitical actors and campaigners – who can almost be seen as influencers as well as objects of fandom. Social media platforms have been incredibly important to people such as Tommy Robinson as well as newer elected politicians, activists and campaigners such as Greta Thunberg or Darren Grimes. Those platforms and their liminal status – are they just technical tools or media publishers? – have enabled a form of free speech and a way to communicate with their fans without traditional mediation. The corporate owners of the platforms have only removed accounts posting content that would be seen as illegal in some countries when it has proved to be negative publicity for the platform. Parapolitical actors such as Milo

Yiannopolous have only relatively recently lost their accounts and funding streams.

Platforms (whether physical or online) are a key site where the limits of free speech are tested by objects of fandom and their fans. Having access to an online platform, sharing a platform at an event or in a broadcast media panel, 'platforming' and 'no-platforming' all become weapons in this context. The LGBTQ+ pressure group Stonewall has a policy that none of its representatives will share a panel, programme or event with transphobic, homophobic or biphobic speakers – which is rarely challenged by producers or audiences with regard to the latter two prejudices, seen as unacceptable for public debate, but frequently is in the case of high-profile anti-trans activists and their fans. The platform serves as a proxy for free speech, and removing or refusing to appear alongside an object of fandom makes enemies of free speech out of those calling for the de-platforming or asking that someone should not be invited.

In the technocratic political era of the 2000s and 2010s, it was not just fans who called for those with bigoted or even fascist views to be platformed on television, radio and at large public events. The phrase 'sunlight is the best disinfectant' remains popular with some liberal commentators, with the common example given of Nick Griffin of the British National Party (BNP) appearing on the BBC's *Question Time*, followed by the party's subsequent collapse. However, Griffin's fanbase as opposed to general support for his views was fairly small, and being personally unappealing affected his success. Nigel Farage saw a ceiling for this approach to socially conservative politics and built a personal and campaign fandom, with financial and media support, that far exceeded that of Griffin and the BNP, and was not only successful in European and local elections but also changed the policies of the Conservative party and won the Brexit referendum. Platforming Farage's more attractive presentation of similar ideas and sentiments acted as a recruiting tool and increased the reach and appeal of his messages – not a disinfectant at all. Dismissing fans of Robinson, Farage and so on does not work, because they react defensively, but pandering to fans does not either – because they do not reflect the public as a whole, and accepting and normalising their views is harmful.

Activism in many contexts often relies on the same logics as fandom. It is the sense of identity, community and the chance to be around and even heard, recognised and appreciated by interesting people, intellectual or literal crushes, that draws people to put in hours of volunteering, as much as their values. A political party that feels like your family, an intense grouping around a single-issue campaign, or an event that raises money for charity – for these to be successful, charismatic and capable people are usually somewhere at the centre and people who are well known, even in a niche and local context, are involved.

It is clear that the logics of fandom also work on a less intense scale for everyone interested in current affairs and issues-based politics. The popularity of Greta Thunberg with her fans and supporters shows that fandom can be a positive if handled well. Political parties and campaigns would struggle with recruitment and retention of volunteers to do canvassing, leafletting or online campaigning without it.

Fandom has always been with us in politics and parapolitics; it has as long a history as celebrity, but social media acts as an intensifier as well as giving a voice for free speech to minority individuals and groups and their fans. While de-platforming harmful actors (in all its senses) is useful and reduces the capacity of fandoms to grow or stay active, and some campaigns come to a natural end, political engagement cannot be as easily dismissed. Where does the energy of fans in this context go once you remove the source of their ardour? Not all fans are young people who will grow out of it or hardcore enough to require a de-radicalisation programme. Mainstream politics should examine how this passion, excitement and investment of time and trust can be harnessed for good without harming the fans or resulting in inappropriate behaviour for anyone concerned.

What does all this mean for 'free speech'? The restrictions on it in UK law in practice do not go far enough, as hate speech is currently too poorly defined – anti-trans and antisemitic groups are organising against the idea of hate crimes and calling their contact with the authorities 'thought policing'. The Equality Act is poorly understood, easily misinterpreted by hate groups in their communications and not enforced. Broadcasters and journalists need to take more responsibility for acts such as interviewing Tommy Robinson, showing the far-right group Generation Identity and white supremacist terrorist content, and inviting anti-trans voices such as Graham Linehan or Kathleen Stock on to programmes or to write articles about their views as if they were legitimate. Free speech is important, hearing the voices of minorities is important – but restricting the reach and legitimacy of the messages put out by their oppressors is too.

Notes

1   Joe Mulhall, 'Modernising and mainstreaming: the contemporary British far right', July, 2019, http://www.hopenothate.org.uk/wp-content/ uploads/2019/07/HnH-Briefing_Contemporary-British-Far-Right_2019-07-v1.pdf (accessed 10 July 2020).
2   Clare Dyer, 'Alfie Evans case: proposed law aims to prevent conflicts between parents and doctors', *BMJ*, 361 (April 2018), k1895, https://doi.org/10.1136/bmj.k1895 (accessed 10 July 2020).
3   Chris Allen, 'The Football Lads Alliance and Democratic Football Lad's Alliance: an insight into the dynamism and diversification of Britain's counter-jihad movement', *Social Movement Studies*, 18.5 (2019),

pp. 639–46, https://doi.org/10.1080/14742837.2019.1590694 (accessed 10 July 2020).

4 Penny Andrews, 'Can I have a selfie, minister?', *Tortoise*, 2019, https://members.tortoisemedia.com/2019/09/10/political-fandom-190910/content.html (accessed 20 April 2020).

5 Daniel Trilling, *Bloody Nasty People* (London: Verso, 2012).

6 Mulhall, 'Modernising and mainstreaming'.

7 Mark McGlashan, 'Collective identity and discourse practice in the followership of the Football Lads Alliance on Twitter', *Discourse & Society*, 31.3 (2020), pp. 307–28, https://doi.org/10.1177/0957926519889128 (accessed 10 July 2020).

8 Nigel Copsey, *'Tomorrow Belongs To Us': The British Far Right since 1967* (Abingdon: Routledge, 2018).

22

Free speech in the online 'marketplace of ideas'

Helen Pallett

The rise of the internet, and social media in particular, has been hailed as the ultimate embodiment of the long-promised 'marketplace of ideas'; an enduring metaphor which has been used as a foundation for interpreting the right of freedom of expression, particularly in the US context. This metaphor has been a seductive one in Western politics, implying the free exchange of views and information between equals in order to reach higher truths. Creating an analogy with the free market trade in goods and services, the metaphor has been applied to diverse domains of public life, from science to the media, arguing that they – and this free exchange of ideas – are fundamental to healthy liberal democracy: indeed the need to foster a free marketplace of ideas has become a central justification in American Supreme Court judgements relating to freedom of expression.[1]

Social media platforms have been championed for enhancing the marketplace of ideas by extending it to include more participants, lengthening the time period available for discussion, and allowing greater exposure to new ideas and information. Since the early days of email exchange, web forums and open source software development, many have enthusiastically argued that digital technologies and platforms could only further opportunities for democratic debate and assist in the establishment of collective truths. Yet many of us who use social media platforms today do not experience these spaces as anything resembling the idealised marketplace of free expression and the pursuit of truth. Rather, the metaphor of the marketplace of ideas appears increasingly unhelpful as a democratic ideal, as it obscures the multitude of ways in which our speech and expression are not free – both online and offline. This chapter will use examples from social media platforms to illustrate how apparently free speech has heavy costs and consequences, is strongly shaped and limited by the broader contexts of actions and actors, and is heavily mediated and controlled through technological and social processes.

The influential German philosopher Jürgen Habermas strongly shaped understandings of democratic public talk in the twentieth century through his arguments in favour of deliberative democracy. He describes a scenario of 'ideal speech' through which citizens with contrasting perspectives come to understand one another's viewpoints through rational discussion of ideas over an extended period of time.[2] Through these deliberations – which might be in person, through newspapers, in online forums – participants are able to come to a consensus and thus settle collective truths, so he claims. From a Habermasian perspective then, social media is the ideal setting for the thriving of deliberative democracy – apparently completely disembodied, transparent, open to anyone, egalitarian. This influential theory centres speech and ideas without attention to the material conditions which may add frictions and barriers to the process of exchange, the broader contexts in which these conversations take place, and the important roles played by people, organisations and technologies in more broadly shaping the scope and form of speech acts. While the idea of a 'free market' in economics is now widely recognised as a myth – no market has ever been entirely free, they are always shaped by powerful actors, they contain inclusions and exclusions, and are constantly shaped by governments – the free market ideal seems to be very much alive and kicking as a metaphor for democracy and free speech.

Costs and consequences

Arguments for freedom of expression often give the impression that such matters are related only to the realm of ideas, the world of the mind. There is little reference to material or bodily concerns. Yet there are countless examples of how acts carried out and justi-fied in terms of freedom of expression can have heavy costs and consequences.

The organisation of social media platforms, particularly the rules structuring conduct and the facilities for monetising social media content, help to lay bare the material consequences of supposedly free speech acts. One example of this is the emergence of so-called influencers who make money from social media accounts, by sell-ing on accounts with a large number of followers, by maximising engagement with their content and through paid partnerships with brands. In this way speech acts can be a way of making a living and providing financial and material security – and were long before the arrival of social media. Organisations with large financial means are increasingly turning to the creation of armies of bots on social media sites in order to further boost their speech acts through enthusiastic engagements and shares. On the flip side, speech acts on social media can also literally incur financial penalties through loss of jobs or access to particular platforms and accounts, or through fines from companies and courts.

The phenomenon of 'hate speech' is now firmly associated with social media platforms, and highlights in a very different way the costs of speech acts. While an imaginary of the free exchange of contrasting ideas implies rational discussion to consensually resolve mere differences of opinion, it does not engage adequately with the weight of speech acts which fundamentally threaten bodily autonomy or emotionally attack certain groups. How can a rational consensus be reached when one or more speakers challenges the right of other speakers to exist, or their legitimacy to speak in these spaces?

Intimidation and threats of bodily harm are good reasons to doubt whether a rational consensus on collective truths can be reached in all cases. In the context of hate speech the perspectives of different speakers would appear to be fundamentally irreconcilable, and tactics might be used to either exclude marginalised speakers from contributing to the consensus, or to coerce them into endorsing a consensus that does not reflect their views. This intimidation and harassment can of course be physical, but has become much more easily traceable and measurable on social media platforms, where it has been established that accounts identifying as women, people of colour or as LGBTQ+, for example, bear the brunt of acts of hate speech. Diane Abbott – who was the first black female MP in the UK when she was elected in 1987 – received more than half of all the abuse directed at female MPs in the run-up to the 2017 UK general election.[3] Such speech acts are often very personal and threaten physical harm.

The practice of 'doxxing' – publishing private personal information about individuals on the internet with malicious intent – is another tactic used to silence particular speakers and groups on social media. Taken together, these practices have meant that many members of marginalised groups have refrained from speaking out on certain issues or have been silenced in the course of debates. Here speech acts hold the potential for bodily or other harms to be sustained, with the consequence that certain groups and view-points might become entirely excluded from the exchange of ideas, or might have their ability to speak curtailed.

These examples also highlight the possibility that the speech acts of some might have material consequences for the safety and financial stability of others. In the UK context debates about the status of people identifying as trans or non-binary have sometimes been treated as conversations in the realm of ideas, especially by 'gender-critical' speakers who are concerned about moves towards allowing self-identification or to support children and teenagers transitioning. Yet given the levels of violence and harassment faced by trans people in the UK, as well as rates of self-harm and suicide, it is clear that this is not merely an intellectual debate. Where free speech is invoked in these debates to defend the rights of speakers to question the status of trans people, the right of one person to offend or speak freely is being set up in opposition to the rights of other groups to personal safety, financial security and mental well-being. Ignoring the material costs and consequences of free speech here seems to further entrench inequalities, and a defence of the right to speak freely implies that this right has the same status as rights to freedom from harm.

Contextual matters

The idea of a marketplace of ideas composed of acts of ideal speech implies that the contexts in which we make our speech acts are unimportant. Yet social media platforms help to illustrate the whole range of ways in which the contexts of speech acts matter for how they are interpreted, received and acted upon, or whether they are listened to at all.

The blunt instruments of follower counts, engagements, hits, likes, retweets, views and more make visible the reality that we do not all speak as equals in the marketplace of ideas. Rather, certain people are more likely to be heard – their speech acts are more widely followed and circulated – and have their pronouncements trusted – indicated by likes and other endorsements. Furthermore, the right to reply to and challenge speech acts is similarly contoured, so an obvious retort or challenge to a widely circulated 'truth' might be far less widely seen and circulated due to the position and standing of the speaker.

The characteristics of a speaker, such as their gender presentation, race and class, are one such factor which affects the extent to which their speech acts are heard, circulated and seen as having legitimacy. On social media platforms, white middle-class men tend to garner more followers and engagements or shares, whereas groups with protected characteristics receive less attention, even from members of these same groups.[4] This is a clear demonstration of what has long been noted regarding the perceived legitimacy of different speakers in the exchange of ideas. Enlightenment theories of democracy, and Habermas's later deliberative model, do not engage with these questions. Rather, they assume that it is possible to have a rational debate between equals. In fact, this assumption that it is possible to define a singular rationality and to reach a rational consensus might be part of the problem. In a political system and public sphere which has been dominated by the voices of white middle-class men for so long, it is not surprising that these voices are still treated by default as guardians of rationality. Dismissals of those from other groups as shrill, emotional and irrational can be read at best as failures to contend with the historical roots of our very definitions of rationality and truth, and at worst as a defence of the ability of certain speakers to define the terms of rational argument, thus excluding certain people from the 'marketplace'.

The legitimacy of speakers not only depends on how others read their characters and characteristics but is also determined in relation to other institutions and sources of credibility. A clear example of this is how those with celebrity status or those who hold positions and qualifications conveying expert status tend to be more likely to be heard and taken seriously on social media platforms. Sometimes these external sources of legitimacy are traded off against one another, as is the case in the wide circulation of statements made by some celebrities about the risks of vaccinating children – which are strongly contested by expert communities. But in the context of other debates, the superior legitimacy of those with expert credentials over other groups such as activists has also produced problematic terms of debate; where essentially political problems, such as how to adequately respond to the problem of climate change and its implications for our lives, can be framed as merely technical issues on which only experts can opine – for example, reduced to the question of whether 'fracking' is a danger to human health, or how best to achieve a full roll-out of electric vehicles.

In her excellent book on the freedom of expression, and the dominance of particular narratives and stories, Nesrine Malik points out that through broader legal frameworks regulating the media, we do not all have equal protections to control what is said about us.[5] Super-injunctions are the preserve of the wealthy and those who have institutional backing, for example, whereas increasing cutbacks in legal aid mean that those on average incomes, and without institutional backing, are very unlikely to be able to mount legal challenges against online speech acts which they believe to be slanderous.

The powers of mediation

The notion of a marketplace of ideas implies the frictionless exchange of ideas through unmediated speech acts. Yet all speech acts are mediated through social and technical processes that have the potential to transform their meanings. At a very basic level there are many barriers to access, whether being able to be in the room for the discussion or having 'a seat at the table', or having access to social media platforms – requiring internet connectivity, digital devices and the fulfilment of certain rules and norms – or even understanding the language in which speech acts are uttered. Social media platforms, as with any other forum for democratic discussion, are shaped by these barriers to entry and thus are likely to reflect the views of certain groups over others.

What is qualitatively different about social media, in comparison to other spaces for speech acts and the exchange of ideas, is the sheer volume of speech acts that are taking place at any one time, and the speed at which they are able to travel across space and between very different communities. This means that it is possible for a single message or speech act to be received and interpreted separately from the broader context – including the conversation it was part of, and an understanding of the position the speaker was speaking from – meaning that the broader argument and context is often lost or obscured, key evidence to validate the claim being made might not be linked to, and often the nuance of the original argument might not be appreciated.

Social media platforms are characterised by rules and ordering devices which further structure and mediate speech acts. The platforms are generally designed to reward engagements such as likes and clicks, and will therefore reorder content other users see as a result, or even boost particular speech acts into others' newsfeeds, timelines and play queues even if it does not have a clear link to a user's network. While consequential, such engagements are an imperfect measure – as are viewing or reader circulation figures of other forms of media – which does not distinguish between engagements which seek to critique or praise a speech act, or attempts to engage with them ironically or sarcastically, for example.

With recent conversations and concerns about fake news, post-truth and the possible creation of 'deep fakes' – videos, photos and audio which appear real but are in fact artificial – consumers of information are likely to receive genuine speech acts differently. On one hand, scepticism about both speaker and message might help to counter some of the challenges of speech acts being taken out of context, or of being interpreted solely on the standing of the speaker. However, on the other hand accusations of fake news are also being used as a way of delegitimising the speech acts of already marginalised groups, and might therefore entrench inequalities further in the marketplace of ideas.

Another significant feature of social media platforms is that they are run by private companies for profit, across multiple national jurisdictions, and thus they raise new challenges for the regulation and management of speech acts, despite the easier traceability and measurability of speech acts on these platforms. This tension can be seen for example in controversies around the failure of Twitter to terminate the accounts of individuals accused of perpetuating hate speech against marginalised groups. What we see emerging here on social media platforms is perhaps a 'marketplace of ideas', but in a different sense. It is not characterised, as was hoped, by a free and equal exchange of ideas through ideal speech acts; rather, our speech acts have now become commodities that are sold back to us by social media companies, compounding existing inequalities between speech acts.

Notes

1 Jared Schroeder, 'Toward a discursive marketplace of ideas: reimaging the marketplace metaphor in the era of social media, fake news, and artificial intelligence', *First Amendment Studies*, 52.1–2 (2018), pp. 38–60.

2 Jürgen Habermas, *Theory of Communicative Action, Volume One: Reason and the Rationalisation of Society,* trans. Thomas A. McCarthy (Boston, MA: Beacon Press, 1984 [1981]).

3 Azmina Dhrodia, 'Unsocial media: tracking Twitter abuse against women MPs', *Amnesty Global Insights,* 4 September 2017, https://medium.com/@AmnestyInsights/unsocial-media-tracking-twitter-abuse-against-women-mps-fc28aeca498a (accessed 16 June 2020).

4 See, for example, J. M. Zhu, A. P. Pelullo, S. Hassan, L. Siderowf, R. M. Merchant and R. M. Werner, 'Gender differences in Twitter use and influence among health policy and health services researchers', *JAMA Intern Med.,* 179.12 (2019), pp. 1726–9.

5 Nesrine Malik, *We Need New Stories: Challenging the Toxic Myths Behind Our Age of Discontent* (London: Weidenfeld and Nicolson, 2019).

Index

Index

Index

Index

Index

Index

Index

war correspondents 147
Watson, Emma 241
Welch, Evelyn 220
Weltwoche 132–3
'Western' culture 196
Westphalia 75
white supremacy 259
Wilde, Oscar 181
Wilson, Woodrow 81–2
Winnipeg Public Library
   48–9

words, power of 8
world views 49, 57, 240

Yaxley-Lennon, Stephen 31, 38
   see also Robinson, Tommy
Yes Minister (TV programme)
   115–16, 120–4
Yiannopoulos, Milo 12, 184–7, 190,
   256–7
Young, Toby 1, 229
YouTube 38